ELEMENTARY
CLASSROOM
MANAGEMENT

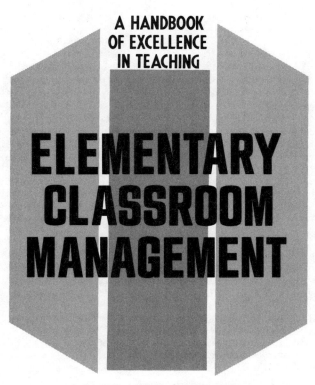

A HANDBOOK
OF EXCELLENCE
IN TEACHING

ELEMENTARY CLASSROOM MANAGEMENT

C. M. CHARLES

Longman
New York & London

Elementary Classroom Management

Longman Inc., 1560 Broadway, New York, N.Y. 10036
Associated companies, branches, and representatives
throughout the world.

Developmental Editor: Lane Akers
Editorial and Design Supervisor: Frances Althaus
Manufacturing Supervisor: Marion Hess
Production Supervisor: Ferne Kawahara

Library of Congress Cataloging in Publication Data

Charles, C. M.
  Elementary classroom management.

  Includes bibliographical references and index.
  1. Classroom management. I. Title.
LB3013.C465   1983   372.11′02   82-13973
ISBN 0-582-28349-3

Manufactured in the United States of America

Acknowledgments

The author wishes to express deep gratitude for the contributions of the following people in the production of this book: Lane Akers, for support and attention throughout; Carolyn M. Evertson, Robert F. McNergney, and Leo W. Anglin for their valuable criticisms of the manuscript; Ruth Charles, for professional contributions and assistance with the manuscript; Charlotte Rodzach, for significant contributions to Chapter 13; Karen Runyon, for significant contributions to Chapter 11; and to the following excellent teachers: Cathy V. McCloud, Carol Mercer, Janet Mulder, Kay Ballantyne, Keith Correll, Frank Barnes, Elizabeth Davies, Roberta Revetta, Carolyn Haslett, and David Sisk.

Contents

1

Basics of Classroom Management

This is a book about teaching. It differs from most because it does not describe philosophy of education, psychology of learning, or methods of teaching the various subjects. Instead, it deals with what teachers identify as their greatest concerns, matters such as discipline, time, pressure, effectiveness—and working with parents. Teachers know that if they are to cope with these great concerns they must make their classrooms operate efficiently, control behavior well, communicate effectively with students and parents, and arrange their lives, professional and private, so as to reduce the heavy stress under which they labor.

But where does a concerned teacher begin? How does one take hold; what does one do? The details that answer those questions fall within the realm of classroom management, and they comprise the contents of this book. The material included is designed to help teachers organize and carry out the innumerable requirements of their work so that they achieve success and derive satisfaction and sense of accomplishment. The presentation is direct in style, without technical language. Occasional references are made to important research, but they are kept few in number. So many ideas must receive mention that parts of certain chapters appear almost to be lists of things to do or remember, but that helps the teacher give attention to important aspects of management without wading through endless pages of discussion.

This first chapter provides an overview of classroom management. It begins with the story of a first-year teacher, who despite excellent training found herself seriously hampered by difficulties of

1

management. Following that story is a description of what she, like all other teachers, needs to know in order to become proficient in classroom management. The needs described therein receive detailed attention in subsequent chapters.

MERCEDES BRIGHT

Mercedes Bright, by midsummer of the year she graduated from college, decided that while it had sometimes seemed otherwise fortune had indeed smiled on her. In a whirlwind of days she completed student teaching, received her B.A., obtained a teaching credential, and then to top it off, after only four interviews she landed a position as a fifth-grade teacher. She accepted the offer without hesitation because the school, if not entirely crème de la crème, was still a cut above average, with a strong staff and some interesting programs.

Of the college students with whom she graduated, Mercedes was the first to obtain a position in a public school. That accomplishment seemed proper to her, though from modesty and consideration for others she would not have said so. She had completed her training program with honors, having always done her best to exceed expectations. Her efforts had not gone unnoticed. "Mercedes is a natural," her master teacher said. "A future star," one professor proclaimed. Her fellow students looked on her with a mixture of admiration, jealousy, and envy, but even they could not dislike her. All the pieces seemed to fall naturally into place—honors, credentials, a good job, self-assurance, and now on to a career that promised immediate success.

Mercedes too believed she had what it takes. She knew she had acquired strong teaching skills. Everyone said so, and the children in her practice teaching had responded well to her. She thought she had a sound philosophy of teaching and learning, and she had been proud to explain it when asked in her interviews. All children, she said, have a right to learn. The schools and teachers have the duty to teach those children, a duty to be kept always foremost in mind. Students for their part have a responsibility to learn, and parents have a responsibility to support the educational process. But the main responsibility lies, she said, with the classroom teacher. It is there in the classroom that learning has to be vitalized through interesting and worthwhile activities, and the teacher has to remain warm, caring, and understanding, ready to nurture the growth of every single student.

Armed as she was with her skills and philosophy, Mercedes saw smooth sailing ahead. The sailing, however, turned out more rough than smooth.

All began well enough. She spent the remaining weeks of summer preparing for the year to come. She went first to her district office and obtained a copy of the curriculum guide for fifth grade. She studied it thoroughly and planned out interesting lessons, projects, and activities. As soon as possible she met with the school principal, talked with the secretary, and went out of her way to meet the school custodians. When other teachers appeared at school, Mercedes talked with them, asked their advice, and showed interest in the plans they had for the coming year. She felt she was going to fit in nicely.

During the week before school she spent every day in her classroom, taking out time only for meetings called by the principal. She arranged the desks and beautified the room with bulletin boards, an art exhibit, and decorations on an autumn theme. She arranged her reference materials, organized a science learning center in a corner of the room, and bought an aquarium which she started with guppies, snails, and plants. She placed growing plants in two areas near the windows. Before the first student arrived, her room was a showplace. She was proud of it, and especially of the pièce de résistance—a hamster center, with three hamsters that fed, climbed, and nested along their transparent plastic tunnels.

On the day that school began Mercedes suffered her full share of nervousness, and she knew that a fearsome headache awaited her at the end of the day. Nevertheless, she felt secure in her ability to direct and work with the incoming students. She greeted the students cheerily, but by the end of the day all that remained of her cheeriness was a wan and wistful smile. As the children swarmed into the room Mercedes began to realize that she had expected many things of them that they obviously didn't know, or else they were deliberately playing ignorant.

She expected them to enter the room in a polite, orderly way. Some did, but others entered pushing, shoving, squabbling, and calling each other names. It took her a long time to get them settled. They appeared ignorant of standards of classroom behavior or even of human decency. What was more, they didn't seem to have any natural respect for Mercedes. That troubled her, and she had to admit it hurt her feelings, too.

As the morning struggled along, Mercedes realized that she would have to work hard to establish regulations for them to follow —in asking permission, sharpening pencils, getting drinks, going to the restroom, and requesting help. When dismissed for recess, the students stormed out and raced down the corridors. Later in the classroom they squabbled when they moved from their seats to the reading circle, to the science center, and to the places where they were to obtain materials, for whose care they seemed to feel no responsibility. When their assigned work was completed, they waved their arms, called out, and even threw pencils and erasers before Mercedes could collect the completed work.

At the end of the first day Mercedes was demoralized but not yet defeated. By the end of the second and third days, she began to feel despair, because her students continued to break rules, even after she had talked with them in her kindest, most sincere way about the necessity for good behavior and for following rules in order that all of them might have the chance to learn. She talked about respect for others and asked if they liked being treated rudely. They said they did not, but after a few minutes of reform returned to their former ways. They were not cruel to Mercedes, or even hostile, but they clowned, giggled, and forever tattled. They were rude to each other and sarcastic. And for Mercedes, the worst cut of all was the way her hamster center backfired. The students were interested all right, in fact to the point of getting up out of their seats during work time to watch the animals. Anyone who sharpened a pencil, got a drink, fetched a book, or threw paper in the wastebasket was certain to take a prolonged detour to the hamster table. Mercedes wished she had never heard of hamsters.

New problems popped up regularly. They began the first day when two parents asked if they could stay for the morning and help in the room. Mercedes was not prepared for that, and instead of thanking them and asking them to wait until next week, she said certainly, she was most eager for their help and support. However, she didn't know what to have them do, so they spent most of the time sitting and watching Mercedes struggle against the students' poor behavior.

Other difficulties surprised her, too. She found that one of her students was identified as learning disabled, and was being mainstreamed from special education into her room half the day. Two of the students were from foreign countries and spoke almost no English. Another student, though of apparently normal intelligence and social development, could barely read from a first-grade reader. Yet another student could read at the high school level, far better than most adults. Mercedes scurried to make provisions for those students whose needs were special.

Normal classroom work presented difficulties, too. Mercedes had trouble monitoring students' seatwork while she was working with small groups. Students continually came to her for help, besieging her several at a time. Usually they asked questions about directions she had so carefully given only minutes before. Practically anything would get students off task, and it was very hard to get them going again. As she struggled through the first days, Mercedes began to see many problems with her own teaching, of which she had previously been so confident. Her lessons did not go smoothly because the students seldom reacted as she had expected. Some of her lessons took too much time and students lost interest; others were too short, and she was left with periods of time too short for beginning new lessons but too long for sitting and waiting.

Student behavior was not improving, and it continued to disrupt even her best lessons. One day a student became ill and vomited in the classroom. Mercedes never was able to get the students back into their math lesson, and finally she yelled at them and made them put their heads down on their desks.

And there were other annoyances. Materials she had counted on came up short or nonexistent. Three pairs of scissors were stolen. One morning she found all the guppies dead. A parent complained bitterly that her son was being bullied on the playground and didn't want to come to school any more. Two of her boys got into a fight and a new shirt was ruined. Naturally the mother called Mercedes to complain about her control.

By the end of that first terrible week, Mercedes' mind was in turmoil and her spirits were at rock bottom. She doubted that she would ever get those ten and eleven-year-old kids to learn, much less behave responsibly. Immersed in this bleakness, Mercedes found an unexpected resiliency. Given the weekend to think, she began to see steps she could take to improve. First, she decided to rearrange the seating, to place students farther apart and separate those who reinforced each other's poor behavior. She saw that she would need to reposition her desk and small-group circle so she would be closer to the rest of the class, particularly to those prone to causing trouble. She decided that when they needed help they would have to stay in their seats and she would come to them. She remembered another teacher's suggestion of a signaling device made of construction paper that students could display when they needed help, rather than sitting with their hands waving in the air. She saw that she would have to improve her means of distributing and collecting materials, and she decided to use student monitors to help. She hit on the idea of assigning specific tasks to most of the students in the class as a way of getting them to be more serious about their responsibilities in and to the classroom. She decided to add more structure and direction to her lessons, at least for the time being, and to teach in a more direct way.

She decided to write all instructions on charts or on the chalkboard. She determined that she would follow through on insisting that students complete their work and fulfill their obligations. To make all these things possible, she realized that she would have to implement a new, more structured system of discipline, one that would allow her to correct student misbehavior immediately, before it spread through the class disrupting everything.

The Weight of Minor Details

Mercedes' trials and tribulations point to one of the most important facts in the lives of teachers, especially those just beginning. That fact is that no matter how much they have going for them in philosophy, knowledge of students, and command of subject matter, they will encounter an enormous variety of relatively minor details that in their totality can overwhelm the entire instructional process.

Such were the problems that beset Mercedes. Fortunately, she did have much going for her, and was able to rely on her background, insight, and skills to devise ways of handling the problems. As she searched for those ways, she recalled brief passages from two books she had read during her training. The first was *The Hoosier Schoolmaster*, recommended by one of her professors. In that book the chief character, a young male teacher who had come out to Indiana to teach in a one-room school, found immediately that he had to contend with a ruffian bunch of older students—boys who delighted in the fact that they had "run off" the three previous school masters. Though they set out to make his life miserable, he determined that he would "be a bulldog," sink his teeth into the situation, and never let go no matter what they tried to do. Mercedes, like the Hoosier schoolmaster, decided that she too would take hold and never let go, no matter what.

Mercedes, also remembered having read in Haim Ginott's book *Teacher and Child* (1972), an anecdote about a river boatman who was ferrying a passenger across the river. The passenger was a scholar, and he asked the boatman, "Do you know philosophy?" "I can't say I do," answered the boatman. "Then you have lost a third of your life," answered the scholar. After a time the scholar asked again, "Do you know literature?" "I can't say I do," replied the boatman. "Then you have lost another third of your life," asserted the scholar. A bit farther along the boat was siezed by the current and dashed against a large rock, whereupon it began to sink. "Do you know how to swim?" asked the boatman. "No," replied the scholar. "Then you have lost all your life," replied the boatman.

Mercedes knew that she could and would swim, and she began

taking care of her numerous minor problems, the combined weight of which threatened to drag her under. She reflected on her situation. She was well trained in preparing and presenting good lessons, but once in the classroom she found that her time was stolen by such things as collecting milk and lunch money, taking attendance, erasing the chalkboard, trying to keep paper and supplies in good order, correcting papers, distributing and collecting worksheets and other materials, and keeping the science and art displays in order. She had to water the plants, feed the fish, and clean the hamster habitrails. She had to take care of obtaining audiovisual materials and getting them returned to the right places. She had to send out notices, deal with visitors in the classroom, and try to instruct students who could not speak English. She spent enormous amounts of time cajoling students and waiting exasperatedly for them to follow her directions. And after days filled with such matters she then had to spend evenings reading papers, preparing materials for the next day, and making necessary telephone calls to parents and other teachers.

These were things for which Mercedes had not been prepared, or even adequately forewarned. They were the minor details that so troubled her in her first days of teaching.

WHAT MERCEDES NEEDED TO KNOW

Had Mercedes known certain things about classroom management, those tough first days would have gone much more easily. Unfortunately, she had to learn them by trial and error as most teachers do, if indeed they ever learn them at all. Especially she needed to know three groups of things: (1) what preparations to make before the school year began, (2) what steps to take during the first days and weeks of school, so that daily matters became routine, and (3) which instructional matters required daily management throughout the year in order that quality instruction might occur.

Before the School Year Begins

Before school starts teachers should take care of three important matters: (1) get acquainted with school personnel and facilities, (2) organize and prepare the physical setting of the classroom, and (3) plan for the psychosocial climate of the classroom.

Getting Acquainted with Personnel and Facilities. Mercedes performed this task well. She went out of her way to establish friendly relations with the principal, secretary, custodians, and most of the teachers, with whom she chatted during the days before school began. She learned the locations of the library, playgrounds and restrooms, cafeteria, nurse's office, custodians' station, workroom, and lounge, and she introduced herself to school people wherever possible.

Physical Setting of the Classroom.   Mercedes did fairly well, too, in organizing her classroom, although the seating was inappropriate and she gave too much attention to appearance and not enough to efficiency and ease of movement. Still by and large she showed that teachers should think first of the curriculum, objectives, and activities expected for their grade level and subject areas, then arrange the environment for best use of the activities and materials that led toward the objectives.

This requires that teachers do many things. Seating, for example, should provide comfort, flexibility, and ease of movement. At the same time the seating pattern should be efficiently compact that the teacher can reach individual students quickly. Work space in the room should be arranged for convenience, with materials easily obtained, used, and returned. Special areas add to the usefulness of the classroom, but they must be convenient, nondistracting, and easily managed. Examples of such areas include science corners, drama area, map and globe centers, reading areas, and for younger children areas where they use puppets and toys. In addition, teachers should arrange display areas such as bulletin boards, student work displays, art displays, and other objects for students to observe.

Teachers need to consider storage areas, too, areas in which materials and equipment are kept. Most elementary classrooms contain physical education equipment, some audiovisual equipment, charts, maps, globes, and reference materials such as encyclopedias and dictionaries. They also contain supplies of paper, pencils, glue, scissors, construction paper, and so forth, that are used in daily activities. These materials have to be stored in such a manner that students may obtain them easily and replace them correctly when finished.

Psychosocial Climate.   Before school begins teachers need to think carefully about the kind of psychosocial climate—that is, the emotional tone—they wish to establish and maintain, together with the procedures that will cause it to occur. Experience has shown that all matters of schooling proceed much more satisfactorily when students have a sense of belonging, when interpersonal relationships are good, and where there exists a sense of joy about learning and pleasure in being a part of the class. In this aspect of preparation, Mercedes did not do so well. While she determined to be kind and considerate of all students, she simply assumed that they would reciprocate, and she did not make concrete plans for ensuring their desired behavior. She did not establish a clear, enforceable system of discipline, and she had no effective means of putting an immediate end to the disrespect, poor manners, and inconsiderate behavior shown by the students. Those conditions must be met before one can move on to providing the sense of joy that comes from work well done, in collaboration with others, that brings progress and recognition.

First Days and Weeks

In the first days and weeks after school has begun teachers must give careful and concerted attention to several matters of key importance in setting the tone and routines of daily learning. Research has shown that what teachers do the first day is crucial in setting the pattern for the rest of the year. The best classroom managers make sure that the first day in school is orderly. They explain rules and procedures, introduce the various parts of the classroom, monitor students closely, and let them know when they behave appropriately (Evertson and Anderson, 1979; Emmer, 1980). These matters should quickly be made fully anticipated and habitual, so that students expect them and move automatically into them. At the same time students must accept responsibility for their own conduct and demonstrate suitable conduct in all class matters. We saw that Mercedes experienced difficulty here. She, like all teachers, should have made arrangements that would have launched the school year well. Such arrangements are described in the following paragraphs.

1. Attendance and Opening Procedures. Teachers wish to start the class day in such a manner that students feel comfortable and secure, and at the same time are doing something productive and worthwhile. This sets the tone for the remainder of the day. Some teachers like to use opening exercises that take attendance and allow students to share experiences. Others prefer to use the first minutes of the day for writing in journals or for reading student-selected materials. Still others prefer to use a "choosing" time in which students are allowed to work for a time at activities of special interest. Any one of these procedures starts the day well, provided it is clarified, student expectations are made plain, and the teacher enforces those expectations.

2. Seating Arrangements and Orientation to the Classroom. On the very first day teachers should explain to students the seating arrangements and the uses of the various parts of the classroom. Some teachers use preassigned seating while others allow students to select their own places, there to remain so long as they behave themselves. The teacher informs students about work areas and the materials contained therein, and points out where group and individual activities are to be pursued.

3. Class Rules and the System of Discipline. Also on the first day the teacher should go over with students exactly what the basic rules for student behavior will be. Four to six rules are considered sufficient, and most teachers have these rules fairly well in mind although they wisely allow students to give input, discuss, and have at least some say in deciding how the rules will be enforced. When students participate in making such decisions, they become more likely to abide by them, see them as fair, and recognize the necessity for rules in helping learning to occur better for all.

4. Orientation to the School. Ordinarily most students will be well acquainted with the school buildings and grounds, unless they are newly arrived. Still, it is advisable to spend some time orienting students to the locations and functions of the various parts of the school plant that they will be using. These include such things as restrooms, drinking fountains, playgrounds, cafeteria, library, principal's office, secretary's office, and nurse's station. Many teachers take their students on a group tour of these places sometime during the first or second day of school. As they learn the locations they also learn any special regulations associated with them.

5. School Rules. Students must follow certain rules that pertain to the school, as distinct from those of the classroom. Such rules tell them how to behave in corridors, on the playground, in the library, in the cafeteria, and at street crossings. Some schools have rules about buses and parking areas. It is the teacher's responsibility to thoroughly familiarize everyone concerned with these school regulations and procedures.

6. The Daily Schedule. The daily classroom schedule should be explained in such a manner that students know what activities are to occur at each part of the day and how they are to work and behave during those activities. Along with a discussion of schedule and activities, the teacher introduces the books to be used and points out materials that will be used on a regular basis—where they are located, how they are obtained, how they are cared for, and how they are returned after use.

7. Monitors. Many teachers use class members to help with the numerous classroom chores. These monitors should be selected during the first week of classes. Some teachers assign monitors to the various duties, while others like to go over a description of the various duties and ask for volunteers or even have elections to the positions. The list of duties for which monitors can be particularly helpful is a long one, and is discussed in detail in Chapter 5. It is desirable to find some special job for every student in the class. Fulfilling such duties causes students to take more interest in school, and it greatly reduces the amount of detail work that would otherwise fall to the teacher.

8. Miscellaneous Needs. Students continually need help while working independently at their desks. They need to sharpen pencils, get drinks, go to the restroom, and go to the office to call their parents. Routine procedures must be established for these matters, so that the teacher can provide help and the students will understand their roles and responsibilities.

9. Traffic Patterns. Students must be instructed on how to enter the classroom, how to leave when dismissed, what to do during fire drills, and how to move from one area of the room to another. Many teachers do not want students to come to the teacher's station. There are other places in the classroom, too, where congestion may occur, such as around special corners or near the sink. Teachers need to instruct students on how they may move about and how many may be out of their seats at any given time.

10. Playground Regulations. Students are on the play grounds at recess and noontime. Often they are there before and after school. They must know what the regulations are regarding behavior, use of equipment, length of time before and after school, and use of the areas on weekends. These things, too, should be clearly communicated during the first few days of school.

11. Paraprofessionals. Many teachers have aides and cross-age tutors who work with them on a regular basis. The duties of these classroom assistants should be made very clear, so each person knows what to do and when and where to do it. If they are assigned clerical work such as scoring papers and keeping records, they should be provided a convenient work station, with files and folders in which to keep their work. Such organization cuts down on wasted time and the feeling of ineffectiveness on the part of the para-professionals.

12. *Parent Volunteers.* Many classrooms have one or more parents who contribute work time on a regular basis. Important work should be assigned to these volunteers and they should have definite duties and a special place to work.

13. *Preparation for Substitute Teachers.* Substitute teachers have a hard life professionally because of the different situations they face and because most students tend to work against rather than with them. For those reasons, and because the classroom should continue to be a place of effective learning when under the direction of a substitute, the regular teacher should take pains to prepare the class to work effectively with substitute teachers. One or two monitors can be assigned to this task. Their function is to inform the substitute quickly of routines, locations of materials, and what has been going on instructionally in each of the subject areas. The entire class should be instilled with sufficient pride that they will work cooperatively with the substitute rather than counterproductively.

Matters Requiring Continual Attention

The thirteen matters previously described should be thoroughly discussed and put into place during the first week of school. In addition to those, there are several other matters requiring management that must have ongoing attention throughout the year. Among them are curriculum management, lesson management, records and reporting, and the management of extracurricular activities.

Curriculum Management. The curriculum is the school's program for learners. Its management entails the selection, organization, and presentation of subject matter content plus the arrangements made for student work and accountability. Because these matters continually fluctuate, they require much planning and reorganization, thus making curriculum management a task that continues throughout the year. Once the routines are established and put in place, however, the amount of work required in curriculum management becomes significantly less.

Seven aspects of curriculum management deserve attention: (1)

subjects and topics; (2) goals and objectives; (3) instructional activities; (4) instructional materials; (5) grouping; (6) teaching method and style; and (7) extension and follow-up.

Subjects and Topics. The subject matter and the topics of instruction are in most cases determined by the school curriculum guide and the contents of the textbooks used. Still, teachers have considerable latitude in selecting topics they feel to be of special value or in which they have had unusual experience.

Goals and Objectives. Within each subject-topic area, teachers identify goals and objectives they intend to have their students reach. It is recognized that instructional efficiency is increased when goals and objectives are made clear, not only to the teacher but to the students and their parents as well.

Instructional Activities. These follow naturally from the combination of subject matter and instructional objectives. Activities are the student work tasks that bring about the skills, attitudes, and understandings specified in the objectives of instruction.

Instructional Materials. These include printed materials and manipulable objects that students use during instructional activities. They range across references, textbooks, charts, models, manipulable objects, paper and pencil, and various art media. Instructional materials enhance and extend experiences and activities for students, and most school activities cannot be conducted without them.

Grouping. This term refers to how students are clustered for efficient instruction. Grouping arrangements vary in accord with interests and needs from single students working individually, to small groups, to larger groups, and on to the total class. Flexible grouping allows instruction to match the needs of topics, activities, materials, and individual students.

Teaching Methods and Styles. This refers to the way the teacher presents information and directs student work. Generally speaking, two types of teaching method and style are widely in use. The first type is *direct teaching*, in which teachers plan and control most aspects of the teaching-learning situation. The second is *facilitative teaching* which calls on students to do much of the planning and organization for work, thus requiring that they assume responsibility for reaching the intended objectives.

Extension and Follow-up. Good instruction calls for repeated attention to the practice, use, and application of the material newly learned. This may include drill, application to the solution of real problems, application to creative production, and extension to activities outside school. Such extension and follow-up are means of making learning more permanent and useful for students.

Lesson Management. Two types of teaching were described as currently in vogue, direct teaching and facilitative teaching. Each of these types calls on teachers to perform several tasks: determining objectives, selecting activities, arranging groups, providing monitoring and feedback, and evaluating students and reporting. These duties differ in nature depending on whether teaching is in the main direct or facilitative, and they are explained in detail in Chapters 7 and 8.

In addition to attending to those elements of teaching, teachers must strive to pace lessons well. This means that the lessons accomplish what they are intended to during their allotted time, moving at a steady pace without rush or delay, and that teachers provide smooth transitions between lessons to avoid awkward periods of time that are so conducive to student misbehavior.

Records and Reporting. Records should be kept that can tell teacher, student, parent, and administrator at a glance a given student's achievement levels, work in progress, strengths and weaknesses, and future needs. This requirement is best met when the teacher keeps a record sheet for the entire class plus a separate records folder for each student. The folder should include a progress form, samples of student work, and progress charts that show growth in graphic form.

When it comes to report cards, each school district has its own system. Most indicate at least two things: levels of achievement in each subject, and levels of effort and behavior displayed by the student.

Management of Extracurricular Activities. Teachers' duties range far beyond those of organizing and presenting lessons. The following are a few of the important tasks they must perform that are rarely considered when teacher functions are discussed:

1. *Plays and performances.* Teachers are called on to organize, coach, direct, and stage these performances. This usually involves organizing a great deal of help from parents and other volunteers.

2. *Field trips.* When the class is able to leave the school to visit

places of special interest, the teacher must arrange transportation, obtain permission slips from parents, secure parent volunteers to help supervise students, and make advance preparation so that the visit will run smoothly and be of maximum benefit to students.

3. *Fairs and carnivals.* Most schools put on fairs, carnivals, and other money-raising activities. Even when these events are under the direction of the parent-teacher organization, teachers are still called on to work in the affair and to help plan and prepare for it.

4. *Open house.* Almost all schools have one or more evenings during the year in which parents and the public are invited to visit the school and the classroom. Samples of student work are displayed, and often presentations made by the teacher describe the curricular program, activities, and expectations for the year's work. Teachers then talk individually with parents about matters related to individual students.

5. *Assemblies.* Teachers are sometimes in charge of assemblies for the entire school, which requires considerable planning and organization. At other times they have to do nothing more than manage the behavior of their students at the assembly and the movement of their class to and from the location of the assembly.

6. *Clubs.* Teachers often have leadership roles in special clubs or other activities, such as cheerleading, athletics, photography, scouting, science groups, after-school recreation, and so forth. Sometimes these extra tasks are done for extra pay. More often they are an expected part of the teacher's overall duties.

CHECKPOINTS

Aspects of classroom management that require attention:

Before the year begins
- acquaintance with personnel and facilities
- prepare the classroom
- plan for the emotional tone of the class

First days and weeks of school
- attendance and opening procedures
- seating arrangements
- orientation to the classroom
- class rules and system of discipline
- orientation to the school
- rules of the school
- the daily class schedule
- selection of student helpers (monitors)

- routines for pencil sharpening, drinks, restroom, etc.
- traffic patterns and regulations
- playground regulations
- use of paraprofessionals (aides and volunteers)
- preparation for substitute teachers

Continual attention through the year
- curriculum selection and organization
- lesson management
- record keeping and reporting
- extracurricular activities

BIBLIOGRAPHY

Blake, R., and Mouton, J. *The Managerial Grid*. Houston: Gulf, 1964.

Eggleston, E. *The Hoosier Schoolmaster*. Magnolia, Mass.: Peter Smith, 1959 (originally published in 1871).

Emmer, E. "Effective Classroom Management at the Beginning of the School Year." *Elementary School Journal*, May 1980.

Evertson, C., and Anderson, L. "Beginning School." *Educational Horizons*, Summer 1979.

Ginott, H. *Teacher and Child*. New York: Macmillan, 1972.

Johnson, M., and Brooks, H. "Conceptualizing Classroom Management." Chapter 1 in Daniel L. Duke (ed.), *Classroom Management*. 78th Yearbook of the National Society for the Study of Education. Chicago: University of Chicago Press, 1979.

2

Managing the Physical Environment of the Classroom

FACTORS THAT DETERMINE PHYSICAL ARRANGEMENT

The physical organization of the classroom strongly influences learning in many ways. It affects for better or worse the attitudes of students and teacher through the extent to which it presents a cheerful, inviting, motivating, and purposeful setting for learning. It determines in large measure how efficient teaching will be because it provides for the clustering of students, movement in the classroom, display and deployment of instructional materials, and areas for effective practice during learning.

All of us maintain a picture in our minds of what a school classroom looks like. The picture often reveals rows of desks, chalkboard and teacher's desk in front, and a shelf of reference books along the side. That pattern of organization has been used by thousands of teachers for teaching millions of students, and it has served well. Yet with today's realities it is not a pattern to be copied in detail.

Now many things must be taken into account when teachers decide how to arrange their classrooms. They must consider the curriculum that they propose to deliver, for its contents strongly suggest ways of organizing the room. In elementary schools one expects the curriculum to include reading, language, mathematics, social studies, science, physical education, art, and music. Many teachers add drama and dance to that curriculum. Classroom organization must make allowances for these different types of activities. Mathematics and language study, for example, may call for students to work at their seats with little movement about the room. Social studies may call for active work at projects involving groups of students. Art requires special work areas, and of course dance, music, and drama require larger open spaces that allow much movement.

The physical environment is influenced by the prime objectives toward which the curriculum is aimed. In programs where basic skills are emphasized above all else, seating arrangements, materials, and distribution of materials must be given first attention. In programs where creative, productive, and interactive objectives receive greatest attention, work and movement areas together with necessary materials must be provided in a different way.

Traditionally elementary and secondary schools have relied on classrooms that provide for one group of students working under the direction of one teacher inside a single room. In recent years many open-space schools have been built. These schools feature classroom space consisting of large areas that contain as many as four separate classes under the direction of a team of perhaps four teachers, who work together to deliver instruction to the students within that area. This kind of arrangement calls for much different storage of materials, giving directions, moving about the room, working in groups, doing creative activities, and so forth.

Still another common type of school arrangement, one that predominates at the junior high and senior high level, and which remains in use in many elementary schools, is that which is referred to as *departmentalized*. With this arrangement students change classrooms between subjects, a situation that mitigates teachers' ability to establish the kind of physical environment they might otherwise prefer.

A final consideration in determining the physical arrangement of the classroom is the teacher's philosophy and emotional comfort. Some teachers believe strongly in direct teaching, in which they control curriculum, student activities, and materials used by the students. Other teachers prefer large amounts of indirect teaching, in which students are given considerable leeway in choosing activities in which they wish to engage, in selecting materials that might be appropriate, and in working with other classmates in ways considered beneficial and enjoyable. Some teachers prefer to have the classroom set and equipped with relatively few materials, using only those seen as directly helpful in the subjects being studied. Others prefer to have their classrooms richly furnished with varieties of materials, charts, pictures, slogans, decorations, and so forth, feeling that such environments are more stimulating to students.

There is little data to establish the superiority of one type of physical arrangement over another. Hence, much discretion is normally left to teachers in deciding how they will arrange and equip their classrooms.

SIX ASPECTS OF THE PHYSICAL ENVIRONMENT

Six facets of the physical classroom environment deserve careful consideration in effective classroom design: (1) floor space, (2) wall space, (3) countertop space, (4) shelf space, (5) cupboards and closets, and (6) general ambience. Let us consider some of the possibilities afforded by each of these six facets.

Floor Space

Floor space in the classroom gives attention to seating, work and activity space; special centers, corners, and areas; the teacher's station; special effect areas; and traffic patterns.

Seating refers to the arrangements of desks or tables that are used by students during times of quiet work. Several points should be remembered when deciding on the seating patterns. Students should not be seated so they have to face a strong light, because looking for long periods into the light makes one uncomfortable and unable to concentrate. They should be seated compactly, near the main chalkboard that will be used for lessons given to large groups. The seating should be arranged so that teachers can move easily among students in order to give help quickly; and it should be made as flexible as possible so that students can rearrange themselves to form a circle for purposes of class discussion.

These conditions are usually best met by seating students in a shallow semicircle near the chalkboard, with their desks three or four rows deep, or by seating students in modular clusters of five or six students each. This is not to discount the value of row seating

> Beth, a fifth-grade teacher, describes how she seats her students:
> "Initially I choose the places where the children sit. Once they become acquainted I let them contract to sit by a person of their choice, but still within their original cluster. By this time they understand about my right to teach and their right to learn without disruption, and they know I will immediately move any person who abuses their contract. In each cluster of desks I try to balance the low students with the high in order to mix minds and provide the slower children with added help during group projects."

which, while often considered old fashioned, has been shown in experiments with second- and seventh-grade students to produce
higher levels of on-task study behavior than does seating at clusters
of tables (Axelrod et al., 1979).

Work and activity space becomes available when one has a compact seating plan and it can be used for different kinds of work
groups. Activities that require movement will need larger spaces;
quieter, small-group, or individual activities will require less. Many
instructional activities—mathematics, spelling, handwriting, and
guided seatwork—are conducted with students in their assigned
seats. Other parts of the curriculum, however, call for individual
and group work that involves physical movement, as is often the
case in social studies, science, art, music, drama, and dance. This
means that to the extent possible open floor space should be maintained or else provided easily by simple movement of student desks.

Many teachers have one or more special centers, corners, and
areas in their classrooms. These learning centers often are located on
tables. In some cases they are placed on cabinet tops or are free-
standing on the floor. They are built around a certain theme, such as
maps, science projects, or art work and are places where students go
and work at least partly on their own, following directions and using
materials provided in the center.

Even teachers who do not use complete learning centers often
have special corners or areas in the room that provide special effects
or instruction. These areas, too, are typically devoted to science activities and materials, reading, instructional games, maps and globes,
and things of that sort, where students can work independently or
in groups of two or three.

The *teacher's station* should be fairly near the students' assigned
seating but not directly in front of them. It has become fashionable
for teachers to have little more than a plain desk or table where they
keep their plan book, manuals, and a few other instructional effects.
There is reason to believe, however, that important benefits accrue from making the teacher's station special and attractive. These
benefits include enhancing the teacher's position as authority-in-
charge of the classroom, making it an exciting and special privilege
for students to be called to the area. There might also be a student
"chair of honor" in this "control center" that serves as a locus out of
which instruction is organized and disseminated.

Teachers' stations can be made special by using a nice desk or
table, with an attractive file cabinet and shelves for the teacher's
personal in-class library. Artifacts, weavings, and art work provide

tasteful ambience. One or two articles of high prestige for students can be kept there, such as a radio, sports team pennant, or large toy animal. A small display area can be used to post pictures of former classes at work on projects, and a special place of honor on the desk or a shelf can display the outstanding work of the week done by students in the class. A special chair or perhaps a small table can provide a desirable area for conferencing with individual students. Photographs of the teacher's spouse, children, or pet can be displayed. Finally if there is a bit of money available, a control module set in the teacher station can be used to turn on and off lights, electric signals, and so forth, in different parts of the room.

Many teachers like to have a special effects area set aside in their classroom where students go either as a reward for having worked well during the day, or as a place to enjoy quiet solitude. Often these areas contain sofas or bean bags and thick rugs. High-interest materials may be provided there, such as popular books and magazines, or headsets where students may listen to the radio or tapes without disturbing the class. Some primary grades have specially constructed lofts with crawl space where students can climb, crawl, and curl up away from the routines of the classroom.

Traffic patterns should be considered so that seating and work areas are arranged to allow students to move about the room, obtain materials, sharpen pencils, go to centers, and so forth, without causing congestion or bothering other students. It is best to arrange seating so that when students rise for dismissal from the classroom they may go directly to the door without having to pass against other students still seated. If students are allowed to sharpen their own pencils, the pencil sharpener should be away from work or study areas, and an electric sharpener is desirable. If they are allowed to obtain their own work materials, the routes to those materials should be clear and open.

Wall Space

The walls of all classrooms provide space rich in instructional possibility—space that is seldom used to fullest advantage. Five portions of the wall space can make effective contributions to the instructional program: (1) chalkboard, (2) bulletin boards, (3) display areas for student work, (4) display areas for maps and charts, and (5) areas for other instructional materials such as work instructions, slogans, graphic models (that show how to do something, as in the steps in multiplying fractions), posters, and special words or symbols to which students can refer while doing writing or other assignments.

The chalkboard remains one of the most valuable teaching devices available to teachers. It can be used to post daily information, assignments, math problems, vocabulary words, and routine information. It can be used for demonstrations and explanations during instruction. And year after year students remain highly motivated to go to the chalkboard and work, during such activities as mathematics and spelling.

Bulletin boards are available in practically every classroom, yet they are seldom used to best instructional advantage. It has become the vogue to use bulletin board space for room decorations, in the form of Halloween themes, autumn themes, spring themes, and so forth. Admittedly these decorations make the room pleasant to look at, but their instructional value is minimal. It is preferable to use bulletin boards for attractively arranged displays of puzzles that draw students' attention and cause them to think, for clippings from newspapers and magazines that have special importance for students and can serve as focal points for class discussions, for posting creative ideas and problem situations that stimulate student thinking, and for displaying models of exemplary student work done as part of the ongoing curriculum.

Display areas for student work give all students the opportunity to have their class work put up on display on a fairly regular basis. Not all work should be displayed, of course, especially if it is not commensurate with the abilities of the student. But when students excell or show marked improvement, their work should be displayed as noteworthy of recognition. This gives students a sense of accomplishment and the feeling that people care about how well they do. These feelings build self-esteem and provide continuing motivation to do quality work.

The classroom environment should contain numerous *art prints, maps, charts*, graphic models, and other illustrative materials related to the curriculum. Some of these materials are contained on rollers or other devices that can be attached to or placed against a wall. Adhesive materials are available that hold such materials securely without damaging the walls.

Other occasional uses for wall space include displays of graphic models that show steps to be followed in skills being taught, words students need in directed writing and vocabulary lessons, inspirational slogans that can be used in class discussions, posting of class rules, reminders for helping substitute teachers, the class motto, special class goals for the year, a class timeline, and so forth.

Cabinet-Top Space

Cabinet-top space is available in many classrooms, often beneath windows where there is a good source of natural light. That makes cabinet tops useful for many kinds of science activities, especially those that involve growing plants. They are also good places for terrariums and aquariums, provided that strong direct sunlight does not strike the animals. Other kinds of science projects find useful placement on cabinet tops as well, including experiments, projects under way, and models of all types—human torsos, sense organs, skeletons, dinosaurs, atoms, molecules, and so forth.

Globes fit nicely on cabinet-tops and they are very important instructional devices. They show the shape of the earth as well as relationships between land masses and oceans, most direct routes between countries and cities, and are helpful in studies of history, geography, anthropology, and science.

Kits of various kinds are usefully placed on cabinet tops. Many classrooms contain commercial kits of high quality and utility to supplement instruction in reading, spelling, social studies, math, and science.

Shelf Space

Most classrooms have shelves built along walls or inside cabinets at various places in the classroom. Often teachers need additional shelf space, which can be provided easily by stacking together inexpensive shelving boards and concrete blocks.

Four kinds of materials are well suited to storage on shelves: textbooks, reference books, popular library, and special materials such as records, tapes, and games.

Textbooks form the central core of most areas of the school curriculum, especially in reading, mathematics, social studies, science, and language. When students have large desks, many teachers prefer to have them keep their textbooks in them along with pencils, paper, crayons, and erasers. When students sit at tables or have desks with small storage capacities, teachers keep textbooks shelved while not in use. When a group is to use its textbooks, they have directions for obtaining their books or class monitors who distribute the books quickly and quietly.

Reference books also play key roles in most school classrooms. Typically, reference books include dictionaries and encyclopedias. In addition, student interest and instructional effectiveness are enhanced by providing almanacs, world atlases, popular interest reference books such as the *Guiness Book of World Records*, Wallechinsky and Wallace's *Book of lists*, and a copy of Roget's *Thesaurus*. In addition to those books, many teachers provide such reference books as the *Golden Library*, which contain illustrated material on a vast array of topics of particular interest to students.

It is useful to keep a small *popular library* shelved within each classroom, if conditions permit, in addition to the textbooks and reference books previously mentioned. It includes easy-to-read books of high interest to students. Most are obtainable in paperback, can be purchased in goodwill stores at low prices, or donated from students' homes. It can also include magazines such as *National Geographic*, plus others written for school-age students. It may contain a daily newspaper. Many teachers like to include materials written by members of the class. These are laminated onto tagboard or bound into small books and illustrated by the authors. When these are read by other members of the class it stimulates interest in both writing and reading.

Most teachers have a collection of *special materials* that they use for motivating, instructing, and extending their students' experiences. These materials include such things as records, tapes, games, puzzles, puppets, toys, photograph collections, collections of shells and fossils, and numerous other items of this sort. Students are made responsible for the materials and are allowed to use them following directions provided by the teacher for their use, interpretation, and care.

Cupboard and Closet Space

Cupboards and closets in the classroom are useful places for keeping supplies of paper, pencils, worksheets, audiovisual equipment, p.e. equipment, brooms, cloths, and other cleaning materials.

Supplies include such things as writing paper, construction paper, pencils, scissors, glue, paints, crayons, rulers, and pins. Supplies are usually stored somewhere in the classroom, with additional quantities in a central area of the school, often in a place called the supply room or teachers' workroom.

Worksheets are used in great quantities in most classrooms. They must be prepared in advance, usually by the teacher or aide, and stored conveniently so that students may easily obtain and use them.

Audiovisual equipment is kept partly in classrooms and partly in a central area of the school from which it is checked out. Classrooms usually retain smaller audiovisual equipment, such as tape recorders and players, record players, large charts and maps, smaller models of various sorts, and sometimes a slide viewer. More expensive equipment, such as motion picture projectors, microprojectors, filmstrip projectors, large models, art collections, and so forth, are housed in a central location from which teachers check them out for short-term use.

Physical education equipment consists in most classrooms of balls and jumpropes that are used in various kinds of games played by students at recess. Many teachers keep these materials in a large plastic garbage can and they made sure that each piece of equipment has the room number marked clearly on it, to keep the materials from getting lost.

Each classroom needs its own cleaning equipment—broom, dustcloths, cleanser, paper towels, and soap. A small vacuum cleaner is useful, as well. These things let teacher and students take care of routine spills, dusting, and other cleaning that becomes necessary regularly, in excess of what one expects custodians to take care of. Student monitors can be assigned to such matters and use the cleaning equipment that is available.

Ambience

Ambience refers to the overall surroundings in the room, as regards esthetics, pleasantness, and general quality of the environment. Many teachers improve the ambience by obtaining quality *art objects* from the central media center and displaying them tastefully in the room. These objects—prints, carvings, sculptures, weavings, drawings, and art-quality photographs—can be displayed on a rotating basis. They not only add to the esthetics, but serve as focal points for excellent discussions on artists, technique, the creative process, and various media. They can also be used as motivational models in art lessons.

Some teachers find *background music* to be an effective and pleasing addition to the ambience, not for the entire day but for certain periods of independent work and relaxation. One study with college students showed that background music in the classroom could have strong positive effects in lowering pulse rate and blood pressure while increasing academic performance (Blanchard, 1979). Background music can be provided by AM and FM radios, tape players, and record players. The latter two give flexibility in choosing music to set moods, and records and tapes are stocked in large supply in most school media centers.

Many teachers like to use special *themes* that add to the ambience, built around professional athletics, popular music, children's literature, and favorite motion pictures such as *Star Wars*, so popular during the late 1970s. These themes include sayings, emblems, and colors. Students help in deciding on themes and selecting materials for display. Some teachers also like to keep an ongoing class mural or timeline that serves as a history of the work and progress of the class. Some like to have popcorn parties on a regular basis, once a week or so as reinforcement for good behavior and good work by the students.

Considering the foregoing six facets of the physical classroom one might imagine it as a hodgepodge overrun with material. Such should not be the case. In fact rather the opposite is preferable. In most subjects for most students and teachers the classroom should appear relatively lean and efficient, without clutter or unnecessary decoration. It should always be organized and clean before and after work times. Students should be given major responsibility in caring for their classroom with the intent not only of keeping the environment orderly, but also of establishing and building values pertaining to ecology, responsibility, and aesthetics. Routines discussed in detail in Chapter 5 should be established for matters that involve use of the physical environment, for moving about in it, and for taking care of it. All of these considerations help teachers and students alike to have an enjoyable, pleasing, efficient, and effective atmosphere within which to work, to have materials and activities that extend their learning, and to develop a sense of community involvement and responsibility that enhances learning for everyone.

CHECKPOINTS

In arranging the physical environment of the classroom, teachers consider the curriculum, the major goals and objectives, and their own preferred activities and ways of teaching. They give attention to six aspects of the classroom:

Floor Space
- seating
- work and activity areas
- special centers
- special effects area
- traffic patterns

Wall Space
- chalkboard
- bulletin boards

- display areas
- prints, maps, charts

Cabinet-top Space
- science projects
- globes and kits

Shelf Space
- textbooks
- reference books
- popular library
- special materials

Cupboard and Closet Space
- supplies
- worksheets
- audiovisual materials
- physical education equipment
- cleaning materials

Ambience
- art objects
- background music
- themes

BIBLIOGRAPHY

Axelrod, S., et al. "Comparison of Two Common Classroom Seating Arrangements." *Academic Therapy*, September 1979.

Berger, N. "When All Else Fails—Get Back to Basics." *Academic Therapy, May* 1980.

Blanchard, B. "The Effect of Music on Pulse Rate, Blood Pressure, and Final Exam Scores of University Students." *Journal of School Health*, October 1979.

Skylar, M. "Movement with a purpose." *Pointer*, Spring 1979.

3

Managing the Psychosocial Environment of the Classroom

MEANING OF PSYCHOSOCIAL ENVIRONMENT

The *psychosocial environment* refers to the attitudes, emotions, values, and relationships that comprise the tone of the classroom. While it is nontangible, it nevertheless exists, as teachers and students can attest. It has even more to do with learning, productive work, and self-concept than does the physical environment. When people are asked to recall their best educational experiences they invariably think of teachers or groups of students who enlivened, invigorated, and supported their educational efforts. Rarely do they think first of the classroom's educational materials, groupings, and physical arrangements.

The psychosocial environment favored by most authorities is one that is warm, supportive, and pleasant. A warm atmosphere is friendly and filled with good nature and acceptance, a supportive atmosphere is encouraging and helpful, with relatively low degrees of threat, and a pleasant atmosphere sets the classroom mood for an enjoyable time working together.

In contrast, a cold environment shows a lack of friendliness and support with an aloof teacher and students. Within a threatening environment students fear making errors, or are preoccupied with minding their p's and q's, obeying rules so that the teacher will not take reprisal against them, or other students harrass or embarrass them. An unpleasant environment shows a general lack of humor in the classroom, where sarcasm prevails and personal animosities and antagonisms are present throughout the day.

It is the teachers' responsibility to establish and maintain psychosocial environments characterized by warmth, support, and pleasantness. These conditions have noticeable positive effects on learning, establishing secure working conditions; helping foster positive relationships among students and between students and teacher; helping establish mutual support in which students can count on each other for help; and building positive self-concepts. It has been pointed out by many authorities that students seek to belong to the classroom as a group; they seek acceptance, or as Glasser (1969) puts it, "love" in the classroom.

Let us recognize that these positive psychosocial environments do not imply an absence of standards, expectations, and control. The best positive environment has structure, expectations, and consistent enforcement of those expectations. The teacher is responsible for establishing and maintaining these conditions, but the entire effort is overlaid with warmth, assurance of support, obvious care and concern, and continuing consideration and helpfulness.

Let us note, too, that productive work can be motivated through fear tactics, indeed oftentimes more easily than through warmth and support. Fear has been used effectively for centuries not only in

---

Cynthia, a second-grade teacher, describes how she attempts to set the tone in her classroom:

"I begin the year with a discussion about my expectations for the year. I tell the children that I consider them my 'school family.' I explain that just as in any family we might not always agree on everything, but that I will always care about them. I say that each and every one of them is very special and important to me, and that I want them to have the best possible school year. Because they are so important to me, I will not tolerate any cruelty or unkindness to each other. I expect them to be the best behaved and well-mannered class in the entire school, both in the classroom and on the playground. I tell them that good behavior is really just good manners, because it shows respect for others, whether children or adults. I also go over the golden rule, and I make a bulletin board on that theme. I refer to the golden rule as our class motto. That is the only rule we have in the class, and I discuss with them how it covers everything. If you don't want to be called names, then don't call other people names. If you want people to listen to you, then be sure to listen to others. And most important, if you want to have friends, then be a friend. The children seem to understand and accept all of this very well. They see it as a fair and sensible way to do things, and I think it helps them know they have a teacher who cares about them."

education but in child rearing, business enterprises, the military, and many other aspects of human life and enterprise. It is doubtful however that fear should ever be used as a motivator in today's classrooms, at least not fear of physical or psychological hurt. Work output can certainly be fostered through its use, but it is known to have deleterious side effects such as stress, frustration, and resentment, which may become manifest in negative attitudes toward school and hostility toward the teacher.

All things considered, it is safe to proceed on the premise that classrooms function best with a positive, structured psychosocial climate, one that reflects warmth, support, and pleasant circumstances with very low levels of fear. The fear that does exist should be limited to a fear of not living up to one's own potential, of letting other people down, of not acting in ways known to be in one's own interest. It should not be a fear of personal danger. It behooves teachers to arrange conditions within their classrooms that result in the positive conditions described. To begin taking these steps, teachers should consider three sets of ideas: (1) human relations skills, (2) responsibilities in fostering optimal psychosocial environments, and (3) steps for maintaining and enhancing the environment. These three groups of considerations are examined in the sections that follow.

HUMAN RELATIONS SKILLS

Human relations skills refer to how people interact, and they are aimed at furthering people's ability to get along together. Good human relations foster those conditions listed as desirable in the psychosocial environment of the classroom—support of others, positive individual and group progress, cooperative work, and the enjoyment that comes from associating with others. There are four facets of human relations skills that merit attention: (1) general skills of human relations, (2) human relations between teacher and students, (3) human relations skills with other professionals, and (4) human relations skills with parents of students.

General Skills of Human Relations

Certain skills in human relations apply to all people in almost all situations. Those general skills include friendliness, positive attitude, ability to listen, and ability to compliment genuinely.

Being *friendly* is a trait admired everywhere, yet many of us have difficulty in showing friendliness toward others, especially when we are in threatening situations or when we are with people whom we dislike. We can be friendly even with people who do not please us by smiling, speaking in a kindly way, calling them by name, asking how they are, asking about family and work, etc. When we do this we find that others tend to respond to us in the same way. Purposeful small talk is a useful asset at these times.

A *positive stance* is a skill of human relations that we should always keep foremost in mind. This means that we look generally on the bright side, or at least for positive solutions to problems that confront us. It means that we do not give ourselves over to complaining, backbiting, fault finding, or hurtful gossip. It reflects the view that while problems and difficulties beset us all, each one of us has some power to control, modify, or avoid conditions that cause us concern. Thus, people with a positive attitude focus on ways to surmount problems or on how to forestall and avoid them if they are insurmountable.

Ability to *listen* is a trait admired everywhere, but seldom well practiced. It seems to be a part of human nature that all of us would rather express our minds than listen to what others have to say. Yet, authorities in communication and personal relations unanimously extoll the virtues of listening carefully to others. Listening produces several desirable effects in establishing good human relations. First it shows that one is genuinely interested in the other person, interested enough to pay attention to what that person has to say. Second, it shows that the other person's opinions and observations are valued, as indicated by the listener's reflecting back, summarizing, or referring to ideas expressed by the speaker. Third, it tends greatly to enhance the quality of communication, by permitting a flow and exchange of ideas.

Ability to *compliment genuinely* is a trait that receives relatively little attention in human relations but is nonetheless a factor of considerable power. Many people are unable to compliment others in a genuine way. This is partly because we feel uncomfortable in doling out compliments, recalling those occasional persons who use compliments in obviously insincere and manipulative ways. And we ourselves have seldom taken the pains to learn how to compliment people on their appearance, speech, behavior, quality of thinking, and so forth, because we have not accustomed ourselves to doing so and also because in truth, receiving compliments makes most people feel ill at ease. Nevertheless, it is clear that most people like to receive compliments, even when they are unable to accept them gracefully, and they react positively toward those individuals who compliment them. Effective compliments should be genuine, and should be explicit. For example, when complimenting someone on a presentation, one might say something like, "I found your talk both entertaining and helpful, especially your suggestions on organizing evaluative conferences between principals and teachers."

While individuals may feel slightly uncomfortable at receiving compliments, this does not suggest that sincere compliments are to be avoided. They are helpful in establishing positive human relations, because we come to feel comfortable with those who compliment us, believing that they consider us worthy and exemplary, and we become more inclined to work and associate with them.

Human Relations with Students

What has been said about human relations in general applies to all situations, whether one is talking with students, other professionals, parents, acquaintances, or with total strangers. These general skills are being friendly, taking a positive attitude, doing effective listening and, when appropriate, providing compliments genuinely.

When working with students, there are additional special skills that teachers should employ: (1) giving regular attention, (2) using verbal and behavioral reinforcement, (3) showing continual willingness to help, and (4) modeling and practicing courtesy and good manners.

Giving regular attention is an important aspect of teaching. It is advocated that the teacher at the elementary level speak personally to each student, on matters not necessarily related to school work or behavior, as often as possible, certainly not less than once each day. Teachers tend to give most of their attention to two small groups of students: those who are hardworking, positive, productive members of the class and those who are behavior problems. This leaves a large segment of students who receive relatively little attention from the teacher, since they provide neither great joy nor great frustration. Some teachers make a point of speaking with each student as the group enters the room to begin the day. Others speak with each student as they take attendance. Still others speak with students individually during small-group instruction, as in reading. Many, when trying to improve the distribution of their personal attention, keep rosters of the class at hand and try to tally the number of times they have given special attention to each student during the day. This personal attention from the teacher contributes greatly to students' sense of belonging and the feeling that the teacher is interested and ready to help.

Verbal and behavioral reinforcers are those words teachers say and the acts they perform to show support, encouragement, and approval of student work and behavior. They increase student attention and work output, and are often referred to as rewards. While some teachers use tangible reinforcers such as stars, tokens, and candy, their use is not necessary in most classrooms. Verbal and behavioral reinforcement suffice. Examples of verbal reinforcers are: "Nice going!" "I can see how much work you have put into your composition." "You must have thought about this a great deal." "You are making improvements in your handwriting every day." Behavioral reinforcers include such things as nods, smiles, winks, thumbs-up, and other movements, expressions, and gestures that show approval, provide encouragement, and indicate support. Teachers, as with giving regular attention, should endeavor to provide reinforcement to all of the students in the class on an ongoing basis, as part of the daily procedures. Caution should be taken in the way praise is used. This point has been stressed by such authorities as Rudolf Dreikurs (1972), Thomas Gordon (1974), and Haim Ginott (1972), who point out that praise tends to inhibit communication, make the student feel uneasy, and even cause a student to lose his own sense of whether his performance is worthwhile. These things tend especially to occur when praise is given to the student's character, e.g. "You are a good boy." "You are very intelligent." When effort is praised, the results tend to be more productive, as in, "I can see that you worked hard. Thank you for that."

Continual willingness to help is a trait admired not only in teachers but in people everywhere and seems in relatively short supply. Yet we laud people as saintly when we see them give it unselfishly, as did Albert Schweitzer who gave up a promising career in music in favor of working as a medical missionary in Africa. Teachers rise in student's eyes, too, when they show this continual willingness to help. Students gravitate to them, work with them, admire them, and remember them in later years as highly significant. How commonly we hear testimonials such as, "Mr. Smith was strict, but he was kind and he always went all out to help us."

Modeling and practicing courtesy and manners is an extremely effective device in establishing and maintaining good relations in the classroom. Teachers should hold highest standards of courtesy and common decency in their classrooms, not allowing students to be cruel or sarcastic to each other or to say and do hurtful things to each other. Courtesy should be held up as an ideal, and it can be modeled and practiced by the teacher who speaks and acts in courteous ways at all times. This does not mean that the teacher cannot laugh and joke, but that the teacher show good manners and be polite. Teachers should insist that students for their part also use politeness and common courtesy. Students often will not understand fully what this means, though most will have a fairly good idea of the basics of courtesy and manners. For this reason it is sometimes desirable to conduct lessons on etiquette and manners to provide direct practice in such things as how to introduce one person to another, how to greet people, how to ask for something, accept it or refuse it in courteous ways, how to use the telephone in a courteous manner, how to address sales persons courteously, and how to deal with each other in the classroom, including ways to apologize sincerely and effectively.

Human Relations with Other Professionals

Much of every teacher's time goes to working with other professionals—fellow teachers, administrators, secretaries, librarians, nurses, and so on. It is important that each teacher be able to work effectively and productively with these people. To make this possible, teachers should be aware of the things they say and do. Again, the general traits of friendliness, positive outlook, attentive listening, and genuinely complimenting should be kept in mind. Added to those traits should be the following: (1) supporting others, (2) sharing the load, (3) participating effectively, (4) compromising democratically, and (5) leading and following when appropriate.

Supporting others refers to what each of us does to assist fellow professionals in what they have to do. This assistance may be very active, as is the case when we help them with their work and participate in finding solutions to their problems. Or it may be more passive, in the sense of psychological support where one accepts, approves, and encourages the work of others. This attitude is contrasted with the conditions that are, unfortunately, seen in overly large proportions among people in educational settings, situations where we tend to denigrate the work of others, make snide comments about their character, and belittle their efforts and accomplishments. These remarks are not made to their faces, of course, but all too often are made behind their backs.

It is interesting that this negative stance toward colleagues should be so prevalent. Research into what is said in faculty lounges, for example, indicates that over 90 percent of the comments teachers make are negative in nature. These comments refer to students, other teachers, parents, programs, administrators, and so forth, indicating that teachers do not, as a rule, support the efforts of their students, colleagues, and others involved in the educational enterprise.

The reason for this situation may be that teachers are becoming ever more frustrated by the plethora of demands heaped on them from all quarters. Frustrated and beleaguered people in all walks of life tend to lash out at others. But since this phenomenon occurs even in times of little stress, it is probable that another factor is also at work. That factor is the implicit belief, commonly held, that we make ourselves look better as we make others look worse. Such, of course, is not at all the case. As we tear down others, so do we tear down ourselves in the eyes of those with whom we work. People who gossip and malign can always count on attentive audiences, but those audiences do not sincerely appreciate the attitude of the person speaking, and they come to distrust that person as the question grows in their minds about what that person says about them when they are not present.

Sharing the load can be an important contribution. In any group endeavor such as running a classroom, a school, or a school district, there are many jobs to be done and many tasks to be completed. Typically, we see a few people carry most of the load, while a number of others do far less than their share. If we are to get along well with colleagues, and indeed that is essential to the quality of our professional effectiveness and our ultimate sense of well-being, then loads must be shared even when they are unpleasant. When committee work must be done, all should participate. When the school carnival arrives, all should participate in making it successful. When work must be done with parents, all should pitch in. In this way, each person takes care of his or her portion of the obligations that fall to all teachers.

Sharing the load in this manner builds positive human relations with other professionals; shirking one's fair share causes resentment and mistrust that are very hard to eradicate.

Participation in school activities is a condition requisite to building strong relations with fellow professionals. In faculty meetings, for example, it is common that some members of the staff participate in policy-making decisions while others prefer to remain silent and leave matters in the hands of others. Active participation is necessary, though one must guard against dominating discussions, which is often counterproductive.

Compromise democratically after everyone has had a chance to speak his or her mind. In any group effort involving professionals we can expect differences of opinion regarding purpose, procedure, work load, and so forth. Proponents of differing viewpoints should state their cases as clearly and cogently as possible, relying on reason as much as emotion. Hostility and intimidation should be avoided. After consideration of ideas, each of us has a part to play in making the decision. People on the "losing side" are obliged to accept the result as a logical outcome of the group process and to continue to work toward the good of everyone, though they may continue to push for the point of view they espouse. Those on the "winning side" are obliged to seek out the help and support of those who opposed them and endeavor to work with them in productive ways.

Both leading and following are roles to be filled in a democracy. If we can be effective in a leadership role we should seriously consider accepting it, and then bring our best efforts to bear in charting courses, obtaining resources, and rallying support for the assigned effort. At other times, other individuals are given the leadership role, while we are called on to follow and support. A leader should be respected and helped in a positive way. This does not necessarily mean following the leader's dictates uncritically, but it does mean helping, suggesting, and working together toward the goals that have been identified.

Human Relations with Parents of Students

Teachers have a great responsibility in communicating and working with the parents of the students they teach. Many teachers accept this responsibility willingly and capitalize on it, while others avoid it. There is good reason for teachers to take pains to communicate and work effectively with parents. Research has indicated that teachers who communicate well with parents are seen as outstanding teachers. There is little doubt that teachers who communicate effectively can count on greater than average parental support in matters of both discipline and curriculum.

Again, teachers should keep in mind the general foundations of human relations when working with parents—be friendly, be positive, listen attentively, and compliment genuinely. In addition, teachers should keep the following in mind: (1) communicate regularly, (2) communicate clearly, (3) emphasize the child's progress while playing down the child's shortcomings, (4) describe expectations clearly, (5) describe plans for future instruction for the child, and (6) be sure to conference productively.

With regard to *communicating regularly*, there is much to be said. Chapter 11 presents detailed discussions of the role and management of communication with parents. Let it suffice here to say that teachers should communicate regularly with parents by means of newsletters, telephone calls, and notes. These efforts show clear evidence of teacher interest in the welfare of the child, and they cause parents to think highly of teachers and be more willing to work with them in the educational plans formulated for the child.

Communicating clearly is highly desirable because we have so much jargon in educational language. Acronyms abound—AGP, SAT, IEP, TET, DISTAR, SWRL—as do labels with special meanings, such as *mastery learning, homogeneous grouping, individualized instruction, inquiry training,* and *loft teaching.* It is necessary when teachers communicate with parents they do so in ways that convey the messages clearly to ensure that parents understand what teachers are discussing with them.

It is important to *emphasize progress* being made by the child, while soft pedaling, but not whitewashing, any difficulties the child encounters. This is a matter of degree, not of exclusion or dishonesty. Ginott (1972) has pointed out that parents' overall views and thoughts about their child are fragile and delicate things, for parents identify with their children, see their failure as failure in themselves, and hold to the idea that their child may yet achieve the things in life that they have wanted but have been unable to attain. To dwell on a child's shortcomings is to probe sorely at the parents. It is preferable to proceed in the following way when discussing student achievements with parents: (1) mention something positive about the child personally; (2) show progress that has been made and is being made; (3) describe instructional and educational plans that will produce still further achievement; (4) mention difficulties that are interfering with the attainment of those future goals, but assure parents that you have a plan for overcoming them and that you need their support in working for the well-being of their child. This procedure causes parents to feel proud, encourage their child, and work cooperatively with the teacher. Parents do want their children to learn and behave well in school, and when they feel the teacher has special interest in their child they become more supportive and willing to help.

Describe expectations clearly and most parents will do more than their part to help. This point is crucial in the effective implementation of systems such as assertive discipline, described in Chapter 4, which is rather detailed and calls for some parental follow-up. Parents are usually eager to support such systems of discipline because they realize that they contribute toward better learning and better attitudes in their children. Yet they must be informed carefully of the details and expectations if they are to offer full support. The same applies to expectations about homework, academic programs, and anything else that plays a central role in the academic program. Parents then become more involved, more appreciative of the teacher's efforts, and much more predisposed to cooperation.

Future plans for the individual student should be described along with the expectations. If the child is encountering difficulty in math, for example, the teacher should have a definite plan in mind for dealing with those difficulties, and that plan should be communicated to the parents. If the child is excelling in science, there should be an instructional plan made to help the child move forward even faster. This might be some sort of individualized plan that would call on the student to work on special projects both in school and at home, a plan that again should be communicated to parents. In short, there should be a plan for future work established for each student, detailed briefly and clearly for parents through conferences, telephone calls, or written communication.

Conferencing productively is closely related to the points already mentioned, but refers specifically to the parent-teacher conferences that are scheduled on a regular basis in most schools. Teachers should have the student's folder in hand. The parent should sit at a table beside, not across from, the teacher, should be offered tea or coffee, and should be made to feel as much at ease as possible. The conference becomes productive to the extent that the teacher first communicates the child's progress, difficulties encountered, and plans for dealing with those difficulties, and second is able to enlist the parent's support and cooperation in carrying out the plans. Details of what should be covered in the conference are presented in Chapter 10.

RESPONSIBILITIES IN THE PSYCHOSOCIAL ENVIRONMENT

The psychosocial environment inside the classroom keys on warmth, openness, and helpfulness, and good organization is necessary to ensure that these occur routinely. Moving toward this kind of climate places responsibilities on both teacher and students.

Teacher Responsibilities

The teacher has the tasks of planning the nature of the psychosocial environment, of establishing the conditions that contribute to it, and of maintaining that environment. There are numerous responsibilities that the teacher must discharge in this function.

Friendliness is a key element in establishing supporting working ties with others. The teacher shows this through pleasant demeanor, by speaking with students, by remembering things about them such as their birthdays and family matters, by going out of their way to speak with them on the playground and when they see them outside school, and by making a point of talking with them about things other than school matters.

All students want their teachers to treat them with *fairness*, to treat all students the same and not some as favorites and others as outcasts, not discipline some while letting others get by with breaking rules. Students support fair expectations, and they support even-handed enforcement of those expectations. They do not like teachers whom they consider to be unfair or to show favoritism. Neither do they like teachers who establish regulations they consider to be unreasonably harsh.

Consistency is important to students because they like to know what to expect from teachers. They want teachers to be more or less the same, day in and day out. This does not mean that students do not like a surprise now and again, but they prefer knowing what to expect, and especially do they dislike unpleasant surprises. They are made uneasy and unsure of their roles in the classroom when teachers are warm one day and cold the next, or when they vacillate between being demanding and tolerant.

People relate well to teachers who show *enthusiasm*; they find it motivating, energizing, and contagious. They like to see teachers show eagerness and enjoyment for what they are doing. This should not be frenetic energy, which works against a stable, productive environment. But enthusiasm in moderation through all parts of the curriculum enhances student enjoyment and sense of progress in the classroom.

Humor is the trait most often identified by students when asked to name what they like in teachers. Students want a sense of enjoyment to prevail in the classroom, and humor contributes greatly to it. They like to laugh, they like jokes, and they like humorous situations. Unfortunately they like to laugh at other people, too, and therein lies a problem. Teachers should not allow students to laugh at the expense of other students or adults in the school setting. If a laugh is being enjoyed together by members of the class, fine. But when it is done in demeaning or cruel ways at the expense of someone who is made uncomfortable by the situation, that is not to be tolerated. Teachers deal with such situations by first pointing out to the class that they will have a good time in the work they do together. There will be laughter, and there will be humor, but there will be no silliness, horseplay, or laughing at others' expense.

A *nonthreatening climate* is conducive to learning. People can work productively under the harshest circumstances, even under real threat to life and limb. They persevere under emotional duress—in some cases work output is heightened in these situations. But as mentioned previously, the side effects of fearfulness, frustration, and great dislike for the situation, whether in the educational setting or elsewhere, override the benefits that might accrue from working in a threatening environment. Therefore, the classroom should be made as nonthreatening as possible. This means that errors are accepted as a part of the normal learning process, and students are not punished overtly or subtly when they occur. Students need to know they can make mistakes without fear of reprisal. They need to know they can make an occasional slip without drawing down upon their heads the harsh disapproval of the teacher. At the same time, this does not mean that anything goes in the classroom. Standards are maintained, and enforcement occurs regularly without fail, in an even-handed way.

Similarly, a *nonpunitive climate* ensures that physically or psychologically harmful punishment will not be leveled on students for what they do. At the same time, they can expect a benign sort of punishment, such as is referred to as *logical consequences*. Logical consequences are established in advance, and students know they will result when rules are broken. Students "choose" to endure unpleasant circumstances when they choose to misbehave. Those logical consequences might include staying after school, being banished to another classroom for a while, or having to call parents to describe what they did wrong. Logical consequences may also include restitution, meaning that students are required to make right what they have done wrong. If they damaged property, they clean, repair, or replace it. If they spoke in cruel, insulting ways to another, they apologize and do a favor for the other person, or atone for their acts in some other way.

This type of punishment does no harm to the recipient, yet it is effective. It is sufficiently unpleasant that students will not wish to experience it again, which helps them maintain a sense of responsibility for their own actions.

Nothing succeeds like *success*, they say, and this adage probably holds true for almost everyone almost all the time. Success is highly rewarding, motivating, and effective in building positive self-concepts. Of course there are times when people do not succeed in certain tasks, times when they make repeated efforts only to find the goals unattainable. These short-term "failures" need not work against one's overall sense of success, especially when teachers take pains to discuss the fact that in life we continually encounter obstacles that stop us short of the mark we hope to attain. Teachers should arrange instruction so that every student experiences success on a regular basis. This leads to a self-view of competence and works against what some psychologists consider the most devastating thing save utter catastrophe that can befall an individual—the conviction that one is an abject failure.

It is helpful to every student's self-image to experience personal *acknowledgement* from the teacher at least once every day. More frequent teacher acknowledgement is desirable, as well as acknowledgement from one's peers. It simply requires noting one's presence on a personal basis, speaking to an individual by name, and giving an occasional smile, nod, or wink. These acts which may appear inconsequential are powerful indeed in helping students feel they are worthwhile individuals, held in esteem by other people significant to them, and accepted within the group.

David, a fifth grade teacher, describes how he uses a class "constitution" to help establish a good climate:

"After discussing our goals and how we might achieve them, we write a class constitution. I explain in the simplest manner how our country is guided by a constitution written by our Founding Fathers. Our class constitution says what we will do and what some of our rights and responsibilities are. The following is a partial draft of a typical constitution (I help the class with the wording, of course".)

We, the students and teacher of Room 408, set forth the following principles and guidelines to uphold our rights as decent human beings. We duly promise to follow these principles earnestly and not to violate the guidelines so mentioned.

Article 1: Knowing that we ourselves would expect the same courtesy, we shall not interrupt others when they are speaking. In classroom discussions we will raise our hands and wait to be called on before speaking, out of courtesy to the speaker.

Article 2: Knowing that all people, great or small, share the right not to be physically abused by others, we shall keep our hands and feet to ourselves.

(and so on)

We, the undersigned, agree to uphold the above articles and their contents to create a fine and upstanding classroom in which to learn.

(all students and teacher sign)

Students want teachers' *understanding* when they have personal difficulties, and when they do not always reach the goals that have been established in the classroom. This understanding removes much of the threat and stress that beset students. Understanding is not to be confused with total acceptance of whatever the student says or does. We can be understanding of people and their backgrounds, of conditions in their lives, and of their personal difficulties and excitements. But we still do not accept and excuse behavior that is inappropriate, whether it involves matters of discipline, work output, or treatment of others, because that would not be acting in the student's best interest.

It is essential that the classroom climate reflect the assurance to students that abundant *help* is available to them, as much as they need, as often as they need it. This provides assurance, security, and support, and fosters positive attitudes toward teacher and school. At the same time, this help should be given in such a way as to prevent the development of a *helplessness syndrome*, a phenomenon through which students become unable to begin and sustain work without constant comment and direction from the teacher. This syndrome develops when students are unsure of themselves, afraid to try on their own, or simply desire the presence of the teacher. When this is the case the teacher's presence and help reinforces the attitude of helplessness on the part of the student, thus compounding the problem.

All students have as a prime goal in life the desire for *belonging*—to the class, to the school, to the family, to a group of friends. When that prime goal is not reached, problems occur. It is easy for the teacher to help students attain a greater sense of belonging, through acknowledgement, friendliness, help, support, and assigned responsibilities in the classroom. In addition, they have to see to it that students are not punished by other students, through sarcasm, cruelty, or rejection.

It is important that all students recognize and accept *responsibility* to foster and enhance not only their own educational program but that of other students as well. One way of providing this sense of responsibility is by giving students tasks, such as those mentioned in Chapters 2 and 5 that contribute to the ongoing wellbeing of the class and classroom. Another way is to develop and sustain through group discussions the idea that every student individually has a stake in making things good for all students collectively, and for the teacher as well, so that finally students see that they have responsibilities to themselves, to fellow students, to the teacher, to their friends, and to their parents. These responsibilities do not weigh them down, but give instead a sense of direction and purpose, with attendant motivation and understanding of the rationale for group endeavors in education and life in general.

As with belonging, every student, as well as every teacher, has a need to experience a sense of *importance*, to know that they are worthy of existence, that they have contributions to make, and that the class would be diminished without them. This feeling of importance grows as students experience success, assume responsibilities in the classroom, and receive acknowledgement from others.

The fourteen responsibilities previously described can be discharged more effectively and efficiently when done in an organized, systematic way. This *organization* provides a controlled procedure for giving attention to every student, for conducting classroom discussions about problems, for seeing to it that each student has responsibilities and successes. Checklists kept in the teacher's planbook are helpful. Teachers should not trust such important matters to chance, hoping they will occur through good intentions. Even the best-intentioned teachers cannot remember to provide all the conditions, on a regular basis, that are known to foster positive, productive environments. Organization ensures that all of these conditions that contribute so strongly to the psychosocial environment are given thorough attention in a consistent manner.

Student Responsibilities

It was noted that students have responsibilities to the psychosocial environment just as teachers do, and the discharge of those responsibilities is very powerful in building the classroom environment. Those responsibilities should be clarified in class discussions and should be reemphasized regularly. Students' main responsibilities include the following.

Learning is the main reason students are in school and they should come to recognize and accept that. They are there to learn the skills, attitudes, and values that will permit them to realize their individual potentials and to function to the fullest in society. They should be reminded that they are obliged to meet this responsibility, and that learning is not just the teacher's responsibility but is that of every student in the group.

All students should recognize and accept a responsibility for the good of the class, whether their *contribution* be through participating in discussions, helping with duties in the class, assisting other students and the teacher, or behaving in the best ways possible. They should discipline themselves to function not as passive floaters, but as active doers toward the common good, helping provide and sustain enjoyment, productivity, and security for all students and teacher alike.

Dependability is something students must understand they are responsible for: doing what they are supposed to do, doing it well, and doing it on time. They can help themselves do this through reminders, or if old enough can keep their own checklists of duties, deadlines, and so forth, and can periodically fill out evaluation forms for rating their dependability.

Students should understand that they are responsible for showing *consideration* at all times. Fellow students, teachers, principal, custodian, and all others in the school have difficulties, egos, and feelings that can be easily hurt. Students should speak often in practical terms of the golden rule, of treating others in ways they themselves would want to be treated. This means being friendly, helpful, and careful of making comments that could hurt other people's feelings.

Students should learn very early that they have responsibilities to *support* the efforts of their classmates and their teachers. Again they are not to be passive captives in the classroom, but active members with responsibilities to discharge. They should be helped to see that they build themselves as they support and help others, that among their classmates and people everywhere they will be held in higher regard and treated better when they show support for the efforts of others.

Relating positively means showing good manners, being polite, being courteous, and not saying and doing things that are hurtful to other people. Students should see that one of their main responsibilities in school is to attempt to get along well with others, a skill that can be learned and improved through effort. Toward this end they should discuss and put into practice the basics of good human relations discussed earlier in this chapter.

MAINTAINING THE PSYCHOSOCIAL ENVIRONMENT

Many responsibilities for students and teachers have been listed as contributing strongly to a quality psychosocial environment. Certain other efforts that merit attention as well are modeling, verbal reinforcement, classroom meetings, and discussions as necessary, both public and private.

Modeling refers to teaching through example and learning through imitation, and the majority of our learnings occur in this way. We see how others act, dress, and talk, and we imitate them.

Modeling is by far the most effective condition for promoting social learning, which is key to the psychosocial environment. Therefore, teachers and students alike should continually model the kind of behavior they know contributes to a positive and productive classroom climate.

Verbal reinforcement was mentioned earlier as a process of providing rewards for behavior we approve of in others. Teachers use it to encourage, guide, and support behavior that contributes to the good of the total class. Students should also be taught how to provide reinforcement, so that when others behave in ways they like they can encourage that behavior. In the same manner they can reinforce teacher behavior that they enjoy and appreciate. They can do this through what they say, including the expressions on their faces and the way they behave.

William Glasser (1969) has devised an especially effective means of helping students to deal responsibility with problems that concern them at school through a technique of *classroom meetings*, and it calls for students to identify concerns and work together to find positive solutions. No fault finding or blaming others is allowed. Students sit in a tight circle for these discussions, giving face-to-face positioning that encourages verbal exchange. The meetings can deal with social problems encountered at school, with academic problems, or with problems that students are encountering outside school. Regular use of classroom meetings can help students carry out the responsibilities they have for perpetuating healthy classroom environments.

In addition to regularly scheduled classroom meetings, impromptu *discussions* held when necessary help students shoulder responsibility for the classroom environment. These may be group discussions held, for example, to consider an incident such as a fight on the playground. Students explore their individual and group behavior against standards they hold for themselves. Some of these discussions may be private between teacher and student, exploring behaviors, difficulties, and solutions that pertain only to the student involved. Not every matter need be discussed, of course. Inconsequential ones should be dismissed out of hand. But when incidents occur that affect the quality of the climate that teacher and students have worked hard to maintain, the problem should be aired and positive plans made for correcting such matters in the future.

CHECKPOINTS

Teachers strive for an emotional tone in their classrooms characterized as warm, supportive, and pleasant, as opposed to cool, rejecting, and unpleasant. Achieving the desired tone calls attention to:

General human relations skills
- friendly
- positive
- listen
- compliment genuinely

Relations with students
- regular attention
- reinforcement
- helpfulness
- best example

Relations with other professionals
- support
- share the load
- participate
- compromise
- lead and follow

Relations with parents
- communicate regularly
- communicate clearly
- emphasize progress
- describe expectations
- describe future plans
- conference productively

Teacher responsibilities in the psychosocial environment
- all of the above
- enthusiasm
- humor
- acknowledgement
- understanding
- organization
- assigning responsibility

Student responsibilities in the psychosocial environment
- learn
- contribute
- dependability
- consideration for others
- support for others
- positive relations

Maintenance of the psychosocial environment
- modeling
- reinforcement
- classroom meetings
- open discussion

BIBLIOGRAPHY

Dreikurs, R., and Grey, L. *Discipline Without Tears*. New York: Hawthorne, 1972.

Ginott, H. *Teacher and Child*. New York: Macmillan, 1972.

Glasser, W. *Schools Without Failure*. New York: Harper & Row, 1969.

Gordon, T. *Teacher Effectiveness Training*. New York: Peter H. Wyden, 1974.

4

Managing Student Behavior

DISCIPLINE: TEACHERS' GREATEST CONCERN

Year after year, classroom discipline heads the list of teacher concerns. It produces more stress than any other aspect of teaching, builds high levels of anxiety and frustration that sometimes lead to a sense of helplessness, and consumes monumental amounts of time intended for teaching and learning. All in all it probably contributes more to teacher burnout than any other factor.

Teachers are not alone in their concern about discipline. Each year the Gallup Poll on opinions about problems in education shows that school discipline ranks at the top for school administrators, parents, school board members, the public at large, and even students themselves. Given this overwhelming concern, one would expect schools to mount massive campaigns for controlling and improving student behavior. And indeed, many school districts have developed new plans that include stricter regulations about drugs, truancy, physical aggression, and defiance of teachers, coupled with stiff penalties including suspension from school for violation of the rules. These new codes, however, while useful in controlling misbehavior that borders on the criminal, have relatively little effect on the minor misbehaviors with which teachers must contend minute by minute through the day. These minor misbehaviors are so numerous in typical classrooms that their collective mass seriously erodes teachers' time, strength, and energy.

Paradoxical indeed is the fact that while everyone wants school discipline, relatively little has been done to help teachers with it. A

48

main reason for the paradox is that until recently nobody has known what to do. Textbooks have made only brief reference to discipline, and that has been of little practical help. Teacher training programs seldom included more than cursory allusion to tricks of the discipline trade, such as be serious, don't smile, get your bluff in, don't be friends with students—time-tested advice to be sure, but advice that told nothing about what to do when students misbehaved. This lack of attention to discipline in the training of teachers, administrators, and counselors has led the public to conclude that discipline is a topic swept under the rug by teacher educators and ignored by teachers and administrators.

No educator, however, would or could sweep such a problem under the rug. We simply did not have, until recently, a systematic way of dealing efficiently and effectively with student misbehavior. Teachers were left to their own devices. Discipline, everyone assumed, was one of those things you either had or didn't have—you either controlled kids or you didn't. It was a matter of strength of personality. But as for organized systems that could be learned and implemented, there was none to be had. Such is no longer the case. We now have excellent methods for maintaining good classroom control that can be taught, learned, and put easily into effect.

SOME FACTS

Before examining procedures for organizing an effective system of classroom discipline, consider the kinds of behavior that teachers find so troublesome. Very close agreement exists among teachers as to student behaviors they find unacceptable and has obtained for decades with little change. What was identified by Wickman in 1928, and reconfirmed by Ritholz in 1959 remains true today: teachers are most concerned about three kinds of misbehavior—(1) behavior that affronts their sense of morality, (2) behavior that is defiant and aggressive, and (3) behavior that disrupts class work.

Teachers do on occasion have to contend with morally offensive behavior such as sexual innuendo, foul language, cheating, and the use of drugs, but such behavior is not the type that defeats teachers. More traumatic for teachers are acts of aggression, defiance, fighting, and very worrisome behavior that, fortunately, still accounts for no more than a minute fraction of all misbehavior. Most frequently, teachers must deal with boisterousness, disruptions, talking out, and unauthorized movement about the room.

It is this last group of behaviors that comprise a mass of "inconsequential behaviors" that in their totality so greatly reduce the time available for teaching and learning. True, teachers are made uncomfortable by immoral behavior, defiance, and aggression, but the classroom misbehavior that ultimately bogs them down is rarely more than talking and moving. Research by Jones (1979) has shown that in typical classrooms, over 80 percent of the disruptions were merely students talking to neighbors, and most of the remaining disruptions were students walking about the room without permission. Jones' findings show that while teachers fear crises, it is the innocuous talking and moving that accounts for over 90 percent of the time that is lost from teaching. Time lost from those two causes is substantial in well-managed classrooms, and it is enormous in those that are less well managed. Most of this lost time, according to Jones, can be reclaimed through the use of some very simple discipline techniques which will be presented later in this chapter.

It is obvious, then, that a good system of discipline must deal quickly and effectively with talking and unauthorized movement which rob massive amounts of time from teaching and learning. However, such a system must also equip teachers to deal effectively with those relatively rare crises that involve fighting, defiance, and open disrespect; behaviors that teachers fear and that cause great anxiety. As mentioned earlier, the traditional advice—mean business, be serious, be consistent, get your bluff in—do not furnish a means for dealing with problems. They may cut down on the number of problems that occur, but they do not, by any means, stop all of them.

SOME NOTABLE ATTEMPTS AT DISCIPLINE

Presently we will see how teachers can build effective systems of discipline, but before doing so it would be useful to review certain attempts that have been made in recent times to construct usable systems of discipline. You will see that each of these attempts, while not adequately efficient in itself, contains valuable elements that contribute to the organization of practical systems for classroom use.

The Kounin System

During the 1960s, Jacob Kounin conducted much research in public school classrooms, comparing practices of teachers who were successful in classroom control against those who were not. He reported the conclusions from that research in his book *Discipline and Group Management in Classrooms* (1970). He found that teachers who were good in classroom control tended to be adept at two things: (1) projecting an image of being in charge in the classroom, and (2) efficiently managing lessons and transitions between lessons.

With regard to *being in charge*, Kounin isolated two important traits which he called *withitness* and *overlapping*. Withitness is knowing what is going on in every part of the classroom at every moment, in a way that is evident to students—perhaps a new name for the proverbial "eyes in the back of the head." Awareness depends on being attentive to all students at all times, but Kounin found that withitness included more than simple awareness. He said that withitness included three additional aspects: identifying the proper student for correction, attending to the more serious misbehavior when two or more occur simultaneously, and timing the correction so that it occurs immediately after the misbehavior. When students see teachers do these things, they know the teacher is aware and in charge.

Overlapping, the second aspect of being in charge, refers to the ability to deal with two issues simultaneously. For example, suppose that while the teacher is working with a small group, misbehavior occurs elsewhere in the classroom. The teacher overlaps by correcting the misbehavior without leaving the small group or even so much as interrupting its activity.

With regard to *lesson management*, Kounin identified several skills that differentiate between teachers with effective and ineffective control. Those skills seem to fall into five groups that we might call focus, pace, momentum, transitions, and avoiding satiation. *Focus* refers to maintaining attention and accountability on the part of each member of the instructional group. *Attention* is obtained through motivation and directing students to do specific tasks of short duration. *Accountability* is obtained by spreading attention among all students, calling on them to respond, interpret, comment, discuss, and demonstrate. *Pace* refers to beginning and ending lessons on time, while covering the material as intended. A sense of pace can be developed by dividing lessons into segments and trying to reach the end of each segment by a certain time, until an inner sense of timing develops. *Momentum* refers to constant progression during the lesson, without slowdowns or frenetic bursts of activity. Slowdowns, or lulls, provide opportunity for misbehavior, while rushed activities can frustrate or be overly stimulating to students. *Transitions* from one activity to another, if not done efficiently, waste time and invite misbehavior. Smooth transitions occur when students know how to end an activity, put away materials, and get to work on the next activity without long explanations from the teacher. Established routines help ensure smooth transitions, which Kounin determined to be more important to good discipline than any other factor.

Finally, Kounin found that teachers with effective control make sure students do not become *satiated*, in other words, do not get bored with what they are doing. Satiation is avoided through good motivation, attention and accountability, interesting activities with challenge and variety, good pacing and momentum, and smooth transitions.

Kounin's ideas make excellent contributions to classroom discipline, through their attention to group and lesson management which greatly reduces misbehavior. However, they do not provide a thorough system of discipline, since no attention is given to effective ways of confronting, stopping, and correcting misbehavior that is sure to occur even in well-managed classrooms.

Neo-Skinnerian Systems

A great deal of experimental work has been done on controlling student behavior through use of the *principles of reinforcement* elaborated by B. F. Skinner (1968). Several systems have grown out of Skinner's work, and they are often referred to as systems of *behavior modification or contingency management*. They all operate on the same fundamental principle: if you reward people for what they do, they become more likely to do that same thing again. In other words, a person's behavior is shaped or modified by its consequences, hence the name behavior modification. What are referred to as rewards are technically called reinforcers, hence the name principles of reinforcement. The way in which the reinforcers are made contingent on behavior affects subsequent behavior, hence the term contingency management.

Practice has shown that effective discipline can be maintained through behavior modification, provided the class is fairly orderly and well intentioned, as is often the case with primary-grade children and high-achieving students at all grade levels. It is also the most effective system for controlling the behavior of certain types of handicapped students, especially the mentally retarded and autistic.

Behavior modification is organized and used in various ways, including rules-ignore-praise, rules-reinforce-punish, contracting, and token economies. The *rules-ignore-praise* system begins with a set of class rules. Students who violate the rules are ignored, while students who comply with them are praised. Teachers obtain control and attention by singling out students for praise when they show appropriate behavior.

The *rules-reinforce-punish* system also begins with rules, and students are reinforced as they comply with them. Violations, however, are punished rather than ignored. While punishment can have undesired side effects, it is sometimes necessary for stopping disruptive behavior.

Contracting refers to agreements between teacher and students given semiofficial status by writing them out and having both parties sign them. The contract calls for completion of specific tasks or amounts of work and spells out the reward that the student will earn on completion.

Token economies have been used successfully for classes that are hard to manage. They use tokens, discs, play money, and occasionally real money for rewards which students earn through appropriate behavior.

These systems of behavior modification have proven to be quite effective and they are widely used at all grade levels. Certain limitations, however, prevent their being the best overall systems of classroom discipline. Those limitations include the following: (1) social reinforcers such as praise are effective for primary-grade classrooms, but less effective for older students; (2) reinforcement shows students what they are doing right, but not what they are doing wrong; (3) reinforcement cannot adequately suppress misbehavior that disrupts learning; and (4) reinforcement is often ineffective with hostile, defiant, abusive students.

Nevertheless, the principle of shaping behavior through its consequences is sound. Most programs of discipline give heavy emphasis to reinforcement, as a key component for establishing desirable behavior.

The Glasser System

William Glasser (1969), a California psychiatrist who developed and popularized *reality therapy* as a means of dealing with personal problems, has made three unusually important contributions to educational practice. The first is in pointing out the highly detrimental effects of failure in school, and how to prevent the sense of failure in students. The second is his push for *classroom meetings* as vehicles for improving communication and solving problems important to the class. The third is his system for improving classroom discipline, which is reviewed in the following paragraphs.

Glasser says that behavior is a matter of choice, choice made right now and not rooted in the past. Students are rational beings; they choose to behave the way they behave. No one forces them, neither does their background, however deprived. Good choices result in good behavior, while bad choices result in bad behavior. It is the teacher's responsibility to help students make good choices, choices that bring success and sense of belonging, rather than failure and alienation.

Glasser says that teachers can fulfill their responsibility by doing the following things:

1. Continually stress student responsibility.
2. Establish rules that lead to student success.
3. Accept no excuses for bad behavior. Instead, focus on what the student must do right now.
4. When students misbehave, direct them to make value judgments about their behavior. Help them identify suitable alternatives.
5. Make sure that reasonable consequences, whether positive or negative, follow the behaviors that students choose.
6. Don't use punishment for negative consequences, as it lifts responsibility from students. Instead use "restitution"—having the student make right what was done wrong. This maintains responsibility and directs students toward good choices.

Glasser's system attempts to produce lasting changes in students' behavior, through the process of calling on them to make value judgments about their behavior. This process begins at the time a student misbehaves. Glasser would have the teacher call the student's name in a matter-of-fact, nonthreatening way, ask, "What are you doing?" and insist that the student answer. Suppose a student is wandering around the room, and when called on so admits. The teacher should then ask, "Is that helping you or the class?" The student will likely say no, and the teacher then asks, "What could you do that would help?" In this case the answer will be clear, but in cases where it is not, the teacher should be ready to suggest at least one suitable alternative. The student may then choose, but if misbehavior is chosen, negative consequences must be invoked. Later, the teacher talks again with the student to formulate a plan that will lead toward responsible self-direction.

Through the entire procedure the teacher stresses a positive approach, devises a simple plan for improved behavior, places responsibility on the student, accepts no excuses for improper behavior, and shows continual willingness to help. It should be re-emphasized that reasonable consequences must follow students misbehavior, in order that students come to see misbehavior as self-defeating.

There is much in Glasser's system that teachers find attractive—student responsibility, behavior as choice, reasonable consequences tied to behaviors, and focus on student value commitment to better behavior. As a total system of discipline, however, it has two limitations: (1) the in-class confrontation, which includes directing students to make value judgments and select better behavior, is time consuming and fragments lessons; and (2) if at a given time more than one student is misbehaving, as is often the case, one student is confronted while the other goes free—in other words, it is nearly impossible to deal with more than one student at a time.

Glasser's system makes strong contributions by viewing behavior as choice, causing students to make value judgments that lead, hopefully, to lasting improvement in behavior.

Dreikurs' System

Rudolf Dreikurs, an Austrian psychiatrist who immigrated to the United States in 1937 and later served as director of the Alfred Adler Institute in Chicago, made two important contributions to the practice of school discipline. The first is his description of genuine goals and mistaken goals that motivate student behavior, and the second is his formula for helping students develop self-control and responsible behavior. He disseminated his views through training programs and books, including the widely read *Maintaining Sanity in the Classroom* (1971) and *Discipline without Tears* (1972).

Dreikurs did not view discipline as a procedure for stifling unwanted behavior, but rather as an ongoing process in which students learned to impose limits on themselves, to be responsible for their own actions, to respect themselves and others, and to take the responsibility for influencing others to behave well. This process would never use physical punishment. Punishment, Dreikurs said, runs counter to the notion of helping students impose limits on themselves, because it is a force applied from outside. It teaches what not to do, but fails to teach what to do.

Instead of relying on harsh punishment, Dreikurs would have teachers proceed in a democratic way, neither permissive nor autocratic, that allows students to have a say in developing standards of conduct and in determining how those standards shall be maintained. Such a democratic classroom requires order, limits, firmness, kindness, leadership from the teacher, student involvement in establishing and maintaining rules, freedom to explore and discover, and the opportunity for students to choose acceptable behavior, together with the responsibilities and consequences associated with it.

Like Glasser, Dreikurs contends that students choose to behave the way they do. They all want the same thing—to feel that they belong to the group, to the classroom, to the school. They desperately want personal recognition, and if necessary they will use misbehavior to get it. Misbehavior occurs when students aim at mistaken goals. Their genuine goal is a sense of acceptance and recognition, but when they feel they are not reaching this goal, they turn, in order, to four mistaken goals—attention getting, power, revenge, and withdrawal.

Dreikurs makes four important suggestions for dealing with student misbehavior. First, teachers should establish a democratic classroom that allows students full opportunity to reach the genuine goal of acceptance. Such a classroom prevents most discipline problems, but of course does not prevent all of them. Second, when misbehavior does occur, teachers should identify the mistaken goal and confront the student with it: "You would like me to pay attention to you, wouldn't you?" Third, teachers must make sure that reasonable consequences always follow student misbehavior. Those consequences should never be physical punishment, but should be something the student finds highly undesirable, such as staying after school to clean the playground or to finish an assignment that should have been completed in class. And fourth, teachers must always remain helpful and encourage student efforts toward improvement.

Dreikurs' work has been widely hailed as contributing, over the long run, to student self-control and responsible behavior. Teachers find it lacking as a total system of discipline, however, because it does not furnish effective methods for stopping misbehavior. Moreover, it seems doubtful that all misbehavior, or even a major part of it, can be eliminated by trying to help students receive attention and a sense of belonging. Nevertheless, through its attention to mistaken goals and responsible student behavior, Dreikurs' democratic discipline can make important contributions to any teacher's personal system of discipline.

Ginott's System

Haim Ginott, who during his career served as professor of psychology at New York University and a professor of psychotherapy at Adelphi University, was one of the first people to popularize the teachings of psychology for the general public. For some time he was resident psychologist on television's *Today Show*, and he wrote a syndicated newspaper column, entitled "Between Us," that dealt with interpersonal communication. The main thrust of his work was on establishing warm, nurturing relationships through quality communication. He died in 1973, but his ideas still enjoy great popularity, and his three popular books—*Between Parent and Child* (1965), *Between Parent and Teenager* (1968), and *Teacher and Child* (1972)—are still widely sold.

Like Dreikurs, Ginott saw discipline as a developmental process to be accomplished over the long term, not as an immediate remedy for bad behavior. He referred to discipline as a "series of little victories" that win over the student and help the student behave acceptably and responsibly. Also like Dreikurs, he cautioned against threats and punishment, pointing out that they cause ill feelings, disrespect, rebellion, and subversion of the teacher's efforts.

Ginott's system of discipline is based entirely on communication, and it can be understood by examining his descriptions of "teachers at their worst" and "teachers at their best." Teachers at their worst, said Ginott, are caustic and sarcastic. They attack students' character, deny their feelings, label them, demand cooperation, use praise to manipulate, and present poor models of humane behavior. Such teachers may on the surface control students by suppressing behavior, but they never develop good working relationships and they never reach the true goal of discipline, which is to help students behave responsibly on their own.

Teachers at their best operate quite differently. They invite cooperation, accept and acknowledge feelings, avoid labeling, correct by directing, and always send "sane messages," messages that address the situation rather than the student's character. In so doing, they present strong models of humane behavior that students tend to imitate.

Several of Ginott's ideas are unique and they merit close attention, especially his concepts of sane messages, labeling, correcting, expressing feelings, and modeling desired behavior. *Sane messages*, according to Ginott, address the situation rather than the character of the student. Suppose, for example, a student is talking when everyone is supposed to be quiet. Rather than saying, "Samuel, you are being inconsiderate again," the teacher should say, "No talking during quiet time." Or suppose two students are fighting. Instead of reprimanding them, the teacher says firmly, "No fighting. Fighting is against the rules." Labeling, asserted Ginott, is disabling. Students who are labeled tend to live up to the label, because it indicates how the teacher sees them and how they, in turn, see themselves. When students must be *corrected*, the best way is to *direct* them, that is, tell them or show them what it is they are supposed to do. Students and teacher alike need to be able to *express feelings*, but both should do so in controlled, productive ways, freely acknowledging their feelings. The teacher can say, "I understand that it makes you angry, but everyone is entitled to a turn." When the teacher has strong feelings, such as anger, joy, or despair, it is good to express those feelings to the class, but in a way that does not attack or belittle students. For example, the teacher might say in a controlled but forceful voice, "I am angry about what happened here. It hurts me to think that cruelty could raise its ugly head in our classroom." Finally, Ginott stresses that teachers must always *model* clearly the behaviors they want students to acquire, such as gentility, consideration, understanding, and helpfulness. This shows that teachers are humane and self-disciplined, traits of higher importance in effective class control.

Ginott makes strong contributions to discipline by providing clear suggestions about communicating with students in ways that are helpful, positive, and constructive and win students over to the teacher. It does not constitute an adequate total system of discipline, however, because it does not provide a means of dealing with highly disruptive, defiant, disrespectful, or aggressive students. It relies to a large extent on the gentle persuasion of the teacher, which to be sure is vital in the long run but may not have sufficient power to stop serious misbehavior on the spot.

POWER SYSTEMS OF DISCIPLINE

The systems of discipline previously described have many elements to commend them, elements of proven effectiveness in the classroom. But each also suffers from one or more major limitations, the most common of which are impotence in suppressing or correcting serious misbehavior at the moment of its occurrence, and loss of teaching-learning time while the teacher deals with offending students. Recently, there have emerged two systems of discipline that overcome both these limitations. They are Frederick Jones's Classroom Management Training Program (CMTP) (1979) and Lee Canter's *Assertive Discipline* (1976). These systems give teachers power to deal effectively and quickly with misbehavior, and for that reason are referred to here as *power systems*.

Jones's System

Frederick Jones, a consulting psychologist from Santa Cruz, California, spent more than ten years researching major problems that teachers face in the classroom, and developing training programs to help teachers deal with those problems. His work is not limited to discipline; it concerns other matters as well, such as classroom organization and management, group discussion, and small-group instruction. Discipline, however, receives greatest emphasis.

Jones's research into student misbehavior yielded some interesting facts. Most teachers fear crisis events in discipline, such as fighting and open challenge to teacher authority. Yet such crises, Jones found, occur rarely, even in hard to manage classrooms. Most misbehavior, accounting for 80 percent of the total, is nothing more than students talking to their neighbors. Of the remaining 20 percent, almost all is comprised of students walking about the room without permission. These two categories of misbehavior often rob teachers of 50 percent or more of their instructional time, most of which can be reclaimed, Jones found, through correct use of four strategies: limit setting, good body language, incentive systems, and giving help efficiently.

Limit setting is a procedure of formulating class rules and establishing the boundaries that separate acceptable behavior from unacceptable. Rules, says Jones, should not be a list of dos and don'ts. Rather, they should describe appropriate work behavior, what to do if materials or supplies are needed, what to do when stuck, and what to do when finished with assigned work.

The boundaries for those rules are established and maintained most effectively through use of *body language*, a set of physical mannerisms that receives paramount attention in Jones's system. Effective discipline, he says, is 90 percent effective body language, the most powerful aspects of which are physical proximity to students, body position, facial expression, tone of voice, and eye contact.

Incentive systems, a second strategy, are used to motivate students to stay on task and complete their work. They use, as rewards for completing assigned work, *preferred activities* such as math drill, competition games, free reading, and free time. Jones describes two techniques that increase the effectiveness of incentive systems—the *stopwatch* and *omission training*. With the first, teachers use a large stopwatch that can be clicked on and off. When misbehavior occcurs, the teacher simply calls the student's name, clicks on the watch, and waits. When the misbehavior stops, the watch is stopped and the lesson resumes. Elapsed time is deducted from the preferred activity to come later. Peer pressure immediately stops misbehavior in most cases.

When misbehavior continues despite the use of the stopwatch, teachers can turn to omission training. With this technique, chronically misbehaving students can earn, for the entire class, extra minutes of preferred activity, simply by not misbehaving for an established length of time. Again, peer reward comes into play, and the formerly misbehaving student gains status through earning preferred activity for the entire class.

Giving help efficiently is a strategy that resulted from another surprise finding in Jones's research. His observations showed that on the average teachers spend four minutes in helping each individual student who is stuck during assigned seat work. Spending so much time with each individual is detrimental in two ways: first, it greatly reduces the number of students who can be contacted during the period, and second, it fosters a syndrome of helplessness on the part of some students, who do not work unless the teacher is standing over them telling them what to do.

Jones shows teachers how to give help efficiently, so that instead of averaging four minutes, they spend an average of no more than twenty seconds per student. This rapid help is possible if it incorporates four elements: (1) A graphic model, if possible, that describes the steps and procedures in the seatwork. Examples might include a model of the steps in doing long division or the steps in writing a haiku. The model is displayed in the room where all can see. (2) The teacher moves to the student needing help and comments positively on anything that has been done correctly. (3) The teacher tells the student exactly what needs to be done next, referring to the graphic model if possible. (4) The teacher leaves immediately, without waiting to watch what the student does next. Students who act helpless get little attention from the teacher, while those who work as expected receive attention and compliments.

The three strategies—limit setting, incentive systems, and giving help efficiently—eliminate the vast majority of behavior problems. For those students who do not respond to the strategies, a back-up system is required, in which the student is isolated or removed from the room. The building administrator provides immediate assistance, if needed.

In summary, Jones's system of discipline calls on teachers to do the following:

1. Establish work-related rules for the class.
2. Establish a back-up system with fellow teachers and building administrator.
3. Arrange room seating to allow the teacher to circulate freely and reach any student with the fewest possible steps.
4. Use body language to establish and maintain behavior limits.

5. Give help efficiently.
6. Use incentive systems.
7. Use positive reinforcement liberally with students who are behaving or working as they should.

Jones's system provides sound techniques for controlling behavior in humane ways, and is yet flexible enough to bend to the teachers' personality and style. On the negative side, its reliance on force of personality projected through body language may prove troublesome for the mild mannered. Teachers who have chronically misbehaving students may find the omissions tactic too cumbersome to apply, and many teachers who otherwise favor the system may find it lacking in nurturance, communication, and warm personal relations. These concerns are relatively minor, however, and should not preclude most teachers' giving serious consideration to Jones's CMTP as a basic system for classroom discipline.

Canter's System

Lee Canter, by training a specialist in child guidance, has put together an approach to school discipline called assertive discipline, a system that during the past few years has taken the country by storm. He is now director of Canter and Associates, based in Seal Beach, California, and he devotes full time to presenting training programs in assertive discipline to school districts throughout the United States.

Assertive discipline has been enthusiastically received because (1) it has a record of proven effectiveness, (2) it provides a rationale for discipline, (3) it provides a system for dealing effectively with misbehavior, whether minor or serious, at the time it occurs, (4) it transfers responsibility for behavior from the teacher onto the student, and (5) it can be quickly learned and easily implemented. Let us examine each of these benefits provided by Canter's system.

Effectiveness. When it comes to discipline, teachers need something that works, that is, a technique that suppresses and redirects misbehavior quickly, without emotional confrontation, while maintaining positive working relationships between teacher and students. Assertive discipline does those things well, according to research evidence from Canter and testimonials from a broad sample of satisfied teachers and administrators. Canter reports that his system reduces misbehavior by 80 to 90 percent in most classrooms and schools. Parents also support the system, and students react to it positively.

Rationale for Discipline.   Canter stresses these points, which form the rationale for assertive discipline, and for that matter for discipline in general:

1. Firm control is not inhumane. Correctly maintained, it is humane and liberating, allowing students optimal opportunity to learn.
2. Teachers have basic teaching rights to which they are absolutely entitled: to teach, to maintain effective learning environments, to expect appropriate behavior from students, and to receive help from administrators and parents.
3. Students have basic classroom rights, to which they are entitled: to learn in an orderly environment, to receive help in limiting their self-defeating behavior, and to receive positive support for their efforts to learn and behave properly.
4. With these facts and rights in mind, teachers should determine that they will let no misbehavior interfere with their right to teach and their students' right to learn.

System for Dealing Immediately with Misbehavior.   Assertive discipline entails the consistent use of the following elements:

1. Clear identification of expectations—class rules.
2. Enforcing limits on student behavior, without confrontation. Canter suggests the following:
   a. Recognize and operate on the basis that all students can behave properly.
   b. Use assertive response styles with students—responses that are short and straight-forward, rather than hostile, verbose, and wishy-washy.
   c. Establish consequences for misbehavior, and show consistently—every time—that a student who chooses to misbehave also chooses the consequences tied to it. Canter suggests the following: First offense of the day —name on the board; second offense—check by name, which means stay in fifteen minutes after school; third offense—a second check and thirty minutes after school; fourth offense—another check, thirty minutes after school, and go to the principal's office; fifth offense—another check and all of the foregoing plus student calls parents on the telephone; sixth offense— student is taken home or parent is told to come get student at once.

    d. Implement a system of positive consequences that accrue to individuals and groups for good behavior.

Responsibility Transferred to Student. Once the rules and consequences are established, students come to see that they choose those consequences, positive or negative, as part of the behavior they choose. The responsibility for control becomes theirs, and the teacher simply invokes the established consequences, impartially and consistently.

Easily Learned and Implemented. Assertive discipline is a straightforward approach, requiring little special training beyond determination to have discipline, establishing rules and consequences, informing students, parents and administrators fully, practicing assertive response styles, and consistently following through. Teachers can acquire the basic strategy in a three-hour training session, and then plan and implement the system within a few days' time.

    Canter's assertive discipline is a total system with proven effectiveness that can be used at all grade levels. While it is popular, not all teachers are comfortable with it. Some feel it is too cold, too structured, too businesslike, and does not give attention to the inner difficulties that affect each student. Others, especially primary teachers, consider it too cumbersome, preferring to use teacher authority combined with positive reinforcement. Still others feel that it places too much responsibility on young personalities, without regard for counseling and developing rapport between teacher and students. Despite these misgivings, no other system of discipline equals assertive discipline as an effective and humane way of dealing with classroom misbehavior.

BUILDING A PERSONAL SYSTEM OF DISCIPLINE

The most important tool any teacher can have is an effective system of discipline, one that stops misbehavior, corrects it, fosters positive relationships, and builds self-discipline within each student. All the systems of discipline described in this chapter were formulated in an attempt to help classrooms enjoy behavior conducive to good learning and positive relationships. None of the systems, however, hits the mark perfectly for all teachers and all students all of the time. What remains, then, is for teachers to construct their own personal systems of discipline, so as to complement their personalities and philosophies while attending, at the same time, to realities of their students, schools, curricula, and communities.

There is no established procedure for teachers to use in composing their personal systems of discipline. However, for discipline to be suitably effective it should contain measures that accomplish the following:

1. Prevention to reduce the amount of misbehavior.
2. Immediate suppression of misbehavior, before it escalates and spreads.
3. Correction of misbehavior, by rechanneling it in positive, productive directions.
4. Student responsibility for their own behavior.
5. Positive relationships between teacher and students, and among students.

Teachers can secure these five conditions by first adopting one of the power systems described—either Jones's CMTP or Canter's assertive discipline—and then supplementing it with favored elements from other systems. Both power systems contain provision for success and positive reinforcement. Jones's CMTP may be the more attractive to primary-grade teachers and teachers of classes that are easy to manage, while Canter's assertive discipline may be the more attractive to teachers of older students or of classes that are harder to manage. Of course, each system has excellent features that can be incorporated into the other.

After deciding on a basic power system, teachers should select elements from other systems that they believe would increase their effectiveness. Such elements might include principles of effective lesson management as described by Kounin, the helpful styles of communication advocated by Ginott, the positive problem solving and good behavior choices advocated by Glasser, and the personal counseling efforts which Dreikurs believes finally lead to student self-discipline.

As part of the basic system and enhancing elements, teachers must decide on class rules, consequences tied to those rules, a support system comprised of administrator and one or more fellow teachers, a communication system for informing students and parents, and a means of ensuring that all students receive attention, success, and a genuine sense of belonging.

CHECKPOINTS

Discipline continues to be the greatest single problem faced by teachers, but in recent years some powerful systems have been developed that greatly help teachers control their classes.

The Kounin system
  • withitness
  • effective lesson management

Neo-Skinnerian systems
  • behavior modification
  • rules-ignore-praise
  • rules-reinforce-punish
  • contracting
  • token economies

The Glasser system
  • behavior is a matter of choice
  • accept no excuses for bad behavior
  • stress student responsibility
  • have students make value judgements

Dreikurs' system
  • use democratic approaches
  • all students want recognition
  • confront mistaken goals

Ginott's system
  • discipline a series of little victories
  • sane messages
  • correcting is directing

Jones's system
  • body language
  • giving help efficiently
  • incentive systems
  • positive reinforcement

Canter's system
  • teacher rights and student rights
  • allow no disruptions to stop teaching or learning
  • assertive responses
  • clear limit setting
  • consistent enforcement

Teachers can build their own personal system of discipline by combining elements of these systems in keeping with their personal philosophies and the realities of the situations in which they work.

BIBLIOGRAPHY

Canter, L. *Assertive Discipline: A Take-Charge Approach for Today's Educator.* Seal Beach, Calif.: Canter and Assoc., 1976.

Dreikurs, R., and Grey, L. *Discipline without Tears*. New York: Hawthorne, 1972.

Dreikurs, R., et al., *Maintaining Sanity in the Classroom* (2nd ed.). New York: Harper & Row, 1982.

Ginott, H. *Between Parent and Child*. New York: Avon Books, 1965.

————. *Between Parent and Teenager*. New York: Macmillan, 1969.

————. *Teacher and Child*. New York: Macmillan, 1972.

Glasser, W. *Schools Without Failure*. New York: Harper & Row, 1969.

Jones, F. "The Gentle Art of Classroom Discipline." *National Elementary Principal*, June 1979.

Kounin, J. *Discipline and Group Management in Classrooms*. New York: Holt, Rinehart and Winston, 1970.

Ritholz, S. *Children's Behavior*. New York: Bookman Assoc., 1959.

Skinner, B. F. *The Technology of Teaching*. New York: Appleton-Century-Crofts, 1968.

5

Managing Daily Classroom Routines

Smooth management of daily classroom routines is central to effective instruction, yet it is a matter usually taken for granted and thus it tends to receive little attention. It contributes as much as any other factor to efficiency, class control, rapid learning, and sense of security in the classroom. It allows students to know what they are supposed to do and when, cuts down on wasted time, and reduces the confusion that detracts so much from teaching and learning. For these important reasons, teachers should spend with students the time necessary for establishing routines to the point that they become almost like habits.

The management of routines requires attention to seven separate matters: (1) opening activities, (2) monitors and their duties, (3) movement management, (4) materials management, (5) providing help efficiently, (6) managing completed work, and (7) managing typical distractions. Details involved in each of these seven areas are discussed in the remainder of this chapter.

OPENING ACTIVITIES

Opening activities are intended to begin the day on a positive note and establish a productive student mind set. Effective teachers use a variety of approaches to begin the class day, there being no single approach established as best. Some like to begin the day with an attendance check, with students sitting quietly. Some call the roll and speak individually to each student, perhaps greeting them personally or saying a word to them in a foreign language, so that each

Liz, a first-year teacher, describes what the beginning of the day was like before she learned how to get the students directly into their routine:

"It is 7:55 in the morning. I have just received and am reading the revised agenda for the school day. There will be a fire drill at 10:15, an assembly for only the best citizens at 10:45, and the nurse will be by to check for lice sometime during the day. In the middle of my desk, amidst the numerous papers, utensils, and cracker-jack toys, an overdue slip from last week's film glares at me. I heave a sigh and look for my attendance sheet. Somewhere a bell sounds, and suddenly thirty-one bright and shining faces, complete with working voices, barge through the door.

'Good morning, teacher!'

'May I open the windows?'

'Guy,' one moans, 'you always get to do that!'

'Teacher! Here is my permission slip for our field trip!'

I stand there in a daze as 25 pairs of hands try to bless me with book reports, late homework assignments, and wilted flowers they picked from neighbors' yards on the way to school."

student is recognized on a personal basis. Others have a seating arrangement that allows them to check the empty seats to see who is absent. Still others establish a system by which students check themselves in upon arrival. One example is to have clothespins with student's names on them. As students enter the room they take their clothespin from where it is clipped by the door and attach it to a chart that shows which group they are in. To take attendance the teacher notes the clothespins that have not been taken. This procedure is helpful when students move directly to work areas in the morning without going first to their seats, or when they begin the day with interesting matters such as reading, journal writing, solving vocabulary puzzles, and so forth, to establish a positive inclination toward work for the remainder of the day.

Sharing is a preferred way to begin the day. Here, selected students are allowed to take a few minutes to tell other members of the class about interesting events, such as a weekend trip or a new baby in the family, or to share interesting objects such as a new book or an autographed picture of a celebrity. It is not a good idea to allow students to share small toys, since such objects become seductive and take attention away from school work later. Neither should students be allowed to share new items of clothing they have received, since that may produce situations potentially embarrassing to the students involved and to their parents. To secure attention and involvement, listening students are encouraged to ask one or two questions of the person who is sharing. The amount of sharing is limited, so that it does not cut heavily into instructional time.

Uninterrupted sustained silent reading (USSR) is another favorite way to begin the day. Students upon entering the room know they are not to talk but are instead to take out a book they have been reading. Then everyone in the class, including the teacher, reads silently without interruption for a given amount of time, usually around twenty minutes.

Journal writing, like USSR, provides a means of beginning the day with enjoyable, productive work. Students keep journals in which they make daily entries for the first several minutes of each day. Opinions differ as to whether this material should be read, corrected, or responded to by the teacher. Some think it should be, as a means of helping students improve writing skills, as well as motivating them and showing that teachers consider the activity important. Others think they should not because they want the writing to be free, spontaneous, uninhibited and, when necessary, private, and they fear that their reading the entries would work against those ends. As a compromise position, some teachers make provisions for students to make private entries, which they clearly mark as private. The teacher is duty and honor bound not to read those passages, but is free to read and react to passages not marked. The journal-writing approach is intended not only to start the day on a positive productive note, but to provide extensive, meaningful practice while building positive attitudes toward writing.

Choosing is a procedure for beginning the day favored by many teachers in both primary and intermediate grades. It allows students when they enter the room to move to areas that contain attractive materials or activities. Different individuals might go to art centers to work with clay, paint, or weaving, or to the reading center to read books, magazines, or newspapers of their choice. Others might go to special work centers that contain carpentry tools and materials, old gasoline engines and tools, or at primary levels, places to play with toys, build with blocks, string beads, and so forth.

Certain rules must be followed during choosing. One is that boisterous, disruptive behavior is not allowed. Another is that students, having chosen their activity, must be responsible for their own conduct and for taking care of the materials with which they are working. Students who break these rules are not allowed to participate in choosing the next day, but must sit at their desks and do other work instead.

Class work nuggets effectively begin the day with short activities out of the normal curriculum. Many teachers like to use "five-a-

Carolyn, who teachers a three-four combination, describes her way of beginning the day:

"The preparation in the morning for an orderly and meaningful prime time for learning begins long before the children arrive, but when they enter the room they follow a routiine that leads directly to learning. After our pledge and song, the children compose a friendly letter, following a model I have put on the board. These letters have to do with what they are learning at school, and the children use their best grammar, spelling, and handwriting because they take them home to their parents. I ask them to write to me if they wish. I have received a few letters, to which I always reply. That thrills the students. Out of earlier errors I compose a minilesson in the form of a letter I write on the board. The children play detective and try to find errors. When they do they raise their hands and we explain the error. In this way, mistakes can be corrected indirectly. The children like this activity even though it is frequently interrupted by requirements from the office: PTA promotions, classroom pictures, survey cards, assemblies, collections for lunch tickets, and other necessary evils that have little to do with school achievement."

days"—five math problems placed on the chalkboard that students try to solve; five vocabulary words on the board that students find the meanings of and learn to spell and use; five cities of the county, state, country, or world that students must pinpoint on the map. Others use puzzles, riddles, or word problems related to some part of the curriculum such as science, language, or social studies. Students try to get the riddles or problems solved before time runs out.

Whatever opening activity is preferred—and some teachers would rather move directly into the curriculum than to bother with opening activities—teachers need to stress positive interpersonal relationships, pleasant productive work, and student responsibility for good behavior and for taking care of materials.

CLASS MONITORS

Most teachers feel very positive effects are associated with the use of classroom monitors. Monitors are students who help with a variety of classroom routines, often assuming complete responsibility for them. Teachers like to use monitors for three reasons: (1) Their help cuts down tremendously on the amount of time that teachers would otherwise have to spend on nonteaching matters. (2) The efficiency of taking care of such things as distributiing and collecting papers and other materials, cleaning up after instruction, keeping track of equipment, and so forth, is greatly improved when trained monitors assist, thereby releasing additional time for instructional activities. (3) The use of monitors calls attention to the class as a cooperative endeavor, in which all students take responsibility for contributing to the progress and well-being of the total group. This develops a sense of community, belonging, participation, and responsibility.

Some teachers use only three or four monitors and frequently rotate the jobs among members of the class, thus giving each student some responsibility during the year. There is reason to believe, however, that assigning duties to every student produces better results. While it may take some effort to make the assignments and to train students in their jobs, payoffs come in commitment and efficiency.

Many kinds of duties must be taken care of routinely during the school day. Monitors can be assigned to most of these duties. One experienced fifth-grade teacher, for example, uses the following monitors:

- *Class president*—in charge of class business and classroom meetings as they are needed.
- *Flag monitor*—in charge of leading the daily flag salute and any other lessons or activities that have to do with the flag.
- *Lights monitor*—in charge of seeing that the lights are turned on and off.
- *Window monitor*—in charge of seeing that windows are opened and closed as necessary during the day.
- *News, weather, and map monitors* (2)—in charge of reporting on two or three news items per day, including weather forecasts for city, state, and nation, and for pointing out on the map where the news and weather events are occurring.
- *Class news reporters* (2)—in charge of making daily entries into the class log about highlights of the day. This material is then kept as the class record, is used as a source for the monthly newsletter which the teacher prepares for parents, and is reread from time to time to provide the class with a sense of history, accomplishment, and growth.
- *Messenger*—in charge of delivering messages to the office, library, and other teachers.
- *Line monitors* (2)—in charge of heading lines and setting a good model for entry into and exit from the room, movement to other parts of the school, and movement during activities outside the classroom, such as field trips.
- *Physical education equipment monitors* (2)—in charge of distri-

buting, recollecting, storing, marking, and otherwise taking care of equipment used on the playgrounds at recess and noon.

- *Table or group monitors* (5–6)—in charge of tables or identifiable groups of students, with such duties as taking attendance, distributing and collecting materials, seeing that the area is kept clean and orderly, and sometimes reporting to the teacher as spokesperson for the group regarding achievement, needed help, and so forth.
- *Plant and pet monitors* (2)—students in charge of watering and caring for plants, pets, or animals in the room, cleaning and caring for aquarium and feeding the fish, and feeding and caring for animals in the terrarium.
- *Materials monitors* (2)—in charge of handling, storing, distributing, and collecting small materials such as workbooks, worksheets, pencils, paper, and scissors.
- *Audiovisual monitors* (2)—in charge of obtaining projectors, operating the equipment, returning equipment and films, and managing the use of films, tapes, slides, microprojectors, records, and models.
- *Librarians* (2)—in charge of the class library and its system for allowing students to check out books and other materials. Library monitors are trained to fill out and stamp cards and due dates to keep track of materials that belong in the library.
- *Substitute teacher monitors* (2)—in charge of assisting all substitute teachers. They know the daily routines, where lesson plans and materials are kept, standards of behavior, and the discipline system used in the class.
- *Visitors monitor*—in charge of greeting visitors to the class, finding seating for them, and informing the teacher of their presence.

These sixteen categories of monitors provide duty functions for at least thirty students. Additional duties can be added if necessary so that all students have a responsible job that requires their attention.

How long students should remain in charge of each assigned duty is a matter of debate. Some teachers prefer to reassign students every two weeks, in order that students might have the opportunity to be involved in various kinds of duties, and so that a few students cannot monopolize favored duties for long periods of time. Others prefer to keep the assignments in effect for two or three months at a time, feeling that it takes students a while to learn their tasks well and become comfortable and proficient in discharging them.

There is difference of opinion also as to how the assignments to tasks should be made. Some teachers merely assign the duties on the basis of personal judgement. Others allow students to choose the duties for which they wish to serve, using alphabetical order or a first-come basis. Still others have students make formal requests for the duties they wish to monitor. In some cases they use application forms that students fill out, and the students compete for positions on the basis of their interests and qualifications. Selection can then be made either by the teacher or by class vote. An example of such an application form is presented in Figure 1.

FIGURE 1: Application form for classroom monitor.

Name _____

Date _____

JOB APPLICATION

1. List jobs for which you are applying. (1st choice, 2nd choice, etc.)

    1st _____
    2nd _____
    3rd _____

2. Why do you want this position?

    1st _____

    2nd _____

    3rd _____

3. What makes you qualified to hold these positions?
    1st _____

    2nd _____

    3rd _____

4. List 3 positions you would like least.

    _____
    _____
    _____

MOVEMENT MANAGEMENT

Movement management may seem inconsequential, but it has much bearing on student behavior and productive work. Unnecessary movement accounts for a large number of discipline problems, either directly or indirectly. Frederick Jones's research described in chapter 4, has shown that most discipline problems are of two types: (1) students talking without permission, and (2) students moving about the room without permission. In this case the movement itself is the misbehavior. Movement can also contribute toward misbehavior by causing confusion, wasted time, congestion, and students' brushing against each other.

Movement management includes such matters as how students are to enter and leave the classroom, move as a group to other places in the school, and move as individuals or groups to locales within the room. It includes procedures for going to the restroom, to the drinking fountain, to the office, to sharpen pencils, for turning in completed work, and for requesting and receiving help from the teacher and other students.

Lines are favored by most teachers as ways for students to enter and exit from the room and move to other locales in the school. Various procedures are used for forming lines. In the past, the most common procedure was to have a boys' line and a girls' line, a practice that is now frowned on because it may contribute to sexual stereotyping. Teachers are now more likely to allow students to form their own lines, or else teachers form the lines in accordance with (1) where the students sit in the room, (2) alphabetical order of the first or last name, (3) arbitrary teacher judgment, with the lines identified by some code name such as a color, (4) by who arrives first, finishes first, behaves best, works best, and so forth, as a system of rewards that helps shape desirable behavior.

In-room traffic refers to movement of individuals and groups within the classroom. If done efficiently, it promotes purposeful work, increases the amount of work accomplished, and decreases the amount of loitering. Teachers should establish rules that call for students to be in their seats and on-task unless otherwise allowed. Many teachers provide a code system, on large sheets of tagboard posted at the front of the room, that tells students what they are expected and allowed to do at different times during the day. An example uses three sheets of tagboard, one with a red circle in the center, another with a yellow circle, and a third with a green circle. These colors are then posted to indicate the kind of work behavior allowed. The red sign means sit in your seat, don't talk except when called on. It is used during directed lessons and quiet seatwork. The yellow sign means that students are to remain in their seats, but they may whisper with their neighbors. This is allowed when pairs or small groups of students are working together at activities such as spelling, math, and similar activities involving drill and practice. The green signal means that students may do group or individual project work, with quiet talking and quiet movement allowed as necessary for working and obtaining materials, references, and other objects.

When it is necessary for students to move in the room, they are expected to do so quietly without talking or touching others. This rule should be established and mentioned regularly during class discussions.

Pencil sharpening is a necessary activity that can, if care is not taken, be very disruptive to the classroom climate. It is good to have an established policy regarding this matter. Some teachers keep all the pencils in a large metal can, all sharpened at the beginning of the day. Students are allowed to take one pencil, or perhaps a monitor distributes them before class. If a lead breaks, the student is allowed to obtain a second pencil. Thus, the pencil sharpener is not used during the day, and there is no instructional time lost because of noise or waiting.

Other teachers feel that this system does not help students to feel responsible for taking care of the pencils. They allow each student to have two pencils which are kept in their desks. Each student is responsible for sharpening them at appropriate times, such as before school or other designated times.

Passes are often used for allowing students to go to the restroom, outside drinking fountains, and the office. Teachers should not allow students to go out of the room without permission, or even with permission unless it is clearly necessary. Some students enjoy leaving the room and will do so as often as possible, thus missing instructional activities.

The passes themselves are useful in helping teachers keep track of where students have gone. Some advocate making the passes from pieces of wood, with sufficiently large dimensions that students cannot inadvertently slip them in pockets or notebooks. Four pass boards should be sufficient, one "drink," one "office," one "boys," and one "girls," the last two for the restroom.

MATERIALS MANAGEMENT

Classroom efficiency depends in large part on how well materials are managed. This is especially so for smaller materials, how they are obtained, used, and replaced. Such materials include textbooks, workbooks, worksheets, paper, pencils, and crayons, plus other materials used occasionally, such as scissors, glue, and paints. The objective is to keep these materials stored efficiently out of the way, yet readily available so they can be easily obtained, used, and replaced.

Materials management requires that teachers give attention to (1) storage, (2) distribution, (3) use and care, and (4) replacement.

Storage of materials will vary. Where possible teachers prefer that students keep in their desks materials used on a regular basis. Desks would contain textbooks, workbooks, pencils, crayons, ruler, and paper. When these materials are kept in desks, teachers have the added task of seeing that the materials are kept neatly arranged in good order so that students can find them quickly and easily. Desk checks help keep materials neatly arranged. Teachers use various techniques for encouraging students to keep their desks orderly, ranging from simple checks on occasional intervals to procedures that are interesting and motivating, such as the "desk elf," an imaginary creature that checks all desks at the end of the day. When desks are found that are especially neat, the elf leaves a surprise such as a special sticker for the student.

Where students cannot keep materials in their desks because of space limitations or where tables are used instead of desks, other arrangements must be made for the storage of small materials. Some teachers provide each student a plastic dishpan, commonly called a *tub*. These tubs hold the students' materials and are kept on shelves. They have the student's name plainly written on them. At the appropriate time students are directed to go to the shelves and take their tubs or what is needed from their tubs back to their desks or table.

Another common arrangement is for most materials to be kept shelved. This includes books, workbooks, worksheets, and paper. As materials are needed, students get them from the shelves or monitors distribute them to individual student work areas.

Distribution of materials is ordinarily accomplished in one of the following ways: (1) Teacher or aide distributes them during recess, noon, and before school, so that when students arrive their materials are waiting before them. (2) Monitors are trained to distribute materials, which they do at recess, noon, or during class activities as the materials are needed. (3) Students themselves get the materials after being instructed about where they are located and how one is to move to and from the storage area.

Use and care of materials presents a good opportunity for

teaching students the principles of conservation as a way of life, as well as ingraining them with the sense of responsibility for the care and wise use of materials. Students should be instructed that they are not to waste materials, but are to make good use of their paper, crayons, and pencils.

The same idea applies to the use of printed materials. Many books, workbooks, charts, etc., can be used repeatedly if one is careful not to damage them, to keep them clean, and to keep them orderly. The amount of use available from each piece of material is thereby significantly increased. The value of taking proper care of materials is important in itself as a means of training students to use natural resources. But in times of fiscal difficulties this value takes on added importance. Budgets for supplies have been shrinking steadily in recent years, requiring that teachers and students use the materials more carefully and sparingly.

Replacing materials after use is as important to efficient management as are distributing and caring for the materials. Restorage is usually done in one of four ways: (1) students themselves quietly replace the materials; (2) monitors collect and replace them; (3) students place materials in folders or containers that are later collected by the teacher, or (4) the teacher or aide collects, organizes, and replaces the materials.

The discussions to this point have focused on the management of small materials used routinely through the day. Larger materials also play key roles in instruction and must be managed and used efficiently. These larger materials include reference books such as dictionaries and encyclopedias, art supplies, globes and maps, and other items such as materials for aquariums and terrariums, physical education equipment, and audiovisual equipment. It was pointed out that monitors can assume most management duties associated with large materials, though many teachers prefer to have each individual student do so, as a way of bringing them into greater involvement in ongoing procedures and responsibilities in the classroom. So far as location of materials is concerned, maps and projection screens should be mounted above the chalkboard so they can be pulled down and used when necessary. An additional use of maps and screens on rollers is to cover material, such as test items and directions, that have been written on the board and are uncovered at the appropriate time.

Physical education materials are best kept in a crate or large plastic trash container near or just outside the door. After school the materials are placed inside the room, in the corner or inside a closet.

Audiovisual materials can be kept on a cart with rollers that can be pushed easily about the room. On that cart can be kept record players, tape players, and listening center, and the top of the cart can be used for the various projectors—motion picture, filmstrip, and slides.

Globes are best kept on cabinet tops or on a special table where all students can see and conveniently approach when necessary. Reference books should be kept on shelves at the side of the main seating area, easily accessible to students. Art supplies are best kept inside cupboards with doors that can be closed, and easels should be kept folded and stacked near the art supplies and the classroom sink. Materials for aquariums and terrariums, materials such as sand, plants, animal food, rocks, and cleaning equipment, should be kept in cupboards and used only by the teacher and monitors given that responsibility.

ASSISTANCE MANAGEMENT

As students work individually at assigned activities such as directed seatwork and parts of group lessons they invariably encounter difficulties that require assistance from the teacher. Effective management requires that the teacher be able to provide this help quickly and effectively, as a means of keeping students on-task while progressing at a rate that allows them to complete their work on time.

Good assistance management requires that one give attention to the following: (1) clear directions that students understand; (2) posted reminders; (3) signal systems for students to use in requesting assistance, (4) teacher movement to students needing help, and (5) providing assistance quickly and effectively.

Directions should be given briefly and clearly. Students should understand exactly what they are supposed to do, when they are supposed to finish, and what they are supposed to do with completed work. Teachers should concentrate on brevity and clarity, and to check understanding they can call on one or two students to repeat the directions.

Reminders, models, and directions may be posted in the room when there are unusual procedures to follow, several steps to remember, or special skills to be used in sequence. Graphic models are helpful in many content areas, such as spelling rules, math algorithms, and steps in conducting science experiments. These models are put on a chart that is posted in the room. Teachers remind students to refer to the chart before calling for teacher help. If directions are complicated, the teacher may write them on the chalkboard in outline form. Other kinds of reminders may be posted, such as "*i* before *e* except after *c*," "keep your area clean," and "invert and multiply." These reminders, models, and written directions should take care of most of the difficulties students encounter during independent work.

Signal systems should be implemented that permit students, when they encounter difficulties they cannot solve on their own, to indicate their need for teacher assistance. Generally, teachers should not allow students to come to the teacher's desk for help. This causes congestion, confusion, and wasted time. Rather, students should remain at their work areas and signal the teacher to come to them. If little help is normally required by a group of students, they may simply raise their hands when necessary. If the class normally requires considerable individual attention, a simple system should be worked out that allows students to signal for help without holding their hands in the air and waving their arms. Some teachers use a piece of red construction paper folded to stand upright on the student's desk. The student signals for help by placing the paper in a vertical position.

While waiting for the teacher to arrive, students needing help should know they are to move ahead to the next problem or exercise. If that is not possible, they take out a book and read silently until the teacher arrives to help them.

Teacher movement is a key factor in assistance management, for the teacher must get to each student needing help as quickly as possible in order to forestall lack of progress, wasted time, and awkward moments that encourage discipline problems. If the desks are arranged in ways suggested earlier, as in modular clusters or shallow semicircles, all students will be in close proximity to the teacher. The teacher may move in a predetermined pattern among the desks and rows to be near students, comment on their work, and give help in regular rotation, or teachers may station themselves at a central area where they can observe all students at work and move quickly toward those who show signs of encountering difficulties.

Assistance should be given very quickly and effectively. It should consume no more than a few seconds' time. Mention was made of Frederick Jones's research, which showed that teachers spend an average of about four minutes per student giving individual help. Jones found that that same help could be given in no more than twenty seconds. The reason for teachers taking so much time is that they typically question the student and then wait for replies, which may be erroneous, fumbling, or nonforthcoming. Jones suggests— and has a program for so training teachers—that they provide help in a different and more effective manner. It is done quickly by following this sequence: (1) comment positively on anything the student has done correctly; (2) give a clear suggestion that will cause the student to resume progress, such as, "Watch the decimal." "Borrow here." "Look at step three on the chart." or "That word means. . . ." (3) move quickly away from the student, being sure to pay brief attention to the work of students who have not requested help. This third step might appear inconsiderate of the feelings of students needing help, but Jones suggests that it has two positive effects: First, rapid movement gives attention to a far greater number of students during work time, and second, it begins to break down the dependency syndrome in which students will not work without the teacher's help or presence.

MANAGING COMPLETED WORK

One of teachers' most time-consuming tasks is dealing with work that students have completed. It is common to see teachers carrying home with them each evening tall stacks of papers that are to be checked, graded, and later returned to students. The following suggestions can help teachers manage this complex and burdensome task effectively.

First, it is not necessary that all work be checked in detail. Much independent work is for practice only, and necessary feedback is given by the teacher who rapidly circulates and monitors student responses.

Second, as much work as possible should be corrected by students in class. There is nothing wrong with allowing students to check their own work or to exchange papers for this purpose. In fact, in-class checking by students is both motivating and instructional, as they are keen to see how many they get right or wrong, and eager to know what the right answers are for those items they get wrong. This gives them immediate feedback instead of their having to wait from one to three days to see how they performed, after which time their interest has diminished greatly. When work requires teacher judgment or very accurate correction, then teachers of course should check the material. There are times available for this task during the school day—before school, during prep periods, after school, and during free reading or choosing portions of the curriculum. Many teachers have aides or volunteers who can do much of the routine checking.

To help in managing these materials many teachers use folders that are kept on students' desks. The folders contain compartments with labels, such as "unfinished work," "ready for checking," and "completed and checked." At the end of each day the teacher examines material in the ready-for-checking compartment, checks it, and replaces it in the checked compartment. Other teachers have monitors collect the completed work, perhaps by tables or groups, and place it in a recepticle. Teacher or aide checks the material and has it ready to return the next day.

Student work that has been done well should be posted occasionally for all to see. This provides a sense of success and is highly rewarding and motivating to the students. In addition, samples of completed work should be kept in student folders to show parents during conferences or at open house. For that purpose, samples of inferior as well as superior work should be kept, to present a well-rounded and accurate picture of the habits and accomplishments of the student.

DISTRACTIONS MANAGEMENT

Sound management of normal class routines eliminates most of the incidental problems with which teachers must contend. There remain, however, certain types of student behavior that if not dealt with provide a source of distraction that interferes with teaching and learning. Those types of behavior include procrastination, messiness, tattling, tardiness, and irresponsibility. The following suggestions should prove helpful in handling and ultimately eliminating such problems.

Procrastination is the exasperating trait of putting things off until the last minute and oftentimes beyond the last minute. All of us have difficulty in beginning tasks that do not excite us, and most of us cannot maintain enthusiasm when tasks are overly complicated or take a long time to complete. But when certain students procrastinate in most of their school program, corrective measures are needed.

When procrastination becomes a classroom problem severe enough to warrant special attention, teachers should find the following procedures helpful:

1. Keep all instructional tasks as short as possible while still attaining the desired objectives.
2. For tasks that remain long, break them down into a series of shorter steps, and place a deadline for the completion of each.
3. Require oral progress reports on longer tasks.
4. For short tasks, emphasize a time limit. Call out the time

occasionally—for example, "Ten minutes; you should be about half finished."

5. Use incentives; for example, "As soon as you have finished this work, you may;..." (some preferred activity such as free reading).

Messiness is a chronic problem for certain students, both in the classwork they complete and in how they care for their school materials. This is annoying to the teacher and it allows unattractive habits to become further ingrained in students. The following suggestions will help relieve the problem:

1. Have group discussions about pride in self, schoolwork, and the classroom, and how that pride is often reflected in neatness.
2. Prepare "neatest" papers to show parents or keep in personal records folder.
3. Establish an incentive system where a series of neat papers earns a reward such as a certificate, sticker, or preferred activity.
4. Allow students to exchange ideas about organizing their desks for maximum neatness and efficiency.

Tattling by students can become a virulent disease that sweeps through the group. It rarely cures itself, and it exacts its toll. It is habit forming causing students to focus on the negative, lose respect for each other, and forever look to an authority to adjudicate minor problems that they themselves should resolve or ignore. For teachers, tattling is a major irritation, and their intervention into petty squabbles often does more harm than good since it takes responsibility away from students while it invariably casts disputants into roles of winners and losers.

Fortunately tattling can be controlled rather easily. The four suggestions that follow are effective and widely used:

1. Discuss with the class the nature of tattling, the bad effects it has on cooperation and good feelings, and the desirability of solving on one's own the minor differences that normally occur. Indicate that it is all right to inform the teacher when another student seriously violates one's rights by stealing, bullying, or inflicting physical harm.
2. Tell the tattler to write out the complaint together with a constructive suggestion for taking care of the problem.

3. Ask the tattler to wait until noon or after school to make the complaint, at which time you will consider it carefully.
4. Have the disputants meet together and discuss the matter until they can come up with a solution acceptable to both, one with which they agree to abide.

Tardiness often occurs for legitimate reaons, but when it becomes habitual in individual students, it can be annoying and disconcerting to the teacher. It can cause the student to miss out on important instruction, and can further ingrain a general lack of responsibility. When left unchecked the habit often becomes worse. Though they may blame their mothers or an unending series of minor catastrophes, chronic late arrivers usually fall into the tardiness habit for one of four reasons: (1) they feel no interest in participating in opening activities; (2) they have not fully understood their responsibilities in their own educational process; (3) they are encountering overly interesting things to do on the way to school; or (4) they have no fear of the consequences of their tardy behavior.

Almost every day a student is going to arrive late, for a variety of reasons, but the incidence of tardiness, especially for the chronic late arriver, can be greatly reduced through the following measures:

1. Discuss with the class their responsibilities in supporting and participating in the school program. Make sure they understand the necessity of arriving a few minutes before school begins.
2. Make the opening activities attractive, enjoyable, and important, so that students will want to participate and will feel left out when they don't.
3. Show you mean business by setting up penalties for tardiness combined with rewards for continued punctuality. Let students help decide on the rewards and penalties.
4. If these measures do not correct tardiness, call the parents, explain the problem, and ask for their help.

Irresponsibility refers to students' general failure to get work done properly and on time; to their misuse or mistreatment of materials, equipment, and facilities; and to their failure to live up to ordinary promises or obligations.

An important goal of basic education is to build within each student a sense of responsibility for the common good as well as for one's own acts. In general this is shown when duties and obligations are fulfilled promptly and correctly, with concern for others. Steps should be taken normally to help instill this sense in students. The following measures help build responsibility and take care of problems that might arise:

1. Discuss periodically with students what responsibility means, how it contributes to the good of everyone, and what students should do, explained in terms of their behavior in the classroom.
2. Assign specific responsibilities to all class members for their parts in managing the classroom. This can be done through the use of monitors as described earlier in this chapter.
3. Have students evaluate their own behavior on several points such as punctuality, completing work, doing one's best, taking care of assigned duties, and helping others when necessary. Have them make contracts for future improvement, and supply appropriate rewards when they live up to their contracts.

CHECKPOINTS

Good management of classroom routines contributes greatly to efficient use of time, class control, rapid learning, and student sense of security. Routines fall into seven main categories:

Opening activities
- attendance
- sharing
- sustained silent reading
- journal writing
- choosing
- classwork nuggets

Class monitors
- help for the teacher
- teaches responsibility
- all students involved

Movement management
- in the classroom
- outside the classroom
- pencil sharpening
- drinks and restroom
- passes

Materials management
- storage
- distribution
- use and care
- replacement

Assistance management
- clear directions
- posted reminders
- signal systems for requesting help
- rapid effective assistance

Managing completed work
- checking
- folders
- monitors
- display of work

Distractions management
- procrastination
- messiness
- tattling
- tardiness
- irresponsibility

6

Curriculum Management

The curriculum is the school's instructional program for learners. It consists of subject matter or courses, together with the activities, materials, standards, teaching techniques, and evaluation procedures intended to produce student progress. It is this sense of the term *curriculum* that receives attention in this chapter, although many authorities prefer a wider definition that extends to such matters as school lunch, health care, and psychological services.

Curriculum management may appear to be a strange term, because most people think of the curriculum as something fixed, a group of subjects written down, relatively stable and unchanging. In practice, however, the curriculum is fairly flexible. While the various subjects and their intended content—and sometimes even the exact teaching procedures, activities, and materials—are written in curriculum guides, there will nevertheless be much variation from one teacher to another in the way the curriculum is implemented. This fact has caused some authorities to conclude that a truer definition of curriculum is "what goes on in the classroom once the door is closed."

Earlier, management was defined as the ways in which any activity or group is organized, scheduled, treated, attended to, kept track of, and evaluated. Such is also the case with curriculum management. In keeping with the general meaning of curriculum as the instructional program for learners—and with the practical definition of curriculum as what goes on once the door is closed—we can see that there is much indeed to consider when it comes to effective management of the curriculum.

"It is important to me for things to run smoothly. I have a daily schedule and expect students to change quickly from one subject to the next. I try to have the first part of a particular period set aside for a whole-class activity. In this way the students all know what is coming and what to do. For example, the first thing in math is always a one-minute timed exercise. The students know that I will quickly say "go," and if they don't have their pencils, scratch paper, and test sheet ready they are out of luck—they can try again the next day.

"The subject matter is also very important to me. Since I teach sixth grade I always have junior high in the back of my mind. Assignments are to be completed. If they are not, a note goes home, filled out by the student, stating what was not completed and why. The work must be made up on their own time. I go over all the assignments ahead of time so students know exactly what is expected. They know the schedule of tests and what they have to do to earn their grades on the report cards. This makes them responsible for their own grades. Occasionally I receive a call from a parent whose child has received a failing grade for the first time ever. Their anger quickly subsides when I remind them that the child knew exactly what work was required for a good grade, and I explain how little the child did.

"This may sound harsh, but I treat the students with great respect and courtesy. I always say 'please' and 'thank you' and 'excuse me.' I admit my mistakes and tell the children I am sorry. They reflect my example. We are courteous, we are considerate, we have an enjoyable time, and best of all we get our work done."

Keith, Sixth-grade bilingual teacher

THE SCHOOL CURRICULUM

The curriculum of the present day, while varying somewhat from one school to another, includes the following subjects:

Elementary School. Almost all students take the same courses: reading, language arts (grammar, handwriting, spelling, composition, listening, speaking), mathematics, social studies (history, geography, current events), science, health and safety, music, art, physical education.

Junior High School. Here students continue to take required courses, but have available some electives. Required courses include English, mathematics, social science, science, health, physical education. Elective courses often include music, art, industrial arts, home economics, foreign languages, and typing.

High School. The high school curriculum becomes much broader and allows for different emphases by students. Required subjects include English, mathematics, social science, science, and physical education. There are in addition numerous elective courses: business education, industrial arts, home economics, vocational education, foreign language, music, art, and others.

How did the present-day curriculum come to include these subjects? The answer lies partly in the usefulness of the contents of these subjects, partly in current philosophy, partly in the psychology of human growth and learning, and partly in the tradition that has endured through the centuries. But even though the curriculum seems to be almost identical from one school to another, one can discern wide differences among schools and even between two teachers in adjacent classrooms. This divergence is often attributable to differences that exist among teachers themselves—differences in philosophy, styles of teaching, imagination and creativity, background of experience, interests, capabilities, and a host of individual differences that exist in their personalities.

We should note first that there are many different outcomes deemed desirable for the various subjects. These outcomes have been described by Benjamin S. Bloom in the book he edited entitled *Taxonomy of Educational Objectives: Handbook I: Cognitive Domain* (1956). Bloom and the committee with whom he worked identified six categories of educational objectives, which they organized from 'lower' to 'higher' in accord with their views of the intellectual processes required for their attainment. The six categories, from lowest to highest are:

- *Knowledge*—possessing information, but without understanding.
- *Comprehension*—understanding the information possessed.
- *Application*—using the information.
- *Analysis*—separating information into component parts.
- *Synthesis*—combining information to produce new ideas.
- *Evaluation*—judging the worth of information.

Bloom and associates, plus countless curriculum workers, have urged teachers to give attention to outcomes at these different levels, with attention to all instead of concentrating on the lowest level of knowledge.

Much attention, too, has been given to objectives in the *affective domain*, objectives that have to do with attitudes, values, and feelings. This domain is seen as important both in itself and as a helpful concomitant to objectives in the cognitive domain.

Carol, as a fourth-grade teacher, uses a combination of what she refers to as "smoothers" and "sparklers" to balance the content in most subjects in her curriculum. Smoothers refer to activities organized to teach basis skills and information in the most efficient way. The following are examples of smoothers in her math program:

- establish skill groups and assign them names.
- develop units for each skill group based on the textbook and the district's scope and sequence chart.
- establish a routine schedule and procedure for math. Begin each lesson with Compucat (a short, timed skill exercise).
- following lesson presentations, allow time for good follow up work
- keep all assignments posted on the board. Give explicit directions.

Sparklers, on the other hand, are activities used to enliven the curriculum and make the learning process more enjoyable for students. Examples of sparklers from Carol's math program:

- use games, flash cards, funsheets, and puzzles for reinforcement and reward for completed work.
- assign monitors to pass out and collect Compucat.
- use one day each week to relate the math skills to another part of the curriculum—examples: length and measurement related to map study; use of geometry with art; use of story problems with sports statistics; use of graphing with science projects.
- post a math riddle or special problem on the board each day.
- use catalogs for students to practice shopping and the use of money.

You can see that the curriculum, in addition to what is written in terms of subject matter content, has multiple outcomes toward which instruction is aimed. This fact helps to account for some of the differences noted from one classroom to anoher even when teachers use what appear to be identical printed curricula.

VARIATIONS IN THE CURRICULUM

Another factor that produces variations from one classroom to another is the teacher's view of learners and philosophy about teaching and learning. To illustrate how these differences can be translated into educational planning, consider the descriptions of a week's plan of instruction prepared by two fifth-grade teachers, both real teachers who teach in the same school district and who use the same curriculum guide and sets of textbooks.

Subjects and Scheduling

Teacher A		Teacher B	
8:30–8:40	Roll and preliminaries, daily	8:30–8:35	Roll and preliminaries, daily
8:40–9:55	Reading, daily	8:35–9:25	Mathematics, daily
Recess		9:25–9:35	Handwriting, daily
10:10–11:00	Mathematics, daily	Recess	
Recess		11:00–12:00	Language, spelling, creative writing, daily
11:10–12:10	Language and spelling, daily		
Lunch		Lunch	
12:55–1:10	Read to class	12:40–1:30	Social Studies/Art
1:10–1:50	Social studies, daily	Recess	
1:50–2:10	Physical Education	1:40–2:00	News
Recess		2:00–2:30	Physical Education/ Creative Dramatics
2:20–2:50	Art MWF Music TTh	2:30–2:50	Music

On paper the curriculum used by these two teachers is similar, and in fact follows rather closely the curriculum guide used in their district. In implementation, however, the "closed-door" curriculum is notably different. To illustrate this point let us examine the nature of the activities used on Monday of a typical week:

Teacher A

8:40–8:55 *Reading*—three groups reading from basal readers; one group with teacher, a second at directed seat work, and a third reading from personally selected library books.

10:10–11:00 *Mathematics*—thirty-minute concept lesson, total group following directions, procedures, and practice directed by the teacher; twenty-minute directed activity working problems included in the textbook.

11:10–12:00 *Language*—twenty-minute grammar and usage lesson; twenty-minute spelling period; twenty-minute application in oral or written language.

12:55–1:10   *Oral reading* by teacher to students from selected book, e.g., *Charlotte's Web.*

1:10–1:50   *Social studies*—ten-minute map skill activity; twenty-minute worksheet and oral reports; ten-minutes wrap up and class discussion.

1:50–2:10   *Physical education*—aerobic exercise

2:20–2:50   *Art*—introduce "crayon sandpaper"; students design project.

Teacher B

8:35–9:25   *Mathematics*—students work at own pace in diagnostic-prescriptive math program.

9:25–9:35   *Handwriting*—Penmanship exercises from teacher-prepared booklet.

9:45–10:50   *Reading*—fifteen minutes teacher reads aloud to students; thirty minutes students work in individual reading contracts that include magazine articles, SRA reading lab, library books, basal text; twenty minutes at reading centers for games, vocabulary development, worksheets.

11:00–12:00   *Language*—Thirty minutes spelling activities working in pairs; twenty minutes expository and creative writing using spelling and vocabulary words.

12:40–1:30   *Social Studies*—map work in groups of five, filling in surface features from legend using atlas; competition for neatest, most accurate work.

1:40–2:00   *News*—Students give newscast, similar to TV broadcast, on areas of local, state, national, world, weather, and sports news (each student prepares from previous day; awards given for best).

2:00–2:30   *Physical Education*—folk dancing.

2:30–2:50   *Music*—music appreciation plus singing from students' favorite songs.

These two schedules were prepared by real teachers teaching fifth grade in the same school district, with similar student make-up, using the same curriculum guide. Both are considered very successful and are highly popular with students and parents. Teacher A, though young, presents a more traditional program, with students working under teacher guidance from textual material. Teacher B presents a curriculum that allows considerably more student latitude and a greater variety of experiences.

AUTHORITIES' OPINIONS

In the examples of Teacher A and Teacher B it is evident that their classrooms are operated in quite different ways. While students were provided the same content areas, the activities, materials, and outcomes were noticeably and measureably different. Which of the two is considered more correct? The answer to that question depends in large part on one's individual philosophy and opinion. Certainly authorities who enjoy large followings disagree among themselves. These differences of opinion are well stated by such eminent figures as B. F. Skinner, Jerome Bruner, Herbert Kohl, Carl Rogers, and Benjamin Bloom.

Skinner (1968) believes that the curriculum should be planned and organized by the teacher and that students should be moved through it in small steps that ensure correct responses. He would have teachers provide systematic reinforcement to speed learning. He has been criticized for allowing little student freedom and latitude for making errors, a criticism which he rejects. It is altogether a myth, he asserts, to consider students "free and happy" in the absence of structure and control, which he believes must be present if students are to make genuine progress in knowledge and skills that bring increased competence in thinking and doing.

Jerome Bruner (1960) would have the curriculum emphasize the structure of the various disciplines, that structure being the internal relationships that give each discipline its own particular identity and ways of seeking knowledge. Math would be approached in terms of its organization and relationships; science in terms of its processes, as scientists use them; the creative arts in ways similar to activities in which creative artists function. This approach, Bruner believes, provides greater insight into the nature and functions of the discipline and thus leads to increased competence by students.

Herbert Kohl emphasizes great freedom and latitude for students, a point of view stressed in his book, *The Open Classroom* (1969). He believes that students take greater interest, participate more, and accomplish much more when they play strong roles in deciding what they are to learn and arranging their own work times and conditions.

Carl Rogers (1969), the renowned counselor who developed the client-center approach to therapy, believes like Kohl that students must have freedom and latitude in determining their own curriculum. He would have teachers play a *facilitative role*, in which they help students clarify what it is they want to learn and in establishing procedures that enable them to attain the outcomes they set for themselves.

James H. Block (1971) has been instrumental in promoting the practice of *mastery learning*. He points out that in typical instruction only about one-fourth of the students reach intended levels of learning, while three-fourths are allowed to fall well short of the mark. This can be corrected, he asserts, by varying time allotted to students, providing very efficient instruction, and not allowing students to move on to other topics until they have mastered the material at hand.

Relatively few teachers adhere strongly to any one of these views, at least not to the exclusion of the others. What we are much more likely to see in the classroom are organized directed activities mixed together with other activities that allow student freedom and choice.

RECENT FINDINGS ON CURRICULUM ORGANIZATION AND STUDENT LEARNING

In recent years considerable research has been conducted into classroom teaching and effects brought about by different methods and approaches to teaching. Barak Rosenshine (1978) has summarized research conducted since 1973 having to do with the teaching and learning of reading and mathematics at the primary-grade level. While we must be careful about generalizing the findings to other areas of the curriculum and grade levels, the findings nevertheless merit serious consideration.

In reviewing and summarizing numerous research reports, Rosenshine makes the following generalizations about student academic gains in primary-grade reading and mathematics:

1. The more content covered, the higher the student gain.
2. The greater the student attention, the higher the gain.
3. Content coverage and student attention are best brought about through *direct instruction*—instruction characterized by clear goals, teacher direction, control, and monitoring, immediate academic-type feedback (i.e., indicating what is being done correctly, what is being done incorrectly, and how to correct errors being made).

4. The best gains were produced by teachers who were strong leaders; the poorest by teachers who made students the center of attention and organized learning around their problems and concerns.
5. When students are allowed to choose instructional activities their learning gains are reduced.
6. Management is a problem of critical importance that has not received sufficient attention. Classes with poor management usually have low academic engaged time and consequently lower academic gains.

These findings have been corroborated by research done in England by Peter Mortimore who for several years studied achievement in inner-city London schools. Mortimore found both good and poor schools in his study sample, as well as good and poor teachers. Schools and teachers that produced highest student gains were those in which teachers related well with students, held high expectations, assigned regular homework, marked the work rapidly, and returned it with helpful comments. They also came to classes well prepared, managed classroom time well, moved smoothly from one activity to the next, and maintained appropriate discipline (Paulu, 1981).

These efforts by the teacher contribute to greater student involvement with school work, a factor now widely believed to produce greater gains in learning. But what specifically can teachers do to foster such student engagement with the curriculum? Tamar Levin and Ruth Long in their book *Effective Instruction* (1981) summarize research that suggests ways to improve both individual involvement and total class involvement. For individual involvement they suggest:

1. Identify and help the students least involved in the activities.
2. Prepare students adequately with prerequisite knowledge and skills.
3. Adapt instruction to individual traits of motivation, self-confidence, and pace of learning.

For increased total class involvement they suggest:

1. Devote more time to instructional activities. (This time is gained through efficient management and delegating non-instructional activities to aides and student monitors.)

2. Increase active student participation.
3. Make fluid transitions between activities.
4. Use adequate and clear instructions and directions.
5. Increase the interest value of instruction.

ORGANIZING AND PRESENTING THE CURRICULUM

Curriculum planning that results in printed guides occurs mainly at the state and national levels, and the work is done by high-level committees. It is there that national and state interests are considered and addressed, and when combined with considerations of students, facilities, and materials, are given form in five main components:

1. Valid objectives, clearly stated.
2. Specification, by grade level, of essential knowledge, skills, and attitudes.
3. Description of major instructional activities and materials.
4. Organization of scope and sequence for daily use.
5. Evaluation procedures that match the stated objectives.

This work is very influential, first because it provides guidelines, suggestions, and sequences, and second because it so strongly determines the nature and contents of textbooks, workbooks, and other instructional materials.

To a large extent, however, the curriculum that is actually presented to students is planned out at the local school and individual classroom level. This is the curriculum referred to earlier as closed-door curriculum. It is there on the firing line that all the realities come together—teacher personality and philosophy, traits and backgrounds of students, financial and material resources, school *esprit de corps*—and there of course the curriculum is presented.

In doing this planning, teachers proceed from the basis of three considerations:

Goals and objectives—what, precisely, one intends that the students will accomplish with regard to knowledge, skills, and attitudes.

Nature and abilities of the students—their readiness, motivation, backgrounds, self-control, and self-direction.

One's own philosophy of education, teaching, and learning—shown in the degree of one's preferences for such things as structure, facilitation, direction, support, interaction, self-direction, responsibility, and active involvement.

From these foundations, which are central in the thinking of every teacher whether or not they are considered explicitly, teachers in order to provide a quality curriculum efficiently managed must also give attention to the following:

Grouping students—large groups, small groups, individual study; arrangement of seating; work space required by groups; varying the groups according to objectives.

Presentation methods—the principal means used in imparting information and bringing students into active involvement with the curriculum. Typical methods include demonstration, discussion, observation, reading, and research. Certain methods are appropriate to certain objectives.

Lesson management—pertaining to how one organizes and initiates lessons, gives instruction, maintains momentum, monitors student work, provides corrective feedback, assists and keeps students on task, provides appropriate practice and application, summarizes, and concludes lessons. Lesson management varies in accord with objectives and group structure.

Material management—using materials of instruction for maximum contribution to information, experience, and practice pertinent to the stated objectives. Materials must be selected, stored, retrieved, distributed, demonstrated, cared for, restored, and replenished.

Evaluation and record keeping—Students should be kept aware of how well they are progressing toward meeting instructional objectives. This knowledge is helpful and motivating, especially when furnished through a combination of objective evidence and personal conferencing. Objective evidence can consist of test scores, objectives attained, analyses of performances, and analyses of products completed. The personal conference provides for subjective evaluation of students' efforts and attitude, and allows students to express opinions and ask questions. Records of objective data and personal conferences are kept in separate folders for each student.

Units of Instruction

These key elements of instructional management are brought into play as teachers organize instruction, which is usually delivered in the form of individual lessons or larger units comprised of a series of related lessons.

A unit refers to a large segment of instruction, often requiring several days or weeks for completion. An example would be a unit of instruction on the weather that might last for several weeks, involve a number of separate lessons, utilize quantities of different kinds of materials, and involve students in many different activities.

Units are useful in many areas of the curriculum, especially in the natural and social sciences. Richard E. Servey (Charles et al., 1978) describes an effective way of organizing units:

1. Formulate a *target objective*, the main overall objective toward which student achievement is aimed. An example presented by Servey in a unit entitled "Maps As Tools" is "The learners will be able to construct a series of maps offering information about a country from which some of their ancestors came."

2. Formulate a few *interim objectives*, subordinate to the target objective, whose attainment moves learners sequentially toward the target objective. Servey advocates using interim objectives that begin with student experiences and lead progressively to their finding personal meaning and becoming able to work productively on their own. Examples of interim objectives in the "Maps as Tools" unit call on students to record latitude and longitude, produce a map of the classroom, and correctly use maps in textbooks.

3. Compose *instructional activities* that lead to attainment of each of the interim objectives. Servey describes three kinds of instructional activities—initiators, explorers, and integrators. *Initiators* are activities that lead students into the topic. *Explorers* are activities that provide new learning experiences for the students. *Integrators* are activities that help students understand and make sense of what they are learning. Materials of instruction and suitable work space must be arranged for the instructional activities. Ordinarily, each of these instructional activities comprises a separate lesson in the unit.

Individual Lessons

Lessons, in the way they are organized and conducted, strongly affect the nature of the in-class curriculum. Lessons are usually outlined in *lesson plans,*—or the blueprints that describe and guide the teacher's activities in presenting the lesson. A lesson plan would ordinarily include the following:

1. Statement of specific objectives—that is a specific outcome usually stated in terms of observable student acts.
2. Activities that will be used, in sequence.
3. Materials needed for each activity.
4. Extension or follow-up of the lesson.
5. Evaluation of the lesson.

Madeline Hunter (1969) has done much work at the laboratory school at UCLA in devising lessons and teaching formats that produce rapid and lasting learning. Her work has been disseminated not only through her own writing but through state and county departments of education across the country. Lesson plans formulated according to her suggestions incorporate the following:

- *Anticipatory set*—which establishes the purpose of the lesson, indicates the objective, and focuses student attention on what is to come.
- *Instruction*—which provides information, modeling, and monitoring of student performance and understanding.
- *Guided practice*—provided after instruction is completed but still under the direction of the teacher.
- *Closure*—which means wrapping up the lesson and often obtaining a sample of each student's performance.
- *Independent practice*—during which students continue to work on the material being learned and apply it to other situations.

Throughout her lessons, Hunter stresses motivation, retention, and reinforcement. For motivation she suggests giving attention to student interests, knowledge of results, success, and feeling tone. For retention she suggests supplying meaning, feeling tone, vividness, and practice. She also emphasizes that positive reinforcement is very helpful for speeding and guiding learning and making it more lasting.

Criteria for Selecting Instructional Activities

All instructional activities are not of equal value. Some help students attain objectives, while others do little more than fill or waste time. To ensure that activities are of benefit to students the following criteria should be considered:

1. Activities selected should *strongly* lead toward attainment of the stated objectives. The objectives might be either "behavioral" and state the observable acts that the learner is to become able to perform, or "experiential" which describe experiences believed to have value for students even when the outcomes cannot easily be described.
2. The activity should be at an appropriate level of difficulty,

neither too easy nor too difficult.
3. The activity should provide active involvement to the extent possible.
4. The activity should be as enjoyable as possible.
5. The activity should build useful knowledge and skills.

Other things being equal, teachers should select instructional activities that do not require great amounts of time for preparation.

Sources of Ideas for Activities

Many teachers are quite inventive and creative in selecting worthwhile, enjoyable activities for their students. Even the best of us, however, sometimes get into ruts. It is helpful to be continually on the outlook for good teaching ideas. Sources for such ideas include (1) teachers manuals and textbooks, (2) observation and word of mouth, (3) curriculum guides, (4) professional journals and magazines, (5) inservice classes and conferences, (6) special sourcebooks, and (7) one's own inventive imagination.

Lesson Management

Jacob Kounin (1970) conducted research in many classrooms to determine the conditions that contribute to better teaching and learning. Among Kounin's findings were several that had to do with how teachers managed their lessons:

Withitness—Kounin found that successful teachers were likely to know what was going on in all parts of the classroom at all times, during a lesson, and that students knew that the teacher knew. He called this trait withitness.

Group alertness—Successful teachers held the attention of all members of the class. This was accomplished by doing such things as looking around the group continually in a suspenseful manner, avoiding a predictable pattern of calling on students, and varying unison responses with individual responses.

Momentum and transitions—Successful teachers maintained consistent momentum within lessons, never allowing dead spots or resorting to frenetic haste. Transitions from one lesson to another were made very smoothly without wasted time or confusion.

Avoiding Satiation—Successful teachers avoided satiation, another name for boredom, by emphasizing progress, providing challenge, and providing variety in activities, materials, and student responsibilities during lessons.

BASICS OF CURRICULUM MANAGEMENT

The following outline provides a resumé of the basic principles of curriculum management. Those presented here have been selected for their value and ease of implementation by the classroom teacher.

1. Follow existing curriculum guides and textbooks. The programs described therein have been carefully planned by people considered expert in their fields.
2. Supplement those guides with your own ideas and expertise. All teachers have experiences and ideas they can bring to bear on instruction that will personalize, enliven, and round out the basic curriculum.
3. Arrange objectives and activities so they are aimed at different levels of Bloom's Taxonomy of Educational Objectives, not always at the lowest level of knowledge.
4. Arrange the daily schedule to allow for:
   a. More difficult or quiet activities while students are fresh.
   b. More physical activity and talk when students are tired.
   c. Alternate quiet activities with those that allow some movement and noise.
5. Plan individual lessons so that:
   a. Direct instruction is used for teaching facts, concepts, and skills.
   b. Indirect (facilitative) instruction is used for teaching process skills, exploration, and creativity.
   c. Attention is given regularly to the affective domain—interests, attitudes, and values.
   d. Emphasis is given to student responsibilities and human relations.
6. Deliver lessons so as to:
   a. Focus and hold student attention.
   b. Conserve time.
   c. Maintain momentum or pacing.
   d. Provide smooth transitions from one lesson to the next.
   e. Call on students to summarize what they are learning.
   f. Provide for follow-up in the form of practice and application.

As you attempt to implement the foregoing principles of curriculum management, the following questions can be used as a helpful checklist:

- What are the specific goals and objectives I want my students to attain?

- What are the students' current levels of ability and readiness? Are they adequately prepared and motivated?

- How, specifically, will I organize, present, and direct my lessons, so as to provide for rapid attainment of objectives?

- What instructional materials will I use in my lessons, and how can I use them effectively and efficiently?

- How will I monitor my students' work and provide needed help efficiently?

- What provisions will I make for my students to practice, in realistic situations, the skills and knowledge they have acquired?

- What procedures of evaluation will I use, that will be most helpful to student learning and to my effectiveness as a teacher?

CHECKPOINTS

Curriculum, defined as the school's instructional program for learners, appears on paper to be fairly standard everywhere. When implemented by teachers, however, it varies considerably, due to differences in teachers' skills, philosophies, and preferences.

Curriculum management refers to how teachers organize and provide their instructional programs. Leading contemporary authorities have different opinions as to how this should be done:

B. F. Skinner—curriculum should be planned and organized by the teacher, to include small steps, success, and positive reinforcement.

Jerome Bruner—curriculum should emphasize the structure of the various subjects, and students should function in ways similar to scholars, using inquiry.

Herbert Kohl—curriculum should provide great freedom and latitude for students. They should choose what they desire to learn and arrange their own study schedules.

Carl Rogers—students should choose what they want to learn, and teachers should behave as facilitators, not dispensers of information.

James Block—curriculum should be carefully sequenced and presented so that most students master the content quickly before being allowed to move on.

Recent research has provided important findings—regarding learning under various instructional arrangements. For example, in primary reading and mathematics it has been found that:

- the more covered, the more students learn
- students who pay better attention learn more
- students learn more when their teachers are strong leaders

Curriculum planning at the classroom level must consider:
- goals and objectives
- abilities of students
- grouping of students
- methods of teaching
- lesson management
- materials management
- evaluation and record keeping

Curriculum is organized into
- units of instruction, especially in science and social studies, that require days or weeks to complete
- individual daily lessons

Both units and individual lessons include notation of
- objectives
- activities
- materials
- extension or follow-up
- evaluation.

BIBLIOGRAPHY

Block, J. *Mastery Learning: Theory and Practice.* New York: Holt, Rinehart and Winston, 1971.
Bloom, B. *Taxonomy of Educational Objectives. Handbook I: Cognitive Domain.* New York: McKay, 1956.
Bruner, J. *The Process of Education.* New York: Vintage Books, 1960.

Charles, C. et al. *Schooling, Teaching, and Learning: American Education.* St Louis: Mosby, 1978.

Hunter, M. *Teach More—Faster!* El Segundo, Calif.: TIP Publications, 1969.

Kohl, H. *The Open Classroom.* New York: Vintage, 1969.

Kounin, J. *Discipline and Group Management in Classrooms.* New York: Holt, Rinehart and Winston, 1970.

Levin, T., and Long, R. *Effective Instruction.* Alexandria, Va.: Association for Supervision and Curriculum Development, 1981.

Paulu, N. "The Surprises of London's Inner-City Schools." *Education Week.* Washington, D.C., December 21, 1981.

Rogers, C. *Freedom To Learn.* Columbus, Ohio: Merrill, 1969.

Rosenshine, B. "Academic Engaged Time, Content Covered, and Direct Instruction." *Journal of Education*, August 1978.

Skinner, B. F. *The Technology of Teaching.* New York: Appleton-Century-Crofts, 1968.

7

Direct Teaching Management

DEVELOPMENT OF CURRICULUM AND TEACHING IN THE UNITED STATES

One major purpose of education in the United States has always been that of building competencies in the 3 R's—reading, writing, and arithmetic. That priority became established with the passing into law of the "old Deluder Satan" act of 1647, which pointed out that Satan intended to lead people away from the paths of righteousness. It was therefore incumbent upon all citizens to learn to read the scriptures as a means of thwarting Satan from his evil intentions.

This emphasis on reading as the prime purpose of early education joined with writing and arithmetic to form the core of basic required education. If students went on to the secondary level they continued studies in reading, writing, and mathematics, plus courses in history, logic, philosophy, and rhetoric.

For two hundred and fifty years the content and purposes of elementary education remained much the same, but in the early 1900s there occurred a shift in emphasis at the secondary level. High schools, influenced strongly by the work of Edward L. Thorndike, whose experiments brought into question the supposed value of "mind-building" subjects such as logic and classical languages, began to add practical subjects to the curriculum, such as business arithmetic, secretarial sciences, and modern foreign languages. The elementary curriculum, however, remained virtually the same, although the 1800s saw the addition of subjects that remain in today's curriculum—such as social studies, natural science, art, and music.

It was not until the 1930s that the elementary curriculum began to move its emphasis, albeit slowly, away from almost total concentration on the 3 R's. Before that time, the curriculum consisted of those basics, and were taught in what is now referred to as a "traditional" way; that is, the teacher was fully and completely in charge of selecting goals, objectives, activities, instructional materials, evaluation procedures, and every other detail of classroom instruction. The teacher directed the students through the learning activities in a forceful, no-nonsense manner. In the 1920s, the work of such educational pioneers as Francis Parker and John Dewey began slowly to transform elementary education, in both content and methods of instruction. Dewey (1916) believed that the school should be a part of the students' lives here and now, as well as preparation for their lives to come. This called on the school curriculum to become atuned to the daily needs, aptitudes, and interests of young students, rather than concentrating solely on preparing them for later adult lives. Dewey further believed that the schools should assume the responsibility for preparing students to function in a democratic society, which could best be done by providing a laboratory in which to develop the skills and attitudes of cooperation, compromise, group decision making, and responsibility in decisions made by the group. Toward that end, teachers were to relinquish some of their absolute authority, though certainly not control of the ship, in order that students might practice and develop these skills of democratic living.

Dewey put his ideas into practice while he served as principal of the laboratory school at the University of Chicago. Disseminated through his many books, those ideas and practices attracted worldwide attention and had tremendous influence on curriculum and teaching practice everywhere. Eventually Dewey received much criticism, not entirely deserved.

Many of his followers, who in their time became influential in shaping educational practice, failed to interpret correctly the ideas that Dewey tried to put forth. They popularized the notion that Dewey intended the school to be a place where students played the lead role in deciding what the curriculum and instructional activities should be. The public believed that Dewey's curriculum would consist of the children doing each day only what they wanted to do, and there arose in the language such terms as "Dewey-eyed educators" to refer to those who would assign responsibility and control to children. This erroneous view was expressed in a famous cartoon in which a child asked his teacher, "Please, Miss Smith, do we *have* to do what we want to again today?"

Dewey never suggested that control of the classroom be turned over to students. He was very firm in his view that the teacher should be always in charge. The teacher, however, was to involve students as much as possible in planning out the details of the activity-oriented curriculum, which Dewey believed best prepared students to think for themselves and to participate democratically.

In 1957 the Russians launched Sputnik, the first man-made satellite to orbit the earth. It was an object the size of a grapefruit that did little besides proceed around and around the earth, but it was nonetheless a scientific and technological accomplishment of tremendous importance. The United States had been attempting to get its own satellite into orbit, but on this occasion came in second to the Soviet Union. That fact produced great anguish in the United States, and there was much fear that the Russians had moved far ahead of the United States in scientific and technological development. Blame was heaped on the schools, as so often happens during matters of national crisis, and the "progressive" school movement, still linked to Dewey's philosophy, came strongly under attack. Its attempts to give students a hand in educational planning, together with its emphasis on activity-oriented subjects rather than the more demanding fact-oriented subjects, were seen as producing generations of "mushy-headed" Americans, unable to deal with complex intellectual matters, thus leaving us far behind the Russians, Germans, Swedes, and other groups against whom American students were compared. Everywhere, people began to question the quality of American education.

Stirred by the outcry, eminent scholars and scientists began to give attention to the school curriculum and make suggestions about how to correct it. While several critics did this on an individual basis, the most significant effort, in terms of its long-lasting impact on redesigning public education, was that of the Woods Hole Conference, conducted in Massachusetts in 1959. There, under the leadership of Jerome Bruner, a group of renowned scholars from various disciplines convened to consider the school curriculum and make recommendations for its overhaul. The group's working propositions, though not its ultimate conclusions, were reported by Bruner in his book *The Process of Education* (1960). Of the several viewpoints forcefully stated in that book, three were to be reflected in the various "new curricula" that soon appeared on the educational scene: (1) The "processes" by which knowledge is acquired are fully as important, if not more so, than the facts and skills that normally result from education. (2) The way to grasp a discipline fully and to become comfortable with it, is to learn its structure—how it is put together and how it works. (3) The young are capable of learning the so-called rigorous subjects such as mathematics at much earlier ages than we had formerly believed.

These three beliefs formed the undergirding of the new curricula that soon appeared—the new math, new English, new science, new foreign language, and new social sciences. All emphasized process as much as factual content, stressed the structure of the discipline, and pushed complicated content lower into the primary grades.

Some of these new curricula proved successful, while others did not. The latter group, including new social studies and new English, have disappeared. The new math, which stressed understanding of the number system, remains in bits and pieces, but by all objective accounts its overall intent of greatly improving mathematics achievement has failed. The new science proved to be successful and it remains in place, though science in the early 1980s has been receiving less and less attention as schools try to bolster achievement in reading and mathematics. The new foreign language instruction, which emphasizes oral communication over the ability to read and know grammar, was the most successful of all in terms of accomplishing its intents. It failed, nonetheless, due to two factors: lack of trained teachers and lack of incentives among American youth to learn foreign languages.

These new curricula proved unsatisfactory for other reasons as well, as for example in believing that the very young could deal with abstract concepts, a belief contradicted by the vast amount of research reported by Jean Piaget (see Charles, 1974). Even more detrimental to their case, however, was the pattern of progressively falling test scores in the areas of mathematics, reading, and language, a decline that has fostered a new push for "back to basics." Many authorities believe that the emphasis put on process and structure has taken away from growth in factual information and the development of functional skills in reading, writing, and other areas of the curriculum.

THE PUSH FOR DIRECT TEACHING

As test scores declined in math, reading, and spelling, the public along with professional educators became further concerned about the quality of education. Fuel was added to this fire through occasional lawsuits filed against school districts by the parents of high school graduates who could not read or write. This mounting concern caused educators to push again for curricula that build basic literacy skills—those same skills of reading, language, and arithmetic that formed the core of the elementary school curriculum for so many decades.

Along with the push toward basics there grew the realization that instruction in those areas is provided best through structured, formalized approaches, with the teacher firmly in charge of the learning process. While earlier it was fashionable to allow students a role in deciding on their instructional activities and schedules for work and study, the movement has swung strongly back to teachers' being in charge of all such matters.

Direct teaching is structured teaching, and its management requires consideration of organization, presentation, and control. Barak Rosenshine (1978) describes direct instruction as follows: "Teaching activities focused on *academic matters*; where *goals* are clear to students; *time* allotted for instruction is sufficient; content coverage is *extensive*; student performance is *monitored*; questions are at a *low cognitive level* and produce many correct responses; and *feedback* is immediate and academically oriented" (emphasis added). David C. Berliner (1980) advises that teachers be trained to increase their ability to provide allocated time, engaged time, student success, content coverage, and direct instruction. With direct instruction, says Berliner, "the teacher controls instructional goals, chooses material appropriate for the students ability level, and paces the instructional episode." This description may sound harsh and dull, but the process need not be. As Rosenshine points out, the interaction among teachers and students is structured, but the atmosphere is not authoritarian, and learning takes place in a convivial atmosphere. This conclusion is supported by Morrison (1979) whose research in fourth-through sixth-grade classrooms showed that highly structured classrooms, when compared to less structured classrooms, produced higher student work involvement together with higher group intimacy and lower amounts of friction.

Direct instruction is better understood when contrasted with indirect instruction, where students take on a significant role in determining what, when, and how they will study and learn. There, the teacher acts as motivator, counselor, helper, resource person, and all around facilitator—a role described by Carl Rogers (1969) as necessary if one is to foster learnings that have personal significance for students. Rosenshine's summary of research conducted since 1973 shows convincing superiority of direct instruction over indirect instruction when it comes to student achievement in reading and mathematics. While Rosenshine's work focused only on reading and mathematics at the primary-grade level, research reported later indicated similar findings at other grade levels. Horak and others (1979) found that sixth-grade students performed better in mathematics in structured situations. Amato (1979) found that direct instruction provided higher achievement for third- and fourth-grade students, and Morrison (1979) reported that sixth-grade students in structured situations showed higher levels of work involvement than did those in less structured classrooms. Such evidence leaves little doubt that direct instruction provides an effective means for reaching some of the major goals that guide the back-to-basics movement in American education: wide basic knowledge and command of fundamental skills that permit one to deal with that knowledge.

In the remainder of this chapter, remember that direct instruction is now the favored method for imparting large amounts of information and for helping students develop the skills for utilizing that information. It is questionable, however, that direct teaching is the most effective means of teaching problem solving, creative thinking, creative production, and processes of inquiry, matters still considered eminently important in education. It is probable that those matters can better be handled through instruction characterized as more indirect—an approach described in detail in Chapter 8.

PREPARING FOR DIRECT TEACHING

Direct teaching requires that the teacher be in control of all parts of the instructional episode at all times. As teachers prepare for direct instruction, they will be called upon to consider the following elements of instruction: (1) objectives, (2) instructional activities, (3) materials of instruction, (4) follow-up work, and (5) evaluation. These five aspects of teaching are considered in the sections that follow:

Objectives

Direct teaching focuses on rapid acquisition of knowledge and skills. Behavioral objectives are very useful in this process. As described earlier, behavioral objectives refer to those outcomes of education that are directly observable in learners. That is, we look for what students say and do as evidence of the behaviors we hoped they would acquire.

When teachers are able to list specific behavioral objectives, a major part of the instructional task has been accomplished. Convincing experiments have been conducted to show that older students, when informed clearly of what it is they are to become able to do and are given the opportunity to acquire those capabilities plus motivation sufficient to cause them to act, will achieve high levels of performance even without instruction from a trained teacher. With the teacher present, learning efficiency is increased still more. Young children cannot be expected to produce such learning in themselves, even when they are clearly informed of desired behavioral outcomes, but their learning, too, is usually improved when they know exactly what it is they are supposed to become able to do.

In years past a great deal of attention has been given to writing instructional objectives. Credit for this push goes first to Robert Mager, who in 1962 produced the enormously influential book *Preparing Instructional Objectives*. Mager pushed strongly for explicitly stated behavioral objectives. His work resulted in a storm of controversy that has since died away. Educators generally accept that behavioral objectives serve a valuable function in many parts of the curriculum—especially those parts that deal with basic knowledge and skills—while recognizing that some areas of the curriculum, such as those having to do with aesthetics and creativity, are not so amenable to behavioral objectives. Much effort was put forth in the middle and late 1960s to train and urge teachers to use behavioral objectives in instruction. Those efforts produced good results, and nowadays teachers think much more than before in terms of the observable behaviors they hope to produce in their students. It is doubtful that it is cost-effective for teachers to expend the time and energy to prepare extensive lists of behavioral objectives for all aspects of the curriculum. When such sets of objectives are needed, they are readily available in most school district offices, curriculum guides, textbooks, and in especially prepared courses of study. Still, teachers do well to *think* in terms of behavioral outcomes more than in terms of the materials and activities they intend to use with their students. The contents of instruction then become the means to the end, rather than the end in itself.

Activities

Activities are those things that teachers and students do in attempting to produce the learning that has been stated in the objectives of instruction. These activities will hopefully produce considerable student attention and active involvement.

Attention is a requisite for almost all types of school learning. It is brought about through motivation from various sources and from teacher direction to pay attention. It is increased when the material and activities are interesting and when the students know they will be held responsible for participating during lessons and for demonstrating afterward that they have learned what was intended.

Active involvement and *active responding* occur when teachers structure activities to cause students to follow along, respond to questions, and make comments. The work of many authorities points to the necessity for student response in order that teachers may, first, judge the appropriateness of the response, and second, provide reinforcement following the response that shapes student behavior in ever more desired directions.

Some authorities, such as Albert Bandura (1969), point out that active responding, at least outwardly, is not absolutely necessary in learning. People can simply observe others perform acts which they, themselves, can later replicate, showing that they have learned without making active responses during the initial learning. Nevertheless, most if not all authorities agree that when students have the opportunity to respond, to move, to talk, or to write under guided direction, their learning occurs more quickly, accurately, and completely.

The activities that serve as the vehicle for instruction must attend not only to student attention and involvement, but to other matters such as grouping and styles of teaching.

Grouping refers to the way students are organized to participate in instruction. Traditionally, the entire class was taught as a single group, although there is also a long tradition of working with smaller groups, a tradition established by necessity in one-room schools where a single teacher taught students of all age levels in all areas of the curriculum, necessitating working with small groups of students most of the time. Where teachers had a single grade level, however, they generally taught the entire class as a single group, with everyone using the same materials and the same activities. As teachers began to find out more about individual differences in interests and abilities, they began to diversify instruction in certain parts of the curriculum, most notably in reading. There we saw the advent of the grouped reading approach, where students were divided into three or more groups and the teacher worked with each group in turn. This provided closer contact with those students while allowing them to work at reading tasks that were more closely matched to their functional reading levels. The other students, meanwhile, did seatwork at their desks, supervised by the teacher at the reading circle.

Rosenshine's work, mentioned earlier, reported research having to do with the size of groupings and with whether those groups required close supervision. He cited work by Stallings and Kaskowitz (1974) that found that teachers who worked with only one or two students at a time had lower achievement gains in their classes than did teachers who worked with groups of five or more. They believed the higher achievement could be attributed to the direct supervision provided by the teacher to more of the students at a given time. Rosenshine cited a study by Soar (1973) that showed that students made higher achievement gains when they worked under direct adult supervision, than when they met and worked in groups without direct adult supervision. Rosenshine believed that one may correctly infer from such studies that students, without direct adult supervision, simply do not remain on-task long enough, and that the larger the instructional group, the more direct supervision available during instruction.

In the past, authorities have urged teachers to form instructional groups suited to differences in ability, interest, speed of learning, background of experience, intelligence, and so forth, known to exist among students. Many teachers have in fact tried to do just that by forming numerous instructional groups within their classes, sometimes as many as five or six in reading, three or four in mathematics, and two or three in spelling; and others have attempted to individualize as much of the curriculum as possible. What they found in actual practice was that one reaches a point of diminishing returns considering the amount of time, effort, management, and manipulation required to make so many different groups or individuals function effectively in the classroom. Generally speaking, the research does not support the value of working with many small groups, as opposed to a few larger groups or even one large group, for most areas of the curriculum.

Nevertheless, there are indeed times when because of interests, abilities, or simply the need to make the instructional task a bit easier, teachers will wish to group students. Those groupings play a role in both the teaching methods teachers use and the instructional activities in which students engage.

Styles of Teaching. When the public thinks of teaching, it still thinks of one teacher standing before a group of students, talking to them in a "telling" way, giving reading assignments, asking questions, and later giving tests. In matter of fact there are many different methods of teaching, each clearly identifiable, and each having its particular purposes, strengths, and weaknesses for dealing with certain parts of the school curriculum. Charles et al. (1978) identified eleven methods of teaching that receive widespread use. Arranged in order from most to least structured, those eleven methods are:

Diagnostic-prescriptive teaching

Expository teaching

Modeling

Read-review-recite

Competency-based education

Simulations

Projects

Group process

Inquiry/discovery

Facilitation

Open experience

The first five methods of instruction involve the direct approach and are characterized as follows.

Diagnostic-prescriptive teaching is a highly structured method that consists of three parts: Diagnosing individual strengths and weaknesses, using a master list of objectives; prescribing for each student activities intended to remedy identified areas of weakness; and conducting postassessment to determine whether in fact the weaknesses have been corrected. This method is used extensively, particularly in schools with previous records of low student achievement in basic areas of reading, language, and mathematics.

Expository teaching is a method in which the teacher explains through words and demonstrations the information and skills that form the content of the subject matter under study. It is a highly popular method of teaching, especially in mathematics and other areas where teacher demonstrations are desired.

Modeling is a procedure that occurs informally for all people at all times. It is synonymous with "imitation learning". We see people do things and say things and we imitate them. When formalized, modeling is a highly effective method for teaching many skills of high importance in the school curriculum.

Read-review-recite is a traditional method of teaching which begins with reading assignments given to the students. After students have read the material, they review the highlights, often by responding to study questions that accompany the material. Finally they are asked to recite, either orally or on written tests, their understanding of the material studied.

Competency-based education is planned, organized, and controlled by the teacher, but in a way that allows flexibility in the instructional activities. It allows students to select from among optional learning activities, while the objectives and assessment procedures are held constant for all students.

Simulations are large-group activities, conducted in class but patterned after real-life activities. They are much less structured than the methods previously described. Examples might include having the class replay the lives of pioneer families during the westward movement, or on a smaller scale, replay situations involving conflict and its resolution in matters that occur on the playground and elsewhere.

You can see that the first five methods of teaching involve much control by the teacher, and they are the methods most often used in direct instruction. Beginning with simulations, we move toward indirect instruction which depends on methods of group process, inquiry, facilitation, and open experience. These methods will be described in Chapter 8.

We may summarize this section on activities in direct teaching by saying that larger groupings are preferred, together with structured teaching methods. These groupings and methods serve to keep students on task, paying attention, and responding at a high rate. They control responses and give the sort of feedback that is most likely to strengthen and improve learning.

Materials of Instruction

Materials used in direct instruction may run the gamut of everything available, but they are selected for certain purposes and used in certain ways. Ordinarily, fewer materials are used in direct instruction than in indirect instruction. In classrooms that are highly structured the environment may have a rather lean appearance, because only those materials directly useful to instruction are kept ready at hand. If diagnostic-prescriptive teaching is used, for example, there will be in evidence only those books and worksheets, together perhaps with a few manipulative materials, involved directly in instruction. If expository teaching is being used, a few charts, models, and physical apparatus needed in the demonstrations may be present. This picture is contrasted with that of the inquiry or open-experience approach where quantities of different kinds of materials are kept at hand to encourage student investigation and manipulation.

This depiction may seem austere, but the classroom environment need not be devoid of color and interest. As described earlier, there is a need for objects such as art prints and other media, growing plants, models, aquariums, and what have you, that serve important purposes in the room. Remember too that the entire day in the classroom rarely consists solely of those structured activities of direct teaching. The point to be made here is that during direct teaching instructional materials are confined directly to the instructional tasks at hand and they are nonexploratory in nature. They are used under direct guidance from the teacher, for clear, definite, precise purposes.

Follow-Up

After instructional activities have been completed under the direct control of the teacher, follow-up activities are provided as a means of practice, strengthening the learning, making it more lasting, and making it more applicable to future situations. Follow-up activities ordinarily consist of seatwork involving worksheets, workbooks, and papers for such things as practicing number combinations, and working on handwriting, directly applying what has just been learned.

This kind of seatwork consumes a large portion of each student's day in most school settings. The way in which it is conducted has large bearing on its effectiveness.

Two points should be kept in mind regarding seatwork. First, if this work is to have maximal value it must pull students forward, insignificant measure, toward the stated objectives of instruction. Seatwork that simply fills time, however enjoyably for the students, is not recommended. It is true that there are many activities that students enjoy a great deal, and they always provide good time fillers and keep the students occupied. There are even times, hopefully rare, when students must be kept occupied at whatever task, as in emergencies that call the teacher from the room. But time is a precious commodity in the classroom, and it is not to be wasted during direct instruction. Therefore, activities that do not contribute strongly toward stated objectives should be avoided. Examples of such work include word searches and seeing how many words can be made from a given set of letters, activities that enjoyably fill time but do little to build or practice new abilities and skills in students.

The second point regarding seatwork is that it should keep students actively engaged. It should not be boring, frustrating, tiring, or useless, because in those cases students will be hard pressed to keep themselves on task. Being on task is one of the factors mentioned by Rosenshine as contributing strongly to student achievement, a factor identified in the Beginning Teacher Evaluation Study (BTES) done at the Far West Regional Educational Laboratory in Berkeley, California. There it was found that "academic engaged time," (that is, time when students were engaged profitably in their intended learning tasks) contributed more than any other single factor studied to student achievement.

Not only do worthwhile activities keep students on task, but the way in which teachers move among students and give help is also of critical importance. This fact was elaborated by Frederick Jones (1979) whose research in classroom management was described in Chapter 4. Jones and his associates asked teachers how much time they thought they spent with each student who called for help during seatwork time. The teachers thought they used about two minutes for each student. Jones found that teachers in reality used over four minutes per student. Because this amount of time greatly reduced the attention teachers should give to individual students during seatwork—a factor that is known to keep students more actively engaged—Jones devised ways for teachers to give help much more quickly and effectively.

Jones advocates that teachers give individual help in no more than twenty seconds, and in his programs he trains them to do just that. Participants are shown how to do the following, and they practice these acts until they become second nature: First, they circulate actively among students who are doing seatwork. Second, when a student calls for help the teacher finds anything the student has done correctly and makes a positive comment about it. Third, the teacher gives a direct hint on what to do next, such as, "Carry here," or, "Look at the rules posted on the board." Fourth, the teacher moves quickly away to another student. Working in this quick, helpful way produces several positive results. The teacher is able to give help and attention to many students, and the students can get on with their work quickly, thus completing greater amounts of work. The rapid circulation among students helps break down a "dependency syndrome" often seen in classrooms, in which a few students, because they like the teacher's presence or because they feel insecure in proceeding without the teacher's advice and approval, call continually for help when they could just as easily be doing the work on their own. When they see that the teacher will not stay long with them, and when the teacher gives even more attention to students who are working well on their own, they begin to see that there is nothing special to be gained from calling continually for help.

So far as the nature of seatwork is concerned, not only should it lead rapidly toward objectives, but it should provide much practice in what is being learned, much review, and much application of the information and skills to the solution of realistic problems or situations. Those three functions enable students to master the material more quickly, remember it longer, and become able to apply it more effectively.

Seatwork, while favored, is not the only means of providing practice and follow up. Other activities include (1) question and answer sessions in which the teacher asks questions that call for short responses—from one to a few words focused on a "correct" answer; (2) brief class discussions following instruction, in which students are called upon to explain the information and processes they have been learning, and perhaps to consider the applications of the material; (3) role playing, in which students act out the procedures, facts, or skills taught in the lesson; and (4) calling on students to replicate the demonstration given by the teacher during the lesson, which is an efficient way of building greater depth of understanding. As has been said so often, if you want to learn how to do something well, prepare yourself to teach it to others.

Evaluation

The final step in preparing for direct teaching is to consider the type of evaluation that will be used. Normally we think of evaluation as pertaining to determining how well students have learned and behaved. Teachers should extend that concept to include an appraisal of the quality of the instructional episode, that is, to make judgements about how well they themselves have taught.

Three aspects of evaluation should be considered in advance. They are product evaluation, process evaluation, and evaluation of teaching effectiveness. *Product evaluation* focuses on the quality of the work that has been completed by the students, on worksheets done, tests taken, models built, and so forth. Ordinarily, direct instruction gives most attention to correct responses given on tests, oral quizzes, worksheets, and classroom discussions.

Process evaluation refers to how well students engaged themselves in the learning activities provided. This is done largely by observation where teachers reflect on how attentive students were, how well they engaged themselves in the learning activities, and possibly how well they were able to apply what they had learned in a follow up setting.

Evaluation of teaching effectiveness is done largely through the

teacher's appraisal of student performance combined with an ex-
amination of the teacher's own behavior. In this regard the teacher
looks first for the quality of product and process on the part of the
students, then thinks in terms of the teaching act, specifically of clarity of directions and presentation, adequacy of motivation, monitoring, and feedback, and how well the teacher was able to attend to
individual students who requested help.

LESSON MANAGEMENT IN DIRECT TEACHING

Lesson management follows in lines that parallel those described in
preparing for direct teaching. This section considers two main
aspects of lesson management—the general and the specific.

General Aspects

When it comes to managing lessons that are presented in direct
teaching, teachers can find much help from authorities in the instructional process. Among those authorities, three provide unusually valuable help. They are Madeline Hunter, David Ausubel,
and Jacob Kounin.

Hunter (1969) has given much attention to management of the
teaching process. She points out the importance of motivation, good
learning set, providing reinforcement, and keeping to the basic plan
of the lesson. Ausubel (1963) contributed the concept of *advance organization* in teaching, a procedure similar to the time-tested advice
given to public speakers—first tell them what you are going to say,
then say it, then tell them what you said. With advance organization
teachers tell students what the lesson is about, indicate high points
that should be noted, explain what the students are supposed to do,
and indicate how they will be evaluated afterwards. Kounin (1970)
has described several general qualities in instruction that contribute
to student attention, progress, and better behavior. Among those
conditions are withitness, smoothness, and attention focusing. The
concept of withitness means that teachers know what is going on in
all parts of the room at all times. The notion of smoothness refers to
the pacing of lessons to maintain constant momentum and appropriately. Transitions into the next lesson must be quick and efficient,
without wasted time that encourages student misbehavior. Attention focusing refers to how teachers keep student attention focused
on the lesson, using such techniques as calling on students to respond, changing tone of voice, pointing out items of particular im-

portance, calling on students to make interpretations, and giving brief interesting side-light commentaries.

Specific Aspects

Many elements of lesson management were described in the section on preparing for direct teaching, and need not be repeated here. Let it suffice to say that attention should be given to six specific aspects of lesson management that further the intentions of direct teaching, which are to maintain student attention, keep students on task, and cover quantities of material efficiently and effectively. These six aspects are:

1. *Larger groups*, with students' eyes to the teacher. Larger groups under the direct control of the teacher make better learning gains than do smaller groups or groups not under the direction of the teacher. Therefore teachers should consider using groups as large as possible that still allow attention to be given to crucial differences in student ability.

2. *Clear directions* with advance organization. Clarity in giving directions is of critical importance in direct teaching. It increases the amount of instructional time available to students. Directions should be given once and not repeated. They should be gone over carefully, however, and where difficulties are anticipated they should be written on the chalkboard or posted on a large chart. This allows the teacher to refer students to the chart instead of delaying all students' work while directions are repeated for a few.

Along with the directions should come advance organization, which further instructs students on what they should do and learn.

3. *Presentation.* Lessons should be presented in such a way that teachers furnish clear models, either through their own activities or through graphic models in books and other materials of instruction. In addition they should talk through the processes modeled, explaining what is done, why, and how. Students may be encouraged to talk through the processes too, as verbalization is known to speed the rate of learning. Modeling and explanation form the heart of direct teaching.

4. *Materials.* Necessary materials should be at hand, students should understand how to use them, and the materials should be easily obtained, used, cared for, and returned after use. Materials should contribute directly and clearly to the basic instruction being given, and not be used for exploration or time filling.

5. *Monitor and feedback.* Student work done as follow-up to the initial lesson presentation should be monitored carefully, and

appropriate feedback should be given as necessary. This requires that the teacher move quickly among students at work, giving help efficiently by making a positive comment, giving a strong hint, and moving quickly on to another student.

6. *Incentives and reinforcement.* Authorities in the instructional process are virtually unanimous in suggesting that teachers use incentive systems and provide as much positive reinforcement as possible. Both serve to motivate students and guide their work and behavior. Incentive systems have been described by many authorities. They are usually preferred activities, that is, activities from the regular curriculum that students most enjoy. Examples include free reading, art activities, and physical education. Students are allowed time at those activities at the end of the day, provided they have worked and behaved well during the day.

Positive reinforcement occurs minute by minute during the day as students respond in appropriate ways. The teacher provides verbal comments, facial expressions, gestures of approval, kind words, and sometimes such things as markers, stickers, points, and certificates for good work and behavior.

CHECKPOINTS

Direct instruction has received much attention in recent years. It is a structured method of teaching that keeps students on task and enables teachers to cover more material. It is described as:

- focused on academic matters.
- goals are clear to students.
- sufficient study time is provided.
- much content is covered.
- student performance is closely monitored.
- questions are at a low cognitive level (short answer).
- feedback is immediate and academically oriented.

Almost all teachers use a combination of direct and indirect teaching. When preparing for direct teaching they give heavy emphasis to:

- clear objectives that students understand.
- clear directions.
- instructional activities that produce student attention, involvement, and active response.
- grouping; usually larger groups are preferred.

- structured methods of teaching, e.g., expository or diagnostic-prescriptive.
- materials of instruction, only as needed for the guided activities.
- follow up—practice and application.
- evaluation, based on product (finished student work) and process (student engagement during the learning activities).

BIBLIOGRAPHY

Amato, J. "Teachers' Achievement Expectations: Effects in Open and Traditional Classrooms." Paper presented at the annual convention of the American Psychological Association, September 1979.

Ausubel, D. *The Psychology of Meaningful Verbal Learning.* New York: Grune and Stratton, 1963.

Bandura, A. *Principles of Behavior Modification.* New York: Holt, Rinehart and Winston, 1969.

Berliner, D. "Using Research on Teaching for the Improvement of Classroom Practice." *Theory Into Practice,* Autumn 1980.

Bruner, J. *The Process of Education.* New York: Vintage Books, 1960.

Charles, C. *Teachers' Petit Piaget.* Belmont, Calif. Fearon, 1974.

Charles, C. et al. *Schooling, Teaching, and Learning: American Education.* St. Louis: C.V. Mosby, 1978.

Dewey, J. *Democracy and Education.* New York: Macmillan, 1916.

Horak, V. et al. "The Effects of School Environment and Student Cognitive Characteristics upon School Achievement in Mathematics." Paper presented at the annual meeting of the National Council of Teachers of Mathematics, April 1979.

Hunter, M. *Teach More—Faster!* El Segundo, Calif. TIP Publications, 1969.

Jones, F. "The Gentle Art of Classroom Discipline." *National Elementary Principal,* June 1979.

Kounin, J. *Discipline and Group Management in Classrooms.* New York: Holt, Rinehart and Winston, 1970.

Mager, R. *Preparing Instructional Objectives.* Palo Alto, Calif.: Fearon, 1962.

Morrison, T. "Classroom Structure, Work Involvement, and Social Climate in Elementary School Classrooms." *Journal of Educational Psychology,* August 1979.

Rogers, C. *Freedom to Learn.* Columbus, Ohio: Charles E. Merrill, 1969.

Rosenshine, B. "Academic Engaged Time, Content Covered, and Direct Instruction." *Journal of Education,* August 1978.

Soar, R. *Follow-Through Classroom Process Measurement and Pupil Growth (1970–71): Final Report.* Gainesville: College of Education, University of Florida, 1973

Stallings, J. and Kaskowitz, D. *Follow-Through Classroom Obervation Evaluation.* Menlo Park, Ca.: Stamford Research Institute, 1974.

8

Facilitative Teaching Management

... truth that has been ... appropriated and assimilated in [one person's] experience cannot be directly communicated to another. ... I have come to feel that the only learning which significantly influences behavior is self-directed self-appropriated learning.

So says Carl Rogers in his classic book, *Freedom to Learn* (1969, p. 153). This proposition explains the belief that underlies facilitative teaching. Those who espouse this approach to teaching believe that the only truly significant learning is that which learners select and work through themselves. They also believe that schoolwork organized and "taught" by the teacher, without prior advice and direction by the learner, will have little lasting effect.

THE MEANING OF FACILITATIVE TEACHING

In terms of actual classroom practice, what does Rogers suggest with this point of view? To understand his ideas we must contrast good traditional teaching with good facilitative teaching. Traditional teaching, says Rogers (1971), has these three characteristics.

1. The teacher decides what would be good for a particular group of students to learn.
2. The teacher then plans lessons, activities, and materials that will motivate students to learn the material.
3. The teacher decides how to examine the students to see whether they have learned the material.

That, says Rogers, is what good traditional teaching is like, but unfortunately it produces inconsequential results.

What would Rogers have teachers do in place of this traditional teaching?

If I had a magic wand that would produce only one change in our educational system, I would with one sweep cause every teacher at every level to forget that he is a teacher. You would all develop a complete amnesia for the teaching skills you have painstakingly acquired (1971).

This statement is taken from Rogers' provocative article entitled "Forget You Are a Teacher." In that article he writes of traditional teaching as being based on the "mug and jug theory." The student is the empty mug to be filled from the jug, which is the teacher. This type of instruction does not, Rogers reemphasizes, produce significant learning.

Instead of teaching in that traditional way, Rogers would have teachers be *facilitators* of learning. Facilitators do not attempt to impart their knowledge to their students. Instead, they do the following things (Rogers, 1971).

1. Continually ask questions of students, in regard to their interests, concerns, fears, and aspirations.
2. Having helped students identify those matters truly important to them in their lives, the facilitator helps them identify resources to which they can turn for answers.
3. Establish a climate that fosters curiosity, permits mistakes, and allows students to learn from all parts of their environment.
4. Use instructional activities that cause students to become involved in asking questions, finding information, and making decisions, activities very unlike the structured activities of direct teaching.
5. Working in an advisory capacity, not a directive one, help students decide how they can best describe the findings, insights, and conclusions that they have achieved through this process of learning.

This process of facilitative teaching, concludes Rogers, gives students the capability of identifying concerns significant in their lives and of finding answers to those concerns in an independent, creative, self-reliant manner. It establishes a means of "learning the process of learning, a continuing openness to experience, and an incorporation into oneself of the process of change" (1969, p. 163).

Although this facilitative approach to teaching is an approach that has been clarified and elaborated only in recent years, the idea upon which it is based has been present in American education for several decades. In part it was put forth by John Dewey in his various writings, one of the best-known of which was *Democracy and Education* (1916). As described in Chapter 7, Dewey would have the teacher strongly in control, but would give students an active role in the educational process, where they would make decisions and assume responsibility for their own actions. He felt that this role would contribute better than anything else to the process of "democratization," a function that he felt could be better accomplished by the schools than by any other institution.

Various curricular plans followed on the heels of such pronouncements by Dewey and other progressive educators. Examples included the Winnetka Plan established in the Winnetka School System in Illinois in 1922, which allowed elementary school students to have much greater say in determining the content and the procedures of their curriculum, and the project method, described by William H. Kilpatrick in 1934, which still enjoys wide use particularly in the social science curriculum.

As years passed, criticism grew that the major curricular decisions were being made by young students who had neither experience nor capabilities upon which to base their decisions. These criticisms rose to fever pitch with the launching of Sputnik in 1957, helping bring about the new curricula advocated and formulated by scholars and scientists in the various disciplines. It was not until people began to see the more undesirable effects resulting from the new curricula—such as lowered achievement test scores and the impracticality of implementing many of the ideas that seemed good on paper—that attention began to refocus on writings of the humanistic psychologists such as Gordon Allport (1955), Carl Rogers (1969), Abraham Maslow (1954), and Arthur Combs (1972).

Rogers, for example, wrote:

I would be at a loss to explain the positive change which can occur in psychotherapy if I had to omit the importance of the sense of free and responsible choice on the part of my clients. I believe that this experience of freedom to choose is one of the deepest elements underlying change (1969, p. 268).

In cautioning against overreliance on behavioral objectives and behavior modification, Combs wrote:

Behavior, it must be understood, is only a symptom; the causes of behavior lie in perceptions and beliefs. Exclusive concern with behavior is not likely to be effective.

Behavior is a product of meaning. The effect of any behavior is also dependent upon the meaning it evokes in the receiver (1972).

This humanistic movement grew with the writings of other psychologists, critics, and practicing classroom teachers. This last group spoke up as they encountered devastating conditions in the schools of the inner cities where it was virtually impossible to instruct many of the students. These students found the curriculum and teaching methods so unrelated to their lives that many were never able to engage in them profitably. Silberman's book, *Crisis in the Classroom* (1970), pointed out the irrelevance of the public school curriculum. Herbert Kohl in his book *The Open Classroom* (1969) explained methods that he found, mostly by accident, to be successful in teaching his formerly incorrigible students. The suggestions were practical in that they explained ways of obtaining order and causing students to learn, and the views were consonant with those of respected psychologists such as Rogers and Maslow.

Somewhat in the background until the middle 1970s was the work of the renowned Swiss psychologist Jean Piaget. His investigations into the nature and functions of the intellect led him to conclude that the intellect grows in predictable ways and that its growth depends not only on maturation but on the kinds of experiences and social interactions that occur in the individual's life. He saw the process of intellectual development as being influenced strongly by exploration, decision making, verbal give and take, and general experiences of trial and error; experiences that allowed the intellect to *assimilate* new information into existing intellectual structures and *accommodate* or modify existing structures in terms of new information that might not fit existing structures. This conception of intellectual development seemed to call for the facilitative teaching advocated by Rogers, Kohl, and others, that allows students to work with self-direction in matters of importance in their lives and to take an active role in locating materials, people, and experiences that provide needed information.

METHODS OF FACILITATIVE TEACHING

Facilitative teaching has not received wide acceptance in the schools despite the urging of Rogers and others of similar persuasion. It has suffered from two rather serious limitations. The first is that it is so unrelated to the traditional organization and functioning of classrooms and teachers that it tends to be rejected out of hand. That is, the chasm between facilitation and traditional teaching, as total systems, is too wide for most people to cross. The second point critics have made is that students will rarely select as matters of central importance those basic skills of reading, language, and mathematics that are critical to academic progress. This limitation is difficult to refute.

Nevertheless, some of the ideas central to Rogers' point of view are present in several methods of teaching that are widely used. These methods provide a ready vehicle for using facilitative teaching to good advantage. They include:

> Inquiry/discovery.
> Group process.
> The project method.
> Open experience.

The Inquiry/Discovery Method

Inquiry and discovery are terms used synonymously. They refer to a method of teaching and learning advocated by many authorities, one that emphasizes process in learning more than products of that learning. This method has been described by Jerome Bruner, the Harvard psychologist who led the 1959 conference in Woods Hole, Massachusetts, out of which grew so many of the new curricula that appeared in the early 1960s.

Bruner's point of view regarding discovery learning was set forth in his 1961 article entitled "The Act of Discovery," in which he wrote:

I urge now in the spirit of an hypothesis that emphasis upon discovery in learning has precisely the effect upon the learner of leading him to be a constructionist, to organize what he is encountering in a manner not only designed to discover regularity and relatedness, but also to avoid the kind of information drift that fails to keep account of the uses to which information might have to be put. It is, if you will, a necessary condition for learning the variety of techniques of problem solving, of transforming information for better use, of learning how to go about the very task of learning. Practice in discovering for oneself teaches one to acquire information in a way that makes that information more readily viable in problem solving.

It is the emphasis upon the process of learning, in a measure equal to if not greater than the emphasis on content, that provides the rationale for discovery learning. Teachers who would use inquiry and discovery must understand what is involved when teaching students in this manner. Bruner explains this approach in his book *Toward a Theory of Instruction* (1966):

To instruct someone in (a) discipline is not a matter of getting him to commit results to mind. Rather it is to teach him to participate in the process that makes possible the establishment of knowledge. We teach a subject not to produce little living libraries on the subject, but rather to get a student to think mathematically for himself, to consider matters as an historian does, to take part in the process of knowledge-getting. Knowing is a process, not a product (p. 72).

Discovery learning, then, is intended to help one learn by oneself and for oneself. Controversy has arisen, however, over whether it is an efficient means of providing instruction, since it requires more time and therefore causes students to cover less material. That controversy has begun to subside as educators have come to see that discovery learning is good for reaching some of the goals of education but not so good for others. For example, discovery learning is an excellent method for teaching students the processes of investigation and creative problem solving, but it is a poor method for teaching the basic skills of addition, sounding out words, and legible handwriting. Such basic information and skills are better taught through direct instruction.

The teacher's and students' roles in discovery learning are as follows: The teacher's role (Ryan and Ellis, 1974) consists of *helping* students select their topics, pose questions that lead into the topic, locate resources, clarify thoughts, express conclusions, and critically examine those conclusions. The students for their part must learn to ask questions, find sources, collect information, construct answers or conclusions, express them, and analyze their own views critically.

The Group-Process Method

One of the most important outcomes of education is the ability to get along with others, to express and receive opinions in clear and nonthreatening ways, and to make intelligent group decisions toward the best interests of the total group. The group-process method of teaching is aimed at developing such skills. It focuses on interactions among members of the class, on processes that help them pursue common goals, and on the give and take of information related to those goals. The teacher plays a facilitative role within the groups, subtly guiding, reflecting, and helping clarify, but not taking a dominant directive stance. When used in classrooms, group process leads to the following (Joyce and Weil, 1980):

1. Establishment of social systems within the classroom based on democratic procedures.
2. Scientific inquiry procedures into the nature of social processes.
3. Activities in solving interpersonal and social problems.

The vital importance of these outcomes has been mentioned, stressed, and restressed through the history of American education. Despite the importance of these outcomes, we must realize that the group-process approach is relatively difficult to implement well. Moreover, it requires amounts of time; time that grows ever more scarce in the present-day curriculum. Unfortunately, it seems actually to waste time as students learn the ways of making group decisions, of arguing pros and cons, and of voting and following group decisions. It is likely that the trend away from group process will continue through the decade of the 80s, since it is not an effective means of teaching subject matter.

On the other hand, it is without doubt the most effective method available for teaching and learning those democratic processes we hold so dear. That being the case, it behooves every teacher to consider seriously the merits and methods in group process.

Herbert Thelen (1969) devised an effective format for providing practice in group process. His format consists of the following:

1. Identification of a real personal or social incident or problem that brings forth strong reactions from the students.
2. Formulation of a statement composed of these reactions that students can investigate.
3. Development of a plan for investigating this problem, including procedures, resources, and duties of individual group members.
4. Investigation in terms of the proposed plan and formulation of a report.
5. Report of findings made by the participants.
6. Evaluation of the solutions, conclusions, or suggestions included in the report.

In a less formalized way, William Glasser (1969) has proposed a procedure for using group process toward constructive ends that he calls *classroom meetings*. These meetings, which he believes should be held on a regular basis and be as much a part of the ongoing curriculum as any of the traditional subjects, would be of three types: (1) academic problem-solving meetings, (2) social problem-solving meetings, and (3) open-ended meetings. Each of these three types of meetings has as its main purpose focusing collective insights toward the solution of specific problems. Academic problem-solving meetings find solutions to problems encountered in academic school work—such as poor test results, not understanding material or directions, or having too much homework to do. The social problem-solving meetings deal with problems that occur among students on the playground, in the cafeteria, and in the classroom, or with adults in the school setting. The open-ended meetings deal with solutions to any problems that are of concern in the lives of the students.

All classroom meetings use the same format and approach. Students are required to focus on positive, constructive solutions. They are not allowed to complain or engaged in fault finding, back biting, or blaming others. The teacher plays an active but indirect role, limiting input to an occasional question, clarification, or answer to a direct student question. They do not tell students what they should think or so.

Glasser has found that the use of classroom meetings accomplishes three important results. First, it does in fact contribute positive solutions to many problems that students encounter; second, it provides the mechanisms for collaborating in positive purposeful ways toward the solution of problems; and third, it establishes an ongoing means for expressing ideas and concerns freely and positively.

The group-process method may be summarized as follows: It encourages participation by all members, focuses on matters of personal and social concern, teaches students how to function in democratic ways, stresses the value of each person's contributions, and allows students to play leadership and followership roles. This method, even in these times of an ever more crowded school day, can be included in the curriculum. It has its own particular contributions to make. It can be used as an integral part of the social studies curriculum, in regularly scheculed classroom meetings, and as a part of the day's opening activities.

The Project Method

The project method of instruction deals with long-range activities that must be organized, conducted, and reported, and that require from a few days to several weeks to complete. It is especially useful in social studies, science, art, and language, and can bring about intensive student involvement.

Though they follow guidelines and suggestions from the teacher, students have the responsibility to plan, organize, and conduct their own work. This work may be done in groups, as is often the case in social studies where group cooperation is a prized outcome, or it may be individual work as is often the case in science and art where individual planning, initiative, and achievement are desired.

The project approach, regardless of the curriculum area in which it is used, is usually aimed at the production of a real, tangible product—a mural, a model, a book, and so forth. Sometimes projects are intended to develop skills rather than products, as is the case with library researches and opinion samplings. Examples of and topics for projects include:

- Produce a class newspaper or literary journal.
- Growing vegetables without using soil.
- Make models of the heart, eye, solar system, etc.
- Set up and maintain cultures of microscopic organisms.
- Set up and operate a class weather station.
- Develop multimedia reports on selected states or countries.
- Plan imaginary trips to selected places in the world, including itineraries, transportation, lodging, meals, places of interest, costs, and so forth.
- Prepare a history of the school, using records, interviews, old photographs, etc.
- Keep a detailed diary of a realistic trip from Missouri to San Francisco by wagon in 1870.
- Have class competitions in simulated investing in the stock market, using daily quotes in the newspaper.
- Plan a model school for the year 2000.

The project method has some great strengths. One of them is intense student involvement. The teacher need do little to motivate students once the projects are under way. The project method gets at a number of diverse objectives, in both the cognitive and the affective domain. Inherent in most projects are objectives having to do with knowledge, comprehension, analysis, synthesis, and evaluation, as well as those having to do with interest, exploration, commitment, and responsibility. These outcomes occur naturally from the processes involved. A third strength of the project approach is that it contributes strongly to self-concept. While group enterprise is stressed as a laudable outcome, the increase in each individual's self-esteem, produced through involvement, responsibility, and genuine accomplishment, is not to be overlooked. Self-concept grows with accomplishment, competence,and recognition by others.

The teacher's role in the project method includes the following: First, the teacher must in advance identify several suitable topics for groups and individual projects in the subjects or topics involved. The most fruitful areas are those of art, communications, creative media, mathematics, science, and social studies, but in fact almost any area of the curriculum can contribute excellent topics for study. Teachers should be prepared to show examples of projects completed by previous students and describe the kinds of things that can be done. They should help students select appropriate topics, and identify goals, procedures, and resources to which they can turn, keeping all within reasonable limits of time. As the projects move toward completion the teacher must find time to talk with individuals and groups about the meanings associated with the work.

As is the case with all facilitative teaching, the project method can make only modest claims as an effective method for teaching basic skills and knowledge. But in keeping with the aims of facilitative teaching, it is unsurpassed as a means of causing students to organize, behave responsibly, follow through, clarify personal meaning, and find significance in what they do. When done as group work it has the further advantage of enhancing interpersonal relations and developing cooperative abilities.

Open-Experience Method

The open-experience method of teaching calls on students to an extent greater than in any other approach to select learning activities, engage oneself with them in a fruitful manner, exercise self-discipline, and in all ways behave responsibly. This method grew out of Herbert Kohl's experiences as a teacher of inner-city students, which he reported in his book *The Open Classroom*, which was mentioned previously. To summarize its beginnings, we may recall that Kohl was teaching students who were largely unreceptive to school learning. Since they were made to go to school they spent most of their energies not on learning but on making life miserable for their teachers.

Rather by accident Kohl found that the students were willing, sometimes even eager, to work at activities they found to be of personal interest. He found, too, that the students would obtain and bring to class many of the materials needed in their activities. From that beginning Kohl organized a program around activities of high student interest. He called this approach open education, meaning that it was open for students to plan. His approach was simple. First, he made sure that the classroom had available activities and materials of high interest to students. Students selected the activities and helped acquire the materials. Second, Kohl allowed students to choose, for a certain part of each day, the activities that each preferred to work at. They could choose any activity and work in any way so long as they did not damage property or infringe on the rights of other students. They could elect to sit quietly and do nothing if they wished.

Kohl found that the students' attitudes toward school quickly changed. Attendance improved dramatically while discipline problems shrank. Before long, students began to take increased interest in the normal school subjects.

The open-experience approach captured wide interest in the early 1970s, and was incorporated into the daily programs in thousands of classrooms. It was quite successful in several respects: It increased participation, interest, morale, attendance, and cooperation. It provided practice in self-direction and responsibility. It gave students a greater stake in their own education.

At the same time it fell short in important ways. Students rarely selected academic work as preferred activities, so that progress was not improved in the areas of school achievement normally assessed. Self-control improved in many classrooms, but grew worse in many others. Parents looked upon open experience as turning the schools over to kids who knew nothing about educating themselves.

The present assessment of open experience is that it can improve student attitude and morale, but it should be used only sparingly since it takes time away from learning in the usual areas of the curriculum. If used under optimal conditions—by serious students working with skilled teachers—open experience might produce the sort of learning envisioned by Carl Rogers and others, who would have school programs consist of students delving diligently into matters of central importance to their lives, assisted by able teachers working skillfully to facilitate the students' progress. To date, few classrooms have successfully achieved this ideal state. Open experience has made its contribution, but it is generally a small one, with little prospect of increase in the foreseeable future.

To summarize the major advantages of facilitative teaching, we may note that it helps students focus on matters of importance in their lives, teaches the methods and procedures of learning on one's own without the direct supervision of the teacher, causes students to be responsible for planning and following through, develops interpersonal relationships, and provides practice in the skills of give and take and effective compromise that are the hallmarks of effective functioning in a democratic society. Facilitative teaching, through individualized, small-group, or large-group activities, always focuses on the personal meaning obtained by the students individually and collectively, and on the contributions that meaning makes to their personal development. Its disadvantages are that it is time consuming and relatively ineffective for teaching basic knowledge and skills.

MANAGEMENT FUNCTIONS REQUIRED OF THE TEACHER

Facilitative teaching is not nearly so precise or structured as is direct teaching, thus management is not so detailed. In some ways this makes good management more difficult because clear steps are not so evident. Facilitative teaching as practiced today usually takes one of three forms: individual inquiry, group inquiry, or group process. Less and less do we see open experience used in formal instruction. The management functions required of the teacher vary somewhat among these three methods, and they are discussed in the sections that follow.

Management of Individual Inquiry

The management of individual inquiry requires the teacher to:

1. Identify many suitable topics for inquiry. These topics should be kept in the background and brought forth as possibilities only when students do not readily identify topics of real concern to themselves.
2. Schedule conferences with individuals. This requires a substantial time investment by the teacher. Some of that time will have to be taken from other parts of the curriculum, as when students are working at free reading, art, or mathematics seatwork.
3. Develop a plan or procedure once topics are identified. This plan should be devised by the student with guidance from the teacher.
4. Designated work space. This will normally be the student's desk or a special table.
5. Identify materials and other resources. This identification

occurs during the conference and the resources are written alongside the plan of procedure. This may be done using carbon paper so that both students and teachers have copies.

6. Observe the students at work and be ready to assist as necessary in accord with the plan devised.

7. Schedule follow-up conferences on a regular basis. Special conferences should be called when necessary.

8. Conduct personal evaluation, with students taking the lead. Ask students to comment on the value of the work, the insights they have developed, future directions they might wish to pursue, and their own effectiveness, diligence, and attention.

9. Put together a formal report, product, or narrative description of the results and deliver it to members of the class and perhaps to other students and parents. Narrative reports may be given orally. Products may be put on display. Performances can be staged for classes, assemblies, or open house.

Management of Group Inquiry

Group inquiry follows some of the same procedures as individual inquiry, especially with regard to prior identification of topics. It is much more likely that a list of topics will be given to a group, allowing them to make their selection, rather than their identifying a topic for themselves without guidance. Group inquiry is normally done in social studies or language where cooperation is sought and the skills of group work are included among the objectives. Once the topics are established, the teacher must do the following:

1. See to the formation of groups. These groups should not be large if they are to work together with maximal effectiveness. Four to five members comprise the most work-efficient groups. Groups are formed on the basis of interests, abilities, friendships, or other special reasons.

2. Provide for leadership. Before establishing the groups, the teacher should discuss with the class the requirements and functions of both leadership and followership. The groups may then select their leaders, unless the teacher wishes to make those appointments.

3. Plan procedures. The group should, perhaps following a

guide furnished by the teacher, plan out the procedures it will follow and put them in sequence.
4. Assign tasks to individual members. Each individual should have a clear task assignment, including what is to be done and how. This ensures that each member fills a responsible role in the process. These task assignments should be decided on by the group.

The remaining steps in group inquiry are the same as those for individual inquiry. Management must provide for work space, materials and resources, teacher observation of members at work, conferences between teacher and group, evaluation of its work by members of the group (a guide-sheet furnished by the teacher is helpful for this purpose, referring to degree to which goals were realized, cooperation, discharge of responsibilities, new learnings, sense of pride in accomplishment, and pleasure in conducting and presenting the work). Finally, the group will have put together some kind of product to present to other members of the class.

Management of Group Process

The management of group process takes a rather different form from that of individual and group inquiry. Process focuses not on the seeking out of information but on the exchanges of information in ways that build skills of cooperation, communication, and compromise. For this reason there will be no product from the group-process approach that will be communicated or displayed for others. Rather, emphasis will be on the activities themselves and their less tangible outcomes: communication skills, attitudes of cooperation and compromise, and predisposition to working for collective as well as individual good.

The forms most commonly used in group process are debate, discussions, and classroom meetings. Each of these forms makes its particular contributions. *Debates* are relatively formal in nature and involve making and rebutting arguments, following a prescribed format. The arguments and rebuttals are formulated by the students and the topics can be selected by them as well, giving attention to matters of special interest in their lives.

Discussions allow for freer exchange of ideas and arguments without having to adhere to rules as stringent as those of debate. Discussions may be in the form of panels with each person presenting a point of view, in round-table with give and take, or in free-form discussions in the style of "Quaker meetings," where people speak when and as the spirit moves them.

Classroom meetings were discussed previously. When carried out as advocated by Glasser they focus on matters of immediate importance to students in areas of academic, social, and personal matters.

Management responsibilities include prior selection of topics to be used as a backup in the event that students are not able to identify topics for themselves. The teacher and the class together must establish rules that will be followed in the exchanges of ideas and opinion. These rules may be prescriptive, yet general: for example, no complaining, no blaming others, everyone has an equal chance to speak and be heard. The teacher participates, but in an unassuming way, taking care not to dominate, exert undue influence, or stifle students' willingness to express themselves. The teacher may need to encourage students and solicit opinions from more silent members. Finally, some kind of evaluation is useful in which students express opinions concerning the value of the experience and whether they considered it enjoyable and worthwhile. They might be called on to summarize the outcomes of the meeting in term of conclusions drawn and skills developed in the process.

THE PUSH FOR PERSONAL MEANING

Facilitative teaching has two goals that set it apart clearly from direct teaching: learning how to learn on one's own, and finding the personal meaning in that which is learned. What we have considered to this point has focused mainly on learning how to learn on one's own. In this section we will examine the second goal, the push for personal meaning.

One can begin to examine personal meaning by contrasting what is learned through facilitative teaching with what is learned through direct teaching. Direct teaching makes great contribution in the learning of basic facts and skills—learning how to spell correctly, use correct grammar, add and subtract, follow directions, attack words, read with comprehension, and so forth. There is little personal meaning to be found in such learnings—that is, insights that help the individual understand self, other people, the world, the meaning of life, and so forth.

On the other hand, in the kinds of learnings toward which facilitative teaching is aimed, personal meaning is at the heart of the matter. When one begins to learn how to learn, begins to learn how to relate to others, and begins to find answers to questions of central concern in life, attention naturally turns to the meaning that each of these things has in the life of the individual.

In this search for personal meaning, it falls the lot of the teacher to assume responsibility fot encouraging students to reflect on their activities and learnings in an attempt to relate them to an understanding of their own lives and to the lives of people in general. This procedure calls on students to go a step further and express their insights in a suitable manner such as through art, written composition, or dramatization. More commonly it is done through discussions and explorations of ideas in groups, with the teacher participating and clarifying but not dominating, and sometimes in individual discussions between teacher and student. In one way or another students are called on to address questions such as: "What does this mean? How does it fit in with other things I know about? What does it mean to me in my personal life? How does it affect me for better or worse, help me understand myself and others, help me relate better with others? How does it help expand and clarify my views? How does it make my life more pleasant, significant, purposeful? How can it help me deal with other people, support them, build them, and at the same time build myself? What new directions does it suggest for me in my life? These are the kinds of questions Carl Rogers and Abraham Maslow are concerned with when they stress the importance of finding personal meaning in those things that comprise the central core of students' education.

EVALUATING FACILITATIVE TEACHING AND LEARNING

Evaluation, of course, means determining the worth of something and in this case involves the degree and value of learning , willingness, and satisfaction for students, and the quality of the facilitative teaching that helped produce the learning.

The evaluation of facilitative teaching and learning must of necessity focus on three things: process, product, and meaning. Process is central to facilitative teaching. It is evaluated in terms of extent of student involvement, clarity of direction, and the degree to which students show initiative, leadership, followership, cooperation, reflection, compromise, responsibility, and self-discipline. Interactions are judged in terms of the degree to which they contribute to effective work and exchange of information.

Products, though assigned no more importance than process, nonetheless are evaluated in making judgements about facilitative teaching. Normal criteria are used, such as quality, completeness, neatness, originality, and the incorporation of elements specified beforehand.

Personal meaning is harder to assess. One must rely on what can be inferred from student diligence, comments, and self-appraisal. The questions posed on the proceeding page for use in helping students clarify personal meaning in their learnings illustrate that point. As students ask and become able to answer such questions about the relation of learnings to their individual lives, we see evidence of their grappling with personal meaning. In more specific terms we look for student ability to put into their own words the general ideas or summarizing statements that reflect the learning they have acquired, and we look for an ever increasing ability to apply learnings toward the understanding or resolution of real problems that occur in daily life.

CHECKPOINTS

Facilitative teaching is used to help students learn to select and work through problems or issues that they find personally significant. It promotes inquiry and discovery, important in learning how to learn on one's own. In the facilitative role the teacher:

- asks many questions about students' interests and concerns.
- helps students identify matters of significance in their lives.
- establishes a climate that fosters curiosity and allows mistakes.
- works in an advisory rather than a directive capacity.

Formalized procedures have been developed that assist facilitative teaching:

- inquiry/discovery (for learning how to learn for oneself).
- group process (for effective democratic interaction in groups).
- project method (for intensive involvement in studies of longer duration)
- open experience (for helping students select topics and manage their own efforts).

Inquiry management functions for teachers in facilitative teaching are:

- help students identify topics.
- schedule conferences.
- help arrange groups, if necessary.
- organize work areas.
- help find resources.
- observe students and be ready to assist if needed.
- help students conduct personal evaluations.
- encourage reports or products shared with the class.

Group process management functions for teachers in facilitative teaching are:

- help with selection of topics or activities.
- help establish rules and procedures.
- encourage participation by all.
- help with group evaluation.

A major goal of facilitative teaching is to help students find personal meaning in what they learn:

- relate findings to one's personal life.
- express insights through creative productions or group discussions.
- reflect on new insights in terms of meaning, value, effect on life, human understanding, human relations, and new directions suggested.

Evaluation of facilitative teaching and learning is done in terms of:

- process—the learning how to learn.
- products that might have resulted.
- meaning that accrues.
- new directions that might be suggested.

BIBLIOGRAPHY

Allport, G. *Becoming*. New Haven, Conn.: Yale University Press, 1955.

Bruner, J. *Toward a Theory of Instruction*. Cambridge, Mass.: Belknap Press of Harvard University Press, 1966.

Bruner, J. "The Act of Discovery." *Harvard Educational Review*, 31:21–32, 1961.

Combs, A. "Some Basic Concepts for Teacher Education." *Journal of Teacher Education* 23:286–290, 1972.

Dewey, J. *Democracy and Education*. New York: Macmillan, 1916.

Glasser, W. *Schools Without Failure*. New York: Harper & Row, 1969.

Joyce, B., and Weil, M. *Models of Teaching*. (2nd ed) Englewood Cliffs, N.J.: Prentice-Hall, 1980.

Kohl, h. *The Open Classroom*. New York: New York Review Books, 1969.

Maslow, A. *Motivation and Personality*. New York: Harper & Row, 1954.

Rogers, C. *Freedom To Learn*. Columbus, Ohio: Charles E. Merrill, 1969.

Rogers, C. "Forget You Are A Teacher." *Instructor* 81:65–66, 1977.

Ryan, F., and Ellis, A. *Instructional Implications of Inquiry*. Englewood Cliffs, N.J.: Prentice-Hall, 1974.

Silberman, C. *Crisis in the Classroom*. New York: Random House, 1970.

Thelen, H. "The Evaluation of Group Instruction," in *Educational Evaluation, New Roles, New Means*. 68th Yearbook of the National Society for the Study of Education. Chicago: The University of Chicago Press, 1969.

9

Records Management

Most teachers dislike keeping records. They look upon the task as a necessary but unproductive aspect of accountability. Some allow the task to overwhelm them, falling prey to the sheer quantity of paperwork, checking-off, storing, and retrieving that seem so often to be a part of keeping records. Accordingly they tend to slight the job, and the result is that they do not keep records in a way that helps teaching, learning, and reporting.

This chapter is intended to show the kinder side of records management, emphasizing its usefulness while showing how good records can be kept without undue burden to the teacher. The chapter is organized into five sections discussing what records are good for, types of records needed for each curriculum area, useful formats for record keeping, how to simplify record keeping, and preparation for conferences with parents and administrators.

WHAT RECORDS ARE GOOD FOR

Good records are valuable to teachers because they help promote efficient teaching, good learning, and effective reporting to parents and administrators. There are other reasons for keeping records, of course, such as furnishing records to other schools and colleges at later dates, keeping attendance for receiving financial aid, showing student achievement as a means of evaluating school districts, and making periodic evaluations and modifications in the school curriculum. Those reasons, however, are not teacher reasons for records; therefore they are not discussed in this chapter.

So far as teachers are concerned, records should enable them to tell, on a moment's notice at any time during the year, where an individual student stands academically and socially, what kind and amount of progress has been made, what specific goals and objectives are still to be attained, what the student's strengths and weaknesses are, how well the student has adjusted socially, and what the specific future instructional plans are for the student. This is a great deal of information, but if records are kept well it can be available at the touch of a finger. Records are kept well when the information they contain is adequate and concise, and when teacher effort in keeping such records is minimal. Let us examine the various aspects of good records management.

Instructional Level

A student's instructional level in any part of the curriculum is the level at which most rapid learning can occur. This is taken to mean that the instruction is neither too easy nor too difficult. Recent research has suggested that most rapid learning occurs when students make correct responses most of the time, but not always. It is important that teachers have a clear idea of students' instructional levels, so that they may plan instruction accordingly, and when necessary can report this information to parents and administrators.

Instructional level is determined through two measures—assessment, which is testing or formal observation to determine what the student is capable of doing, and on-going appraisal, which is a monitoring of the student's performance in the learning tasks provided by the teacher. These measures are recorded and become part of the teacher's records. Means of recording include entering into the records *scores* made on assessment and other tests, keeping *samples* of work completed by the student, and jotting down *comments* based on on-going observations made by the teacher. How these are entered, and on what kind of format, is explained in the section on forms and formats.

Progress

Parents, students, and teachers appreciate evidence that shows that the student is making genuine progress in the school curriculum. While progress is exciting and motivating, a lack thereof must be noted as well, for it is there that replanning and remediation must begin.

In the minds of parents, students, and teachers, progress is equated with success—a condition that produces self-esteem, good attitude, and high motivation. It can be shown in several ways. One of the most common ways is to record *pre- and posttest scores* in areas such as math, spelling, and reading. A pretest is given prior to a segment of instruction (usually lasting several weeks). When that segment of instruction is completed a posttest is administered. The pre- and posttests are quite similar, or even identical, and the increment in scores from first to second administration is a measure of progress entered on student records.

Another means of showing progress is by marking off the attainment of specific objectives included in a continuum of objectives such as those frequently used in reading, mathematics, and language. (See Figures 2 and 3 for examples.) This procedure shows at a glance where a student entered the continuum, what progress has occurred, and what remains to be accomplished.

A third means of showing progress involves samples of work that can show a before-and-after comparison and is especially useful where scores are difficult to assign and interpret, as in handwriting or art. Before-and-after work samples are kept in individual student folders, as will be explained later in the chapter.

A fourth means of showing progress is through the use of graphs that show progressive increments in scores attained, progressive decrements in the amount of time needed to complete certain tasks, frequency of desired behavior, number of books read, and so forth. Keeping charts and graphs for this purpose is highly recommended because graphic evidence is particularly reassuring to parents and exciting to students. Further, students themselves can be put in charge of maintaining the graphs, which are kept attached inside the student's individual folder.

Remaining Goals and Objectives

Parents are interested not only in progress their child has made but in what remains to be accomplished as well. Well-managed records provide this information at a glance, especially that part reflected in the continuums of objectives. Where a continuum is not involved, written and oral comments by the teacher together with indications of material to be covered in the textbooks provides adequate indication of what lies ahead for the student.

Strengths and Weaknesses

Many student strengths and weaknesses will become apparent as teacher and parent examine the curriculum continuums, test scores, and work samples kept with student records. Verbal clarification is often needed. Scores made on objective tests, for example, may require explanation. Where norms are used the scores will usually be converted to one of four types: (1) grade norms, which show how a student stands in relation to grade level; (2) age norms, which show how a student compares to students at different age levels; (3) percentile norms, which show a student's ranking "in the pack" of others who have taken the same test; and (4) stanine norms, which show relative standing similar to percentiles, but within broader limits.

Error patterns often present more useful evidence of particular strengths and weaknesses. When one knows exactly what a student is doing right and where certain kinds of errors are being made, precise instruction can be provided to correct the problem. Error patterns are revealed by certain types of tests, especially in mathematics, reading, and language. They are also noted as teachers observe students doing guided seatwork. Where such patterns become evident, evidence can be entered in the student's records, in blanks furnished for written comments. This evidence is especially helpful in reporting to parents, in organizing remedial instruction, and in conferencing with curriculum specialists who may wish to provide specialized instruction.

Social Adjustment

Certainly one of the most important outcomes of schooling is the ability to relate acceptably and to work cooperatively and productively with others. These areas of social growth constitute significant parts of the objectives of the social studies curriculum, and many teachers emphasize them throughout the school day. Evidence of social growth or problems is obtained on an informal basis by the teacher, who notes how a student gets along with others; if a student uses manners and shows courtesy; whether a student is inclined to cooperate, takes turns, and shares responsibility; if a student gets work done on time; and whether a student shows a tendency to abide by the rules of behavior established for the class.

Observations related to these matters are entered as brief notes in the social behavior blanks on the student progress form, a copy of which should be kept in each student's personal folder. The contents of the progress form are shown in Figure 3.

This information is of great importance to parents, whose first concern is their child's behavior in school. Their interest in this matter shows how intently parents want their children to behave, to be cooperative, and to learn as much as possibble.

Future Instructional Plans

Somewhere between the middle and the end of every parent-teacher conference there needs to be a description of future instructional plans for the student. Sometimes these plans will be carried out by the teacher and student; sometimes they will involve the parent's active involvement or tacit support. In either case, parents are entitled to be informed about the instructional plans designed to help the academic and social growth of their child.

Such future plans are suggested by the evidence included in the records. The general instructional plan is used for all students. Special attention is added for each individual student as needed within the general plan for all. This special attention is derived directly from the profile of strengths, weaknesses, instructional level, remaining goals, and social behavior revealed in the records. The teacher should comment briefly on the implementation of plans suggested by the data at hand, and should indicate how parents can assist with those plans. Notes of such intentions should be made, and the teacher should be sure to follow through on them and make parents aware of the special attention being given to their child.

RECORDS NEEDED FOR DIFFERENT CURRICULUM AREAS

Different areas of the curriculum call for different types of records. Those differences are explained in this section, and desirable types of records are indicated. Remember again that while lengthy explanations are provided here, they are for the purposes of clarification. The actual record keeping is, as ever, intended to provide adequate coverage in a concise form, with a minimum of effort required of the teacher.

Mathematics

Records most useful in mathematics include assessment scores, objectives continuum, work samples, and a progress graph. *Assessment scores* can be used to indicate instructional level, progress made, and certain areas of strength and weakness. Refer to Figure 4 to see how they can be entered in the records. The *objectives continuum* with areas of student attainment checked off provides a concrete illustration of the overall mathematics program together with indications for the individual student of progress, objective attained, and objectives not yet attained but toward which instruction will be aimed. A few selected *work samples* should be kept to show typical errors, work pace, and ability to solve word problems. To reveal all this information in two or three samples, the teacher may have to construct a worksheet that contains several different types of math problems, including word problems, and administer the work under timed conditions. The teacher can explain the intent, results, and implications during the conference with the parent. Graphs should be kept for certain parts of the math curriculum where they can show progressive increments in a dramatic way. Areas of most promise include timed exercises in basic facts of addition, subtraction, multiplication, and division, as well as growth in ability to solve word problems.

Reading

Records of most value in the area of reading include assessment scores, objectives continuum, and where applicable a personal reading list that names books and other materials read by the student. As with math, *assessment scores* provide a good indication of the level at which instruction should be of most benefit for the student. But even more than in math, reading assessment scores indicate special needs of the student in such aspects as word attack skills, comprehension skills, interpretative reading, and ability to recall what was read. There are numerous kinds of assessment or diagnostic tests in reading. A progress form such as the one shown in Figure 4 indicates the areas in which measures are most often sought. The *objectives continuum* serves the same function also, revealing specific objectives reached and not reached by the student, but ordinarily there will be more objectives included in the reading continuum than in any other area. Work samples seldom furnish helpful data for conferencing with parents or professionals, except as they might indicate a failure to get work completed on time or with acceptable neatness. In their stead, a *personal reading list* is helpful, showing books and other works selected and read by the student.

Spelling

Spelling is an aspect of language that can be treated almost like math facts, insofar as records are concerned. For each student, the records should include *assessment scores*, a list of *scores made on weekly spelling tests*, and indications of *special programs* or bonus word lists with which the student is working. The assessment scores show entry level, progress, and functional level. A list of scores made on weekly tests shows continuity of achievement and effort. Where the student is involved with special word lists or is working with bonus words above the regular spelling list, such should be indicated.

Students themselves can keep spelling records updated. They can record the final score made on each week's spelling test, together with the date, and they can write in bonus words or attach copies of special word lists used in personalized spelling programs. Keeping these records provides added incentives to practice good penmanship and increases motivation and involvement in the learning process.

Grammar and Vocabulary

With this part of the language curriculum records management moves from recording scores to entering *notational appraisals and comments*. Refer to the progress form in Figure 4 to see how this is done. The word *grammar* is used to refer to general language usage, both oral and written, including sentence structure, subject-verb agreement, correct verb tenses, and so forth. The teacher notes errors that seem to reoccur for a given student and makes written comments, if needed, on the record form. The same procedure is followed for vocabulary unless the teacher has included a vocabulary development segment in the language program. In that case, students can keep a list of words whose meanings they have mastered, as was the case for the special spelling words. In some cases, the two are combined; that is, the special spelling list and the new vocabulary list are one in the same.

Writing

In this part of the progress form, written comments are entered that have to do with handwriting and composition. Composition is further divided into expository and creative writing. The main emphasis in the first is on expressing ideas clearly and sequentially, involving skills in organization, topic sentences, subordinate sentences, paragraphing, and so forth. Creative writing stresses the artistic side of writing, striving for beauty of expression, novelty of presentation, and varied forms of prose and verse. In both cases *samples* of such writing should be kept in the records folder. These samples should be made to do double duty, first to exemplify the student's best efforts in creative or expository writing, and second (having been rewritten if necessary) to reflect the student's best handwriting. Teachers can show student *progress* by including before-and-after samples, though in truth the resulting contrast is somewhat suspect since immense variations in composition and handwriting can occur from moment to moment as a reflection of the student's intent to do especially well.

Social Studies

The social studies program follows different paths according to grade level. Numerous topics are covered in a given year, usually including current events plus the history, geography, economics, customs, and so forth for particular communities, states, nations, and continents. Skills with maps, globes, charts, and graphs, plus innumerable construction activities are usually involved in the program, and often the art, music, clothing, and other cultural items of particular places and times are stressed.

All this makes record keeping difficult in the social studies, except for entering *notational appraisals and comments*. Some teachers use a series of examinations, and *scores* made on those tests can be kept where desired. Samples of work done in social studies are usually too cumbersome to be kept as records, although sometimes group murals or construction projects will be on display in the class room when teachers conference with parents. At such times, the individual student's contributions to such work can be pointed out.

Science and Health

Class work done in the areas of science and health is similar in nature to that done in the social studies. Large units of study characterize the curriculum, and group projects are often undertaken. Some teachers like to have students complete one or more individual projects in science, and those projects when completed are put on display for a time. So far as records are concerned, *notational appraisals* are entered in the blank spaces provided, indicating the type of work done and the student's level of involvement, quality of participation, and any special work that might have been done.

Art

Art programs usually consist of two aspects, appreciation and production. Art appreciation is an area that is difficult to measure, and records are usually inappropriate except for notation of experiences in which the student has participated. Productive art, on the other hand, makes strong contributions to the student's record file. It provides excellent *samples*, at least two of which should be included in the folder. Legitimate before-and-after samples permit recognition of artistic growth, and attention can be drawn to the inclusion of various elements such as line, form, texture, composition, and balance. Specific art techniques are also revealed in the samples. Inclusion of the art samples also helps demonstrate balance in the curriculum in a graphic way, that is, evidence that the curriculum includes not only the basics but is balanced with experiences in aesthetic areas as well.

Music

Meaningful records are difficult to keep in the area of music. Neither music appreciation nor music production yield scores or products that show relative standing, growth, or attainment of objectives. *Notational appraisals* can be entered on the progress form to indicate experiences in which the student has participated, special talents noted, and contributions made in this part of the curriculum.

Physical Education

In elementary schools, physical education is rarely presented through formal instruction. Students are taught to play various games and more or less fend for themselves while the teacher supervises them at play. A quality physical education program, however, can contribute to students' well-being in many ways. Their status and progress are measurable, and students can demonstrate the attainment of specific objectives. Teachers should obtain a *continuum of objectives* for physical education and attempt to help students reach as many of the objectives as possible. In addition, recent years have seen the implementation of excellent programs in running, cardiovascular fitness, and individual sports that build coordination and fitness. In running, jumping, throwing, exercising, and other types of activities, *scores* can be kept that allow students to compete against their own past records. These scores show times, distances, number of repetitions, and so forth. The scores can be graphed, and the resultant picture is highly motivating.

FORMS AND FORMATS FOR GOOD RECORD KEEPING

The previous section described the types of records that are most useful for different parts of the curriculum. The descriptions referred to several kinds of forms and formats for keeping records, including master continuums of objectives, individual student folders, progress forms, graphs, and work samples. This section describes the nature and uses of these forms and formats, and in addition gives attention to three that were not mentioned previously—incentive record systems, cumulative record forms, and report card forms.

Objective Continuums

Objectives are written statements that describe, as precisely as possible, what the outcomes of instruction are to be. They are now written in behavioral terms, which means that they describe what the student is to become able to do that is observable by the teacher. Technically, behavioral objectives should contain an action verb—write, sing, jump, and so forth—that describes an act one can see or hear the student perform, and often though not always results in a product—composition, drawing, definition—that can be examined and appraised by the teacher. In addition, experts say that the objective should specify the amount of time allowed, the conditions under which the act is to occur, the criteria of acceptable performance, and any other factors that help clarify the act and product.

Teachers seldom state behavioral objectives so elaborately. It takes too much time to prepare objectives in that way, and when they are written they take up so much space that they do not fit easily into plan books or other materials used by the teacher. Still, teachers have accustomed themselves to thinking in terms of rather specific student acts, criteria, and conditions. Thus, well-stated behavioral objectives can be reduced to the absolute essentials of original action verb plus its direct object, which may be a physical act or a product. This reduction permits a great many behavioral objectives to be indicated in a small space, as at the head of a sheet of paper or folder.

"When I begin a school year, I prepare a set of goals or a continuum of skills. I list these across a grid. Down the side I list the names of the children. Since I teach kindergarten there are relatively few skills compared to other grades. I have prepared paper-and-pencil tests for those skills that can be tested in this way. Examples are: writing name, writing numerals, writing letters, circling the object that is above, below, larger, smaller, etc. These tests can be administered by parents who have been instructed or by my aide. The aide records the information. I look over the tests and the results. If there seems to be a need for further testing I do it myself. These tests simply document what I have already discovered in working with the children. If the school report card is correlated with the continuum of skills, so much the better. In recording, I use carbonized paper to make copies for myself, the parents, and the office."

Ruth, a kindergarten teacher

When such objectives are put into a particular order or sequence, especially when one objective leads to the next, which in turn leads to another, we have what is called a *continuum*. Such a continuum of objectives describes the intended outcomes—some of the main outcomes at least, if not all of them—for a particular subject or part of the curriculum. Continuums are very helpful to teachers, for they describe a sequence of outcomes, arranged in an order to promote most rapid growth, and they name acts or products that can be observed, assessed, or measured. Those observations, assessments, and measurements can be put into a code—either checkmarks or various kinds or numerical scores—and entered on each student's records. Thus the continuum provides a clear and direct guide to the curriculum, suggesting the kinds of activities that the teacher ought to provide, and a well-organized vehicle for keeping records. Examples are presented in Figures 2 and 3. Figure 2 shows a portion of a mathematics continuum appropriate for kindergarten. Figure 3 shows a portion of a reading continuum used in fifth grade.

Various kinds of coding systems are used for making entries on the continuum format. One of the simplest is entering a slash (/) to indicate that the concept or skill has been introduced. When the student has mastered the concept or skill, the slash is crossed to make an (×). Other systems indicate the date on which the objective was reached, the number of trials attempted before mastery, and the degree to which the objective was attained—e.g., mastery (*m*), satisfactory (*s*), improvement needed (*i*).

When continuums are used only in reading and mathematics, the recording can all be done by the teacher at times when students are doing independent seatwork. If more continuums are used, or if there is much recording to do, teacher aides or volunteers can be assigned to enter checkmarks on the list. The teacher should strive to use a simple marking system, and should keep the amount of time required for entering checkmarks to a minimum.

Individual Folders

The master continuums of objectives are kept by the teacher in a secure place. In addition to those records, each student should have a personal record folder that contains many important records together with samples of work. These individual folders are indispensible for use in conferencing with parents, administrators, and students themselves. In addition, they contain documents and forms that are highly motivational to students, and they allow students, from third grade upward, to take responsibility in assembling, car-

FIGURE 2.
A portion of a kindergarten math continuum.

Student Names	iden & complete pattern	match set members	iden set with most	match set of 6 to numeral	iden set 1 less than 5	iden set 1 more than 2	iden greatest numeral	iden least numeral	iden counting order (1–4)	iden counting order (11–13)

FIGURE 3. A portion of a fifth-grade reading-skills continuum.

| | Word attack | | | | | | | Comprehension | | | | | | Vocabulary | | | |

Student Names	consonant sounds	short vowel sounds	blends and digraphs	long vowels, final	long vowels, double	vowels modified by r&l	variant & irreg. vowels	affixes	main idea	facts	cause-effect	sequence	prediction	inference & conclusion	bases, prefixes, suffixes	antonyms, synonyms	contractions	compound words

ing for, and presenting their own records of school performance, a responsibility that contributes to student sense of involvement in the educational process.

Student folders can be arranged in various useful ways. The following suggestions will result in attractive, useful folders:

- *Folders*—use legal size manila folders. The extra length will accommodate oversized art work and other samples.
- *Front Cover*—teacher affixes student name, room number, teacher name, and grade level. Students decorate the front cover with own design or art work (be sure to practice first).
- *Inside Front*—teacher attaches progress form sheet, described in Figure 4.
- *Inside Back*—teacher affixes graph forms to show progress in math, spelling, and other areas.
- *Loose Inside*—this area is used to hold samples of student work in handwriting, composition, and art. Special vocabulary and spelling lists plus individual reading list can be included. Before-and-after samples, intended to show progress, can be stapled together. The samples should be updated periodically, four to six times per year.

Students from third grade on can assume much of the responsibility for recording, graphing, and updating their folders. The folders, however, should not be kept in student desks, but in a central depository where they will remain neat and clean and out of the way except when in use.

Progress Form

We have frequently mentioned the progress form, which is to be attached inside the front of the folder, and on which so much information can be succinctly recorded. A sample progress form is shown in Figure 4. It is suitable for second grade and above. Slight modifications are needed for use in kindergarten and first grade.

Graphs

Graphs can be used to great advantage in record keeping in areas where performance can be quantified, where essentially the same task is done week after week, and where there is likelihood of progressive improvement. Such is the case for timed tests with number facts in mathematics or for the number of consecutive chin-ups done

FIGURE 4. Sample progress form.

Name _____

	Pretest	*Midtest*	*Posttest*

Reading
    San Diego Quick—level
    Oral Reading Test—level
    Silent Reading Test—level
    Word attack needs _____

Mathematics
    Math grade-level test—
    Basic facts (see graphs)
    Word problem application _____

Language
    Spelling placement
    Word lists and scores—(see graphs and samples)
    Capitalization, punctuation, grammar _____

Composition & Handwriting (see samples) _____

Social Studies _____

Science & Health _____

Art (see samples) _____

Music _____

Physical Education (see graphs) _____

Other _____

Social Behavior _____

FIGURE 5. Sample graph sheet for various curricular areas.

Math: Additional facts, number correct out of 50 in five minutes time.

No.	*Week* 1	2	3	4	5	6	7	8	9	10	11	12
45 –												
40 –												
35 –												
30 –												
25 –												
20 –												
15 –												
10 –												

Spelling: Scores on midweek tests, number correct out of 20.

20 –
19 –
18 –
17 –
16 –
15 –
14 –

in physical education. One graph can be made to show performance for an entire year, on a weekly basis. When sectioned a single graph page can accommodate several different subject areas. Figure 5 shows a sample of such a graph sheet.

Work Samples

Along with graphic representations, samples of completed class work are very useful for judging student performance and for reporting to parents, other professionals, and students. The work sample can be made to incorporate and reflect many different skills and concepts, and the sample can be analyzed in terms of those individual elements.

Not all school work yields samples that can be included in the folder. Samples of most benefit would include:

1. A math worksheet, specially organized to require different skills, such as regrouping, subtracting, adding, and maintaining correct alignment; to reveal certain common types of errors that might occur; and to require knowledge of basic number combinations.

2. A written composition that has used many of that week's spelling words. This composition can then reflect organization, sentence structure, spelling, and handwriting.
3. A piece of art work such as a drawing intended to incorporate techniques having to do with line, form, color, contrast, and overall composition, elements that can be analyzed both in isolation and as a total composition.
4. Personal reading and spelling lists, where supplementary or bonus work has been undertaken.

Every two to four weeks, a new work sample can be stapled to that already in the folder. This provides an on-going record of progress, which can be very satisfying for students, parents, and teachers.

Incentive Record Systems

The forms and formats described to this point are used to record and report curricular progress during the year. They are used for conferencing with parents, students, and other professionals, and for developing a sense of responsibility in students for participating in their educational program.

Three other record formats make strong contributions to the curriculum. Two are required—cumulative records and report cards. The third, incentive record systems, are used in the classroom primarily as a means of motivating students to do more work in such areas as reading and work at learning centers.

Incentive formats are charts with students' names displayed in the classroom to provide recognition for quantity of work accomplished. A common example is that of a master chart onto which a star is affixed beside each student's name each time that student completes a library book. Some teachers use "book worms" for this purpose, beginning with a worm face with the student's name on it and adding a segment, showing the title of the material read, each time a new book is completed. The objective is to see how long a worm one can make before the year is over.

Other incentive formats are displayed on individual student's desks. One example is a "money card," where the teacher uses a rubber stamp to stamp coins of different denominations on the money card in accord with fixed amounts the students can earn for completing various learning activities, for good behavior, or for showing courtesy and good manners to other students. The money card has the student's name on it, and the "coins" are stamped on, so there is no problem of losing discs or having them stolen. The card is kept on the desk and may, when filled, be dated and placed in the student's personal folder.

These types of incentive formats serve the dual functions of motivating student output and easily maintaining records of accomplishments and behavior. Teachers must keep one caution in mind: it is illegal under the right to privacy act to display publicly comparative student performances which may show a student in bad light when compared to others. If there is any question in this regard, teachers should check with the building principal to make sure they are not violating existing regulations.

Cumulative Records

Each student, from the time of entering kindergarten until graduating from high school, has information entered yearly on a *cumulative record form*. This constitutes the core of a student's educational record, as regards both academic learning and social behavior. At one time cumulative folders were private, not to be examined by either students or parents. That is no longer the case, and the cumulative records are available for inspection by parents, legal guardians, and past a certain age by the students themselves. Since the forms are open, teachers have begun to exercise care in what they write in them. Teachers must be able to back up anything derogatory that they write. Generally speaking the cumulative folders include the following categories of information about the student: *identification date; individual adjustment* (interests, activities, leadership, family relationships, out-of school responsibilities, attitudes and feelings about self, peers, school, and referrals to school services or community agencies); *growth and development through school experiences* (this includes curriculum units and degree of success in all major areas of the curriculum). *Group scholastic test scores, individual test scores, group achievement test scores,* and *personality and interest inventories* may also be included in the cumulative folder.

Report Cards

Report cards are record formats best known to parents and the public. They are summaries, however, end points that report status of achievement but do not help with further planning of instruction.

Report card formats almost defy generalization because they come in so many different sizes, with so many different contents, marked in so many different ways. Yet they do have some things in common, and they are a task with which all teachers must contend, although few teachers feel a sense of pleasure in the task.

Report cards list the separate areas of the curriculum in which the student has had instruction. They have provisions for marking how well the student has achieved in each of those areas. Some are marked with the familiar A,B,C,D,F, while others are marked with S (satisfactory) and U (unsatisfactory), A (achieved) or N (needs improvement), and other such systems. In a few places, report cards have only written comments from teachers, with no letter grades or marks. There has occurred a rather marked swing in recent years back toward the use of A,B,C,D,E, mostly in reponse to requests from parents.

In addition to reports of achievement status, some report cards provide a space for marking the effort made by the student. This allows an average student who tries hard to make good grades for effort. Very common everywhere are spaces for marking the social behavior or "citizenship" displayed by the student. These marks are often given using the letters O (outstanding), S (satisfactory), and U (unsatisfactory).

Aside from these commonalities, and the fact that the report card includes student's name, school, teacher(s), and date, the physical appearance of report cards, as well as the means of marking them, vary greatly from place to place.

SIMPLIFYING RECORDS MANAGEMENT

The point of this entire chapter was to show how good, complete records can be kept and used with a minimum of effort so that record keeping does not become an overwhelming burden for the teacher. After so much discussion it may appear that this chapter has merely reemphasized the burdensome nature of records management. Consequently, now let us see how records management can be simplified so that it becomes a relatively minor task. The four suggestions that follow show how that can be done.

1. Relate all records to goals and objectives stated in the school's curriculum guide. Stipulated there are the student learnings for which teachers and students are accountable. It is those things that the teacher must keep track of and report to parents and administrators.

2. Use record-keeping forms that require a minimum of marking. Combine and summarize them, so that one form contains the records for many activities. Supplement the forms

with samples of student work that show progress toward stated objectives.

3. Make almost all of the record entries during school time, not at home in the evening. Let aides help with this task. To the extent possible involve students. Use them for scoring, recording, and charting. Such participation is good for students; it motivates, gives practice in responsibility, and makes them feel a genuine part of their educational program.

4. Make the individual record folder a source of pride for students. It shows their accomplishments, what they can do, and how they have progressed. It is an extension of themselves, and as they contribute to its quality so do they reflect their own quality.

PREPARING RECORDS FOR CONFERENCES

Most teachers conference personally with parents at least once each year. Some conference more often, and there are times as well when conferences about particular students must be held with administrators and specialists. The quality of input that teachers bring to such conferences is increased sharply through good records. The contents direct what teachers should say and the evidence at hand backs them up. The following pieces of material will help the teacher feel securely prepared for any conference.

The individual student record folder. This is the most useful set of materials for conferencing about a student that can be shown to the parent or administrator. The progress form inside the front cover describes the curriculum in a nutshell, with scores and comments about how the student is doing in each of the areas. Inside the back cover are the graphs that show evidence of progress, and included inside are work samples and lists that provide concrete evidence of student effort, accomplishments, and progress.

A note about future plans. Student strengths and weaknesses are revealed in the record folder, but a main purpose of the conference is to describe future instructional plans for the student. Teachers should take a moment before the conference to make notes concerning such plans, which they then discuss with parent or administrator.

A note about suggestions for help at home. Together with future instructional plans, teachers will wish to indicate to parents how they can help with the child's instructional program. This help might consist of setting definite study times uninterrupted by radio or television, working for short periods of time with drill or spelling, or discussing with the student the plot of a story or book that is being read. Involving parents in this way engenders support and causes the student to see that parents as well as school are actively concerned about educational progress.

Ancillary materials. Near at hand, but not referred to unless needed, one should have the school's curriculum guide plus copies of objectives continuums, textbooks, workbooks, and sample worksheets. If an instructional kit makes up a significant part of the reading program, for example, it should be at hand for possible reference as well. These materials should be referred to in the conference only if there are questions about objectives, materials, or activities. Otherwise, the record folder and notes are sufficient.

CHECKPOINTS

Good records can be very helpful, but most teachers do not like to keep them because they require so much work. Procedures exist, however, that allow teachers to keep complete, useful records with a minimum of effort.

Good records can reveal for any student at any time
- academic instructional levels
- specific strengths and weaknesses
- progress that has occurred
- social behavior
- future plans for the student

Records for mathematics
- diagnostic and assessment scores
- objectives continuum
- selected work samples

Records for reading
- diagnostic and assessment scores
- objectives continuum
- selected work samples
- personal reading list

Records for spelling
- assessment scores
- weekly test scores
- special word lists
- progress graphs

Records for grammar and vocabulary
- notational appraisals and comments
- personal grammar difficulties
- personal vocabulary list

Records for writing
- handwriting sample
- sample of expository writing
- sample of creative writing

Records for social studies
- notational appraisals and comments
- scores on scheduled exams

Records for science and health
- notational appraisals

Records for art
- samples; legitimate before-and-after comparisons

Records for physical education
- continuum of objectives
- performance scores and times

Formats for keeping good records easily
- objectives continuums (these are simply checked off)
- progress form
- graphs to show progress
- work samples, few in number, specially selected
- individual student folders, in which to keep the forms and samples

Incentive record systems (for motivation)
- displayed in the room or on students' desks to show quantity of work completed by each student
- must *not* be used to show any student in a bad light

Cumulative record forms and report cards must be done as directed by the school.

Simplifying records management
- relate all records to objectives in the school curriculum guide
- use record forms that require a minimum of marking
- make most entries during school time
- make the individual record folder a source of pride for students

Conferencing with parents
- use individual student folder to describe strengths, needs, and progress
- make a note about future plans for the student
- make a note about how parents can help at home

10

Communications Management

By the time she had been teaching for two years, Janet had become aware that some teachers enjoyed exceptional reputations among parents in the community while others, often as skilled and insightful, were hardly recognized by parents. She decided to investigate the cause of this difference. Before entering teaching she had spent several years as a buyer for a large department store, and she had strong feelings about the value of communication in establishing credibility and building working relationships. Suspecting that the same factor might help account for teacher reputation she devised a study which she completed for her master's degree (Mulder, 1979).

Janet proceeded by approaching the principals of several elementary schools in a large metropolitan area and asked each to identify teachers who were held in high esteem by parents in the community. She arranged personal interviews with the teachers identified. When she analyzed her findings Janet was able to conclude that without exception those teachers with laudable reputations were excellent in communicating with parents, going out of their way to make contact and keep parents informed about their children and the educational program provided. Janet found too that these teachers were not hesitant to ask for help from parents, to contact them when problems arose, and to show that they valued the parents as partners in the education of the children. No evaluations of teacher quality were made. Thus there was no certainty that the teachers interviewed produced better learning than those who were relatively unknown. But so far as parents were concerned those teachers were excellent. Parents believed that they were working strongly on behalf of the children. They supported the teachers, and through that support a great part of the instructional battle was won.

Subsequently, Charles (1981) undertook a study that related student achievement to certain techniques emphasized by teachers. One of the aspects involved was frequent, systematic communication with parents. The study showed that teachers who followed certain guidelines produced greater than expected gains in the areas of student self-concept, good manners, and achievement in reading and mathematics. Those guidelines emphasized many traits and factors discussed in previous chapters of this book—learning activities that move students strongly toward objectives; keeping students actively on task; teaching through modeling; and emphasis on good manners and common courtesy. An additional point of view stressed in Charles' study was that parents were to be considered teachers' best allies in the education of their children, and as such they were to be kept fully informed about objectives, programs, and progress. In addition, their help was to be sought in various matters, partly because the help was valuable and partly because it brought parents into closer involvement with the academic program. While parent involvement was prized, teachers remained firmly in control of the programs and made all the professional decisions.

Teachers used various means of communicating with parents. For example, Kay, a kindergarten teacher, prepared a weekly newsletter that included information about the academic program, activities at school, student comments, and so forth. Though the newsletter required some effort, Kay reported gratifying results. She found that parents not only read the newsletter avidly, but also went out of their way to respond personally and in writing. It seemed that every parent was reading each newsletter word for word. They seemed to see the newsletter as proof positive of the interest Kay took in their children.

The teachers who participated in the study were asked to solicit comments from parents and to keep records of those comments. The following are typical of the written comments received:

I really appreciate the way you have helped me with teaching my child manners, discipline, and respect for others. You have made my job a lot easier.

The children treat each other with respect. There is no bickering, verbal byplay, name calling, scapegoating, or fault finding. They have demonstrated courtesy to me as a visitor in the room.

You've excited our son about school. We thank you for improving his self-image.

Thank you for your kindness, thoughtfulness, interest, patience, understanding, and caring.

These comments illustrate what many teachers have known for a
long time, that when teachers take pains to communicate with
parents, the parents become staunch allies, interested in the school
program and willing to help. All parents want their children to learn
and behave well in school. Many of them do not know exactly what is
expected of their children, and few know that their support and help
are wanted, or even what they could do to help. Very few take the
initiative in such matters, feeling that they would be too forward if
they offered to assist with classroom activities. But a great many are
willing, even eager, when called on to help.

THE VALUE OF COMMUNICATION

Websters Intercollegiate Dictionary defines communication first as
imparting or conveying information, and second as the process of
exchanging information and ideas. Both these meanings explain the
sense in which communication is used in this chapter. For the most
part communication by teachers consists of imparting or conveying
information. This information emanates from the teacher and goes to
students, parents, administrators, other teachers, and even in some
cases to the community at large. Sometimes, especially during instruction and conferencing, communication is used to exchange
ideas, and often the teacher takes the role of drawing out the other
person, obtaining ideas, reflecting, and helping the other person clarify thoughts. Students and parents, after all, have the right and need
to provide input in the educational program..

In addition to rights and needs for two-way communication,
everyone when kept informed about educational matters tends to
make better progress, be more supportive, provide more help, and
place higher value on education. Good communication helps by
informing, clarifying, keeping matters above-board, forestalling
unpleasant surprises, and enhancing the impression made by the
teacher.

COMMUNICATE WITH WHOM, ABOUT WHAT?

If good communication is to occur it will be due to the efforts of the
teacher. Teachers must take the initiative in conveying information
and, when necessary, of drawing it out. With whom does the teacher
share and convey information? For the most part communication is

directed to students, parents, administrators, and colleagues; occasionally information is conveyed to the public. Efforts are made to communicate about a number of things.

The curriculum—that is, the total program and what it entails.

Rules and expectations regarding discipline and homework.

Information concerning student progress.

Positive commentary about student behavior, work, and effort.

Personal communication concerning special problems encountered by students.

Any special needs or help required.

Casual information or advance notice of activities forthcoming.

Active solicitation of support or help from parents.

Simple information about pleasant matters.

Thomas Baker (1981a) urges teachers to "toot their own horns" as well. He suggests the following as good possibilities for publicizing one's efforts: Notify newspapers of interesting activities, take advantage of the requirement that radio stations must present public service announcements, keep and publicize an open-door policy, and meet with local politicians and invite them to visit the school.

Students should have clearly communicated to them the various aspects of the educational program in which they are involved, how instruction is to be given, what their responsibilities are, how they are expected to behave, and what system of control will be used to ensure proper behavior. The communication should show that the teacher is concerned, friendly, and helpful.

Parents, as previously noted, have the right to be informed about their child's school program, to know what is expected of their child and themselves, to know how they can help at home. When problems occur, they have a right and responsibility to know about them and to participate in the plans and procedures designed to correct them.

Atkeson and Forehand (1979) describe research that shows how parents can effectively participate in improving disruptive behavior and academic progress of their children. Baker (1981b) provides suggestions for making positive contact with parents, including telephone calls, personal letters, information bulletins, personalized invitations, and after-school play activities in which both parents and students participate.

Parents often do not know what they can do to help their children in school. Edward L. Stranix (1978) has prepared a list of twenty-five suggestions that can be sent to parents or discussed with them. The list includes items about health, communication, praise, patience, home study, attendance, television, and reading.

Administrators should be continually informed about the programs provided in each teacher's classroom. This information can be communicated informally, either orally or in written outline form. The system of discipline should be explained, unless the entire school is using the same system, and a copy of the plan should be kept on file in the principal's office. Plans for upcoming parties, programs, and field trips should be approved by the principal in advance. Most principals want to see written communications such as newsletters before they are sent out to parents. Teachers have the right to request active support from the principal concerning program, discipline, and special activities. If the principal is not able to support any portion of the program, the principal is obliged to help the teacher devise a modification that can be supported.

Carol, a fourth-grade teacher, sends the following suggestions home to parents to help them work more effectively with their children:

1. Praise your child for his or her accomplishments and efforts.
2. When your child misbehaves, talk about the act not the child's personality.
3. Express how you feel when you have been upset, as: "I feel annoyed," or, "I feel upset."
4. Don't make threats that you won't follow through. Instead, make consequences a natural part of the offense. For example, if the child rides a bike where it shouldn't be ridden, take the bike away for a reasonable period of time.
5. Don't bribe your child to get him or her to do homework and other tasks, but do give little rewards when they do the work.
6. Don't use sarcastic remarks and put-downs. Teach your child respect by showing respect.
7. Give your child some responsibilities around the house. Homework is a natural responsibility.
8. Set limits of acceptable behavior. Make sure the child understands. Stick to the agreements.
9. Listen to your child with attention and sensitivity. The child is worthy of your respect.

Colleagues—other teachers, clerical staff, para-professionals, librarians, nurses, psychologists, and others—should be kept informed of any activities or needs that concern them. No one likes to be taken by surprise in the performance of their professional duties. When the teacher takes pains to communicate such matters fully, help and support are likely to be given willingly. Such efforts to communicate promote a sense of friendliness, cooperation, helpfulness, and mutual support. The result is greater *esprit de corps* and better teacher morale.

PROFESSIONAL ADVICE ABOUT COMMUNICATION

In recent years many writers have suggested communication skills for teachers and have explained certain aspects and functions of good educational communication. Among those writers are Thomas Gordon on opening communication, C. M. Charles on clarity, Haim Ginott on using sane messages, William Glasser on group problem solving, and Eric Berne and Thomas Harris on parallel communication. Each of these writers acknowledges the strong benefits that accrue to teachers from effective communication and each contributes toward improving the overall quality and effectiveness of communication. Their ideas are described briefly in the paragraphs that follow.

Opening and Promoting Communication

Thomas Gordon, the author of *Teacher Effectiveness Training* (1974), wrote extensively on increasing the effectiveness of teachers through good communication. Among his many suggestions are several for opening up and encouraging communication where exchanges of ideas are desired and where one of the communicators might be ineffective or reluctant to express himself. Gordon would have teachers use such techniques as door openers, making reflective comments, acknowledging the other's responses, avoiding roadblocks to communication, and using a no-lose approach to resolving conflicts that might arise during communication.

Door openers are used to help a person begin to express ideas or feelings. They include comments (made by the teacher) such as, "I can see that you are upset about something." "Would you like to tell me about it?" Such comments make it easier for the other person to begin talking.

Reflective comments can be made by the teacher once the other person has begun to talk. These comments reflect back to the speaker what has been said, a technique developed as a central part of client-centered counseling popularized by Carl Rogers in the early 1950s. Instead of giving advice or making evaluative comments, the teacher attempts to reflect back the feelings being expressed by the other person, which in turn helps that person to identify problems more clearly and eventually to find solutions. Examples of reflective comments are, "That makes you pretty angry." "It makes you feel bad when you are not included." "It seems to you that I am picking on you."

Acknowledging responses are also helpful in this reflective mode. They include such comments as, "I see." "I understand." "Uh-huh." "Go on."

As communication begins to progress, the teacher takes care to avoid what Gordon calls "roadblocks to communication." He lists twelve such roadblocks that tend to shut off communication rather than encourage it. Examples of roadblocks include giving advice, questioning the other person, moralizing or criticizing, and diverting the person from the subject at hand. Teachers tend to make interpretations for other persons and give logical arguments pro and con the other person's problem. These too are roadblocks that shut off communication.

Finally, when a conflict is at the center of communication, Gordon advocates using the *no-lose* approach to resolve it. This involves finding a solution that allows both parties to emerge as winners, instead of the usual picture in which one person wins (usually the teacher) and the other person feels that he or she has lost (usually the student or parent). The no-lose approach calls on participants to identify several possible solutions to their disagreement, select one to which both participants can agree, and try it out to see if it will work. If it does not, a second solution is tried.

Clarity of Communication

While Gordon focused on communication as a means of clarifying and solving interpersonal difficulties, C. M. Charles (1976) looked at a different aspect of communication, one that has to do with the clarity of the message being delivered. This aspect of communication is important in instruction, since so much of the teacher's responsibility lies in imparting information to students and in giving them directions about how they are to work and behave—information that should be given in a clear, straightforward manner.

Charles suggests that teachers keep three things in mind if they wish to improve the clarity of instructional communication. The first is to identify the key components of a brief and accurate communication in much the same way that news reporters do—by identifying who, what, when, where, why, and how. The second step is to organize these key components into a logical sequence that is easily followed and understood. The third step is for the teacher to monitor students and others following the communication to be sure they have understood accurately what was said. One way of obtaining this information is through having students repeat, using their own words, the message that was delivered by the teacher.

Sane Messages for Person Building

Yet another aspect of communication important for teachers has to do with building within each student a sense of self and belonging. This aspect has been addressed extensively by Haim Ginott and best expressed for teachers in his book *Teacher and Child* (1972). Ginott looked at communication not so much as a way of conveying logical ideas as a way of conveying care, consideration, and support. He presented instructions for teachers on using communication to build student self-concept, sense of competence, and sense of belonging in the classroom. His basic proposition had to do with *congruent communication*, which referred to communication that is harmonious and authentic, where words match feelings yet do no psychological harm to others.

The key principle in congruent communication is *sane messages*, whereby the teacher addresses situations rather than students' characters. Suppose in the classroom there occurs an accident, high noise level, discourtesy, or failure to finish work on time. Teachers often address such situations by attacking the character of the students—"Let's try not to be so clumsy." "You are very wild today." "Your manners leave something to be desired." "You are lazy, I'm afraid." Instead of using such comments that denigrate the student, teachers do much better, says Ginott, to use sane messages that address the situation rather than the student—"We need to clean up the spilled paint." "It is so noisy I can't do my work." "Disrespect has no place in this classroom." "Our work is not finished on time. How can we take care of this matter?"

Among the many suggestions furnished by Ginott the following are also helpful in improving communication. Instead of giving commands to students simply comment on the situation—"There is work to be done." When correcting student misbehavior, dwell not on what was done wrong but on what they should do right— "Remember we raise our hands before speaking." He urges teachers not to harangue students but rather to make statements that are brief and to the point, and that help students get back to work as quickly as possible—"We fouled up because we didn't follow the rules. Let's try it again. I think we will do better this time."

Solving Group Problems

While Ginott's suggestions are aimed at building the individual person, other writers have focused on the role communication can play in solving group problems and building group cohesiveness. Such is the case with William Glasser, whose book *Schools Without Failure* (1969) has contributed so much to effective classroom practice. One of his contributions is the concept and practice of classroom meetings as means of bringing group communication to bear on solving matters of concern to the class.

Glasser felt that most of the major problems that confront teachers and students in the classroom could be resolved by using certain techniques of discussion. These discussions he called *classroom meetings*. They were to be conducted with students seated in a tight circle, which made it easy for students to see and talk with each other. The teacher sat as part of the circle and participated with the students, but did not direct the discussion or make criticisms or judgments of the comments made by students.

There were to be three kinds of classroom meetings, and all had the same purpose, which was to find constructive solutions to problems. The three kinds of meetings were (1) academic problem-solving meetings, having to do with concerns about school work; (2) social problem-solving meetings, having to do with personal and interpersonal problems such as disagreements with other people at school; and (3) open-ended meetings, in which students were allowed to discuss any problems of group concern.

Certain rules were required to make the classroom meetings function as intended. First, only positive, constructive solutions could be sought to the problems. There was to be no complaining, blaming, fault finding, or back biting. Second, every person had a right to express an opinion without being slighted or put down by others. Third, the teacher was to play a subdued role, participating in a way that clarified and encouraged but did not dominate, lead students, or criticize their contributions.

Glasser believed that these meetings should become a regular part of the curriculum. He said they should be considered as important as the three R's or any other part of the curriculum and should be scheduled on a regular basis.

Parallel Communication

We have all had experiences in communication where one person assumes a domineering, superior position and the other person or persons take a subservient position. While this condition may serve effectively for one-way communication, it works against two-way communication where exchanges and clarifications are sought. Eric Berne (1964) drew attention to three *ego states* that people employ when communicating with others. Those three states, corresponding to the psychoanalytic id, ego, and superego, were called *child, adult*, and *parent*. When communicating with people whom we consider to have status equal to our own, we use the adult ego state. When we feel superior to others, we may use the parent state, and when we feel inferior we may use the child state. Berne described these states as follows:

- *Parent*—talking to someone as our parents talked to us when we were children, that is, giving advice, correcting, admonishing, and controlling.
- *Child*—in using this state we talk, act, and think as we did when we were children, deferring to authority, behaving emotionally rather than rationally, and showing hurt feelings and pettiness.
- *Adult*—this is the ego state that best promotes effective communication, and the one therefore most valuable in communication. In this state we think, act, and reason in logical, rational ways. We do not moralize, preach, or admonish. Neither do we automatically defer to others, agreeing with everything they say. We communicate in a controlled manner, considering all the facts, sorting them out, organizing our thoughts, and expressing them firmly though not in a hostile manner.

Berne's ideas were coordinated into a system found useful in analyzing communication by Thomas Harris and explained in his book *I'm O.K.—You're O.K.* (1967). When people use the adult state in communicating with each other, all seem to reflect the opinion that "I am okay and so are you." When they use a state other than the adult they seem to be saying, "I am okay but you are not," or else, "You are okay but I am not." The resultant mixed communication, that is communication that is not parallel, restricts communication and produces bad feelings on someone's part.

TIMES THAT CALL FOR GOOD COMMUNICATION

Throughout the school day, as well as before and after, numerous instances occur in which good communication can greatly enhance a teacher's effectiveness:

- *Daily routines*—taking care of routine matters such as taking roll, calling for lunch count, and talking informally with students and parents.
- *Giving directions*—essential that clarity be a main concern. Directions normally should be given only once, with the expectation that students will listen to them attentively. Where directions deal with preplanned segments of the curriculum it is helpful to write them on the board or on a chart posted in front of the group.
- *Providing instruction*—essential that clarity be a main consideration. Much instruction involves imparting information from teacher to student, without student response. But much other instruction calls on students to respond. They too should be taught how to organize and express their thoughts clearly and succinctly.
- *Class discussions and meetings*—valuable discussions that often follow instruction, and particularly in discussions such as those advocated by Glasser in his classroom meetings. Individuals should note and put into practice some of the points suggested by Gordon (opening communication), Ginott (person building), Glasser (group problem solving), and Berne and Harris (using parallel ego states).
- *Individual conferences with students*—in regard to academic matters or personal matters such as emotional difficulties or poor behavior. Teachers should be sure to use Ginott's suggestions about addressing the situations rather than attacking the student. Gordon's suggestions are helpful, too, as regards encouraging and facilitating communication.
- *Staff meetings*—with principal, teachers, and other professionals. It is important that teachers express themselves clearly and concisely, and at the same time avoid putting others on the defensive through criticism, attack, or disregard. When it is necessary to disagree with another person, as is often the case, one must do so without causing the other person to feel that the attack is personal.
- *Meetings with parents*—one of the most delicate and crucial

areas of communication for teachers. Much has been said in this chapter about communication as a means of enlisting parental support and cooperation. One never knows in advance just what tack a parent will take in a personal conference, especially when the subject is something as sensitive as the education, treatment, and behavior of their child. The parent may show deference or hostility. Hopefully, it will be a calm, reasoned, productive attitude, but teachers must be ready for whatever comes. Parents who are docile and withdrawn may require encouragement if they are to express the thoughts that are in their mind. Those who are beligerent will require a teacher attitude consistent with the adult state —one of calm, reason, poise, and acceptance of the parent's state of mind.

- *Individual meetings with administrators and teachers*—teachers often show deference or belligerence, either of which puts them at a disadvantage. It is necessary that teachers use the adult ego state, think of themselves as being on a professional and personal level equal to that of the administrator, and use a calm, reasoned attitude when expressing and considering ideas.

TECHNIQUES FOR COMMUNICATING WITH PARENTS

A special section is included here on communicating with parents since it plays such an important role in the overall well-being of the teacher. As described earlier, parents have a right to know what is going on in the education of their child, to provide some input, though by no means dictate the program, and to help in the educational program should they so desire. Parental support is a condition much prized by enlightened teachers and in most circumstances is to be sought and nurtured.

In communicating with parents it is important to remember that they do not speak what has been referred to as "pedagese," that special language spoken by educators filled with code words and acronyms. One should use plain English. Where acronyms are used, such as ECE, DPT, or USSR, the names should be given and explained. For example, ECE means early childhood education and its use in the school requires certain activities and measures of accountability. DPT means diagnostic prescriptive teaching, in which children are tested for strengths and weaknesses in certain areas and then receive instruction designed to strengthen areas of weakness. USSR refers not to the Soviet Union but to an aspect of reading called uninterrupted sustained silent reading, in which every person the classroom including the teacher reads for a period of time silently and without interruption. In addition to clarity, teachers should attempt when communicating with parents to be as brief and professional as possible. Six vehicles should be considered in plans for effective communication with parents.

1. *Newsletters*. Recall the description of the efforts of Kay, the kindergarten teacher who prepared a weekly newsletter for parents and the excellent response that it brought from them. Newsletters take time to prepare, but they pay off. They should be kept short and to the point, giving attention to such matters as goals for the year, special activities, methods of helping students behave responsibly with consideration for others. They may include notes about field trips, dates of conferences, feast days, and other special events. They should be written in a personal tone, and should emphasize how much parent support is appreciated. Parents take even greater interest when the newsletter includes comments about individual students and includes samples of student work. Older children can contribute to the newsletter and even take on its production as part of their language arts program, since it requires skills of organization, outlining, vocabulary, expression, grammar, spelling, and expository and creative writing. Newsletters should not be gossip columns, but rather should deal with matters of academic importance.

2. *Notes*. Personal notes sent from teachers to individual parents are helpful in many ways, especially in calling attention to good and poor behavior of students and to any other problems that concern the student. Unlike the newsletter, such notes are quite personal in nature. They should be hand written, or may be done on preprinted forms personalized with additions made in the teacher's own handwriting. An example of such a note form is shown in Figure 6. Notes can also be used to remind parents about snacks, money for lunch or admissions, permissions for field trips, and other such matters.

3. *Telephone calls*. Parents rarely get telephone calls from the teacher except when their child is in trouble. Phone calls take relatively little time, especially when used to transmit a brief friendly message. The calls should not ask for parent commentary unless it is necessary, else it may turn into a lengthy chat. The teacher should thank the parent and express appreciation for support and cooperation. Calls of this type are well worth the time they require, and every parent can easily be contacted once each month. They show teacher interest in the child and a desire to work together with the parent for the child's benefit. An efficient format for the phone call is to introduce oneself, state pleasure at the opportunity to work with

This is to certify that

_____

has completed all assignments this week.

_____   _____

Date   Teacher's Signature

FIGURE 6.

"Bill" this year, remark very briefly on some incident that shows Bill's positive nature, and mention one thing that will be emphasized in Bill's academic or personal program in the days to come. The teacher then thanks the parent for cooperative concern about Bill's progress, says goodbye, and hangs up. The entire session takes no more than two minutes.

    4. *Conferences*. Most schools have regularly scheduled conferences that bring parents and teachers together about individual students. Sometimes in addition to the scheduled conference, the teacher may

need to call the parent to school for a special conference about a matter of concern. Whatever the case, the conference can be made very productive if properly arranged. This requires careful handling by the teacher, who must set parents at ease, convey a message without causing affront, draw out the parent's ideas, and formulate or express a considered plan for bringing about desired improvement in the child's educational program. The following are suggestions made by an experienced teacher recognized for her ability to conference productively with parents (courtesy of Ruth Charles):

Responsibility for the success or failure of the conference rests with the teacher. Plan each conference well.

Greet the parent in a friendly, relaxed manner.

Don't sit behind a desk. Sit side by side with the parent at a table. This helps establish a cooperative relationship.

Begin by chatting about the student as a worthwhile person. Mention good traits. This reassures the parent.

Guide the parent through the student's file, commenting on samples of work included there.

Encourage the parent to talk. Listen carefully. Be accepting. Do not argue or criticize. Parents cannot be objective about their own child. Arguing and criticizing cause resentment.

Keep in mind that parents are your best allies. Let the parent know you feel this way. Show that you both want the best possible education for the child.

End the conference by describing your plans for the student's future progress. Earnestly request the parent's help in supporting your efforts. Thank the parent for talking with you about the child.

When preparing for conferences, keep these things in mind:
- Have a folder for each child, with the child's name written on it in an attractive, impressive manner.
- Include a profile of skills covered, skills mastered, and skills to be introduced later.
- Include samples of the student's work, with tests that back up your evaluation.
- Make notes that remind you of anecdotes that provide insight into the child's behavior and progress.
- Think of yourself in the parent's place. Always be tactful and polite.

5. *Open house*. Once or twice each year most schools have an open house with parents and children invited to visit the classroom during a scheduled evening. There they see the teacher, the classroom, samples of student work, and books and materials in use. Often they hear a formal presentation by the teacher describing the year's program, typical activities, duties of aides, student expectations, the discipline system, and kinds of help that can be given at home. After the formal presentation parents have the opportunity to speak informally with the teacher, ask questions, and make comments about child and activities. This presents a different picture from the parent-teacher conference since it is relaxed, nonthreatening, and not focused on a particular student's strengths and weaknesses.

6. *Performances and displays*. Some teachers, though certainly not all, like to put on displays, performances, and exhibits, to which they invite parents and relatives of students. These activities allow students to show what they have accomplished and they provide an additional opportunity for teachers to describe objectives and activities of the educational program. Examples of such activities include musical productions, plays, choric verse readings, readers' theatre, science fairs, art exhibitions, and athletic events. Parents usually turn out in numbers for such events, eager to see their child perform or view products produced by the child. Teachers who make the effort to conduct such activities find that the parents become more involved in the academic program and more supportive of the teacher.

COMMUNICATIONS REMINDERS

Teachers who wish to communicate more effectively with parents can check themselves regularly against four points. Those four points are listed and described below.

The Four-Way Test

Before saying anything of substance about a student, a student's work or behavior, a parent, a teacher, an administrator, or anyone else, a teacher should apply the "four-way test" which consists of these four questions:

Is what I am going to say true?

Will my saying it help anything?

Will my silence hurt anything?

Will my speaking build positive relationships?

Specific Strategies

Specific strategies for use in effective communication have been described throughout this chapter. Some of them were:

- *Clarity*—saying what you mean to say in an organized, logical way.
- *Professional demeanor*—being friendly yet business-like, not given to gossip or talk for talk's sake.
- *A positive approach*—one that builds persons and feelings.
- *Documentation*—backing up with records what you need to say.
- *Assertiveness*—making sure that you express your points, in a friendly, insistent way, not giving in to others when you need to stick to your ground.
- *Flexibility*—the ability to change one's mind when necessary and admit mistakes.
- Using the *no-lose method of resolving conflict*—the method described by Thomas Gordon wherein positive solutions acceptable to both parties are sought and implemented.

Frequency of Communication

A chart can be a useful device for keeping track (and as a reminder) of contacts made with parents. One useful form is shown below:

Date and Type of Communication*

Surname

_____

_____

_____

_____

*NS =newsletter
T =telephone
No =note
C =conference

What Would I Want to Know?

In thinking about contents of scheduled communication, teachers find it helpful to put themselves in the place of parents and reflect on what they would want to know about their own child. Questions that typically come to mind include:

- What is my child doing well, correctly?
- What is my child's overall behavior like?
- How does my child get along with others?
- Does my child cause problems?
- What is the daily curricular program like?
- What books and materials does my child use?
- Is my child progressing as well as expected?
- What are my child's notable strengths?
- What are some of my child's specific needs?
- What are the current educational plans for my child in this class?
- What can I do to help with my child's progress?

CHECKPOINTS

Students, parents, and teachers have the right and the need to be fully informed about the educational program that affects them. This depends on good communication, and where such communication exists, students tend to make better progress and parents and others tend to support the teacher's program.

What should be included in communication
- description of the curriculum and program
- rules and expectations regarding discipline and home work
- information about student progress (a positive commentary)
- special needs or problems of the student
- information of general interest
- solicitation of help from parents

Times that call for good in-school communication
- daily routines
- giving directions
- providing instruction
- class discussions
- individual student conferences

- staff meetings
- meetings with parents

Vehicles for communicating with parents
- newsletters
- notes
- telephone calls
- personal conferences
- open house
- performances and displays

Reminders for good communication
- the four-way test—true? helpful? hurtful? build relationships?
- specific strategies
  - clarity
  - professional demeanor
  - positive attitude
  - documentation
  - assertiveness
  - flexibility
  - conflict resolution—no-lose
- what would I want to know?
  - what is going well
  - what needs improvement
  - specific needs of the child
  - future plans
  - how I can help

BIBLIOGRAPHY

Atkeson, B., and Forehand, R. "Home-Based Reinforcement Programs Designed to Modify Classroom Behavior: A Review and Methodological Evaluation." *Psychological Bulletin*, November 1979.

Baker, T. "Got A Minute? Toot Your Own Horn." *Instructor*, August, 1981a.

Baker, T. "Got A Minute? Build A Bridge to Parents." *Instructor*, August 1981b.

Berne, E. *Games People Play*. New York: Grove Press, 1964.

Charles, C. *Educational Psychology: The Instructional Endeavor*. St. Louis: C. V. Mosby, 1976.

Charles, C. "Education for Dignity and Rapid Achievement." Research in Education (ERIC), document number SP 016751, January 1981.

Ginott, H. *Teacher and Child*. New York: Avon Books, 1972.

Glasser, W. *Schools Without Failure*. New York: Harper & Row, 1969.

Gordon, T. *Teacher Effectiveness Training.* New York: McKay, 1974.

Harris, T. *I'm O.K.—You're O.K.* New York: Harper & Row, 1967.

Mulder, J. "Effective Communication: Successful Tool for Positive Teacher Image." Unpublished Master's Paper, College of Education, San Diego State University, 1979.

Stranix, E. L. "How Can I Help My Children Do Better in School?" *Teacher,* September 1978.

11

Management in Open-Space
Classrooms

Ninety kids? Yes, I really have ninety kids in my room. And no, it's not bed-
lam—there are three of us teachers to work with them. We call this system a
Loft, while others call it Open Space. Does it work? Administrators say yes,
but most teachers who have not tried it say "Teach in a loft? Never!" All I
can say is I have tried it for eight years and it has been wonderful for me
(Runyon, 1979, p. 2).

What is open space, what are lofts, and what is there about them
that merits attention in this book? Open space refers to large areas in
the school building that can accommodate about four normal-sized
classes, without interior walls that separate one group from another.
In this arrangement there exist many opportunities for team
teaching, with various arrangements and groupings of students.
This type of setting came into prominence in the early 1970s, when
many such schools were built. They were somewhat less costly to
construct than traditional buildings. From an educational stand-
point, it was believed that the arrangement might improve education through forcing team teaching and multiple groupings of
students.

Little evidence supports the educational superiority of open
space over the traditional classroom. Both seem to produce about
the same academic gains in students. Teachers have been somewhat
reticent to enter into open-space teaching, with its instructional
teams and varied groupings. Where they have done so, they have
often pulled moveable partitions, erected tall bookcases, and found
other ways of walling themselves off so that they have retained, in
effect, their single class of students within a single classroom, shar-

ing nothing with the other classes except the excess noise that drifted over, around, and through the barriers they had erected. While such steps might be viewed as counterproductive, the fact remains that most teachers are far more comfortable with a single group of students under their sole direction. They prefer not to work in team situations where they are responsible for large groups of students and where they have to spend extra hours in planning.

But what of lofts? The terms *loft* and *open space* are almost synonymous. They differ only in shades of meaning; open space refers to the type of organization while loft refers more to a specific open-space area within a school building. Thus teachers refer to "our loft" rather than to our open space.

And what is there about lofts that merits attention in this book on management? First, lofts are not isolated phenomena. There are thousands of them in which students and teachers work every day. Second, they require special treatment. They cannot function effectively as four separate classes, since all students can see and hear what is going on everywhere in the loft. They usually have four teachers who have to coordinate activities; one can't have singing while another has directed math instruction. There is a very large number of students located together, and they must be controlled, monitored, helped, and otherwise attended to. Materials management can be much more complicated when working with up to 140 students at a time. Work areas for projects, quiet activities, and so forth, must be arranged on a large scale. And finally lofts provide— even require—that teachers be flexible in groupings, use team teaching, share responsibilities, and provide individual help to students.

ADVANTAGES OF OPEN SPACE

Open-space teaching provides certain conditions that are generally recognized as advantageous to the educational program. These advantageous conditions carry strong implications for classroom management:

1. *More individual attention is given to students.* This point may seem incorrect since there are such large numbers of students within the loft. Specific individual attention is available, however, and is made possible through flexible grouping and shared teaching responsibility. One teacher can work with most of the students at a given time while the other teachers work with small groups or individuals.

2. *A better variety of good teaching activities is provided.* Four heads are better than one when it comes to thinking out, organizing, and presenting educational activities. This collective reasoning provides genuine inservice education, since the various members obtain valuable ideas from others and see their colleagues working in effective ways.

3. *A high level of professional support is present.* When teachers work together to devise and deliver an educational program, each has a stake in the performance of the others. Thus, there is likely to be much active support among the members of the team. By contrast, teachers in self-contained classrooms function on their own. Other teachers rarely have a clear idea of what those teachers are doing. Sometimes there exists general support among teachers of self-contained classrooms, but all too often the tendency is for teachers to criticize the work of their colleagues.

4. *Shared responsibility provides much work flexibility.* When three or four teachers work as a team, using various groupings and each performing certain functions, they must share responsibilities in many ways—in instructing, planning, disciplining, and taking care of the numerous incidentals that occur in any classroom. This sharing of responsibility provides a greal deal of flexibility, since each teacher does not have to be responsible for each and every portion of the daily work. This allows teachers to work with individual students, conference with parents while others are teaching, plan, prepare materials, and take care of other matters during school time. If unavoidably detained on the way to work they can even arrive late at school without causing problems (though late arrival is not suggested as a benefit of loft teaching), and when they must be absent the team can carry on the usual program without the disruption that so often occurs with a substitute teacher.

5. *Multigrade combinations and continuous progress are easily possible.* Lofts lend themselves well to the inclusion of two or more grade levels, with instructional groups organized on the basis of ability. When several such groups are used, *continuous progress* is made easy, in which a given student progresses through various levels of academic difficulty in reading and mathematics, for example, without regard to grade level. Many authorities believe that this is beneficial for students and allows teachers to match work more precisely to the students' levels of ability. Individual students may stay in the same loft for two or three years while making steady progress in achievement. Lengthening the time spent with a given group of students and set of teachers is believed to have good effects on many students, particularly those who are timid and slow-starting.

6. *Teacher strengths are multiplied.* With flexibility in grouping and teaching, teachers in the team are allowed to capitalize on their individual strengths while down-playing their weaknesses. For example, a teacher strong in science can take on the science program for the entire loft while allowing another teacher strong in language to do the same. Thus students receive instruction in all subjects of their curriculum from teachers who are skilled and enthusiastic.

DISADVANTAGES OF OPEN SPACE

While open space provides many advantages for students and teachers, it suffers from certain disadvantages as well:

1. *The noise level is higher.* When you put 120 students together in a single space, albeit a large one, it is virtually impossible to keep the noise level as low as in a self-contained classroom. The normal movements and whispers will be four times as great as in a single class, and when talking and physical movement are permitted the level of background noise reaches limits that are distractive to many teachers. In truth, the noise factor seems to be a matter that affects teachers more than students, for research has shown that student learning can be just as high in the presence of noise as in silence, provided students are kept on-task. Noise, however, can sometimes depress learning for primary-grade children because they fail to hear directions clearly.

2. *Student movement may appear to be excessive.* One advantage of team teaching in the loft is flexibility of grouping. But students must move from group to group and from place to place for materials, work space, and so forth, and this movment can be distracting to students and teachers alike. The amount of movement in fact is more than four times what it would be in a normal classroom, since there are more instructional groups and greater distances between work and study areas.

3. *Team teaching requires sharing duties.* Sharing duties was mentioned as a strength of loft teaching, since it provided flexibility and allowed teachers to capitalize on their individual strengths. But many teachers do not like to share duties. They enjoy teaching the entire curriculum, and they enjoy being in charge of all that goes on in the classroom, feeling that too many cooks spoil the broth and too much waste time and misbehavior occur when one teacher is not firmly in charge.

4. *Activities in the loft must be coordinated.* Many teachers object to the necessity that all activities in the loft be coordinated, which they must because of noise. A group of students who have become fa-

tigued may need to stand and stretch or even sing a song, but that activity cannot be done since it would be distracting to the other groups in the loft. Many teachers feel that total coordination detracts too much from the spontaneity needed to enliven teaching; one is not able to move, discuss, sing, or whatever seems most appropriate at a given time. Moreover, work times must be filled out. For example, in a given twenty-minute time segment, all groups must work for twenty minutes and finish at the same time, which makes a kind of Procrustean bed that cuts off the feet of some while stretching the limbs of others.

5. *Much planning time is required.* Even teachers of self-contained classrooms feel pressed for time when it comes to planning, keeping records, conferencing, and attending to the myriad duties of teaching. Teachers who team in loft settings must spend even larger amounts of time, because planning done as a group requires considerably more time than does individual planning. This is due to the fact that ideas must be thrown out for discussion and then chewed over until consensus is reached, after which a division of labor and duties must be planned and time schedules set. While this group planning may be very helpful and stimulating, it cuts severely into the total time available to teachers—a commodity that is already in short supply and growing ever more scarce.

6. *Too much togetherness may become a problem.* A special blend of personalities is required if teams are to be able to work together effectively for long periods of time. Very close association, especially when individuals have equal professional status—that is, when one is not clearly the boss and the others under that person's direction—can result in petty annoyances that over time escalate into proportions detrimental to cohesive team work. It is very difficult to specify what the best mixture of personalities should be, but one thing is certain: being good friends does not eliminate the problem. People who are very close friends should think carefully before entering into team teaching, because the annoyances and frustrations may in time injure the friendship. Runyon (1979) strongly suggests that team members select themselves together and then understand that the first year will be a trial period only, to see if the group is compatible and complementary.

THE INSTRUCTIONAL TEAM

The instructional team is the key factor in determining whether open-space instruction is effective. All other aspects of organization and management can be brought about easily enough if the team is compatible and task oriented. If there is friction among team members, and if some or all of the members are prone to procrastination, the entire instructional effort will be seriously if not fatally damaged.

For that reason special attention should be given to the team, especially to its selection and the manner in which it is to function. In that regard, four aspects of team work require specific attention. They are selecting the teachers, establishing leadership, building a communication bond, and maintaining morale. These four aspects are discussed in the sections that follow.

Selecting the Teachers

Instructional teams present many problems not encountered by teachers working in isolation. In the single-teacher classroom, for example, there is little need to worry about taking charge, dividing the labor, assigning responsibility, reconciling different teaching methods, coordinating discipline systems, or meshing differing philosophies of teaching and learning. With the instructional team, all these matters become important, and all must be resolved successfully if the team is to function well.

For that reason, the overall best way to establish instructional teams seems to be through the process of self-selection. That is, the teachers themselves decide whether and with whom they would like to work in a team-teaching arrangement. It was mentioned earlier that close friendship is not a good basis upon which to select instructional team members. Often good friends have quite different personalities, philosophies, and work tempos. Teamwork may put a severe strain or friendships of this type, causing members to find fault with each other over ways of doing things and schedules that have to be met.

What sorts of people are likely to function well together in teams? First, they should have similar philosophies about the purpose of education, the way it should be organized and delivered, and the way to work best with learners. Second, they must each be willing to play many background roles; all cannot be prima donnas at the same time. This is a significant contrast with the regular self-contained classroom where the teacher is always center stage. Third, they must be work and task oriented. They must be willing to put in longer hours than other teachers, due to the extra planning that is required, and they must have a pressing desire to reach closure, that is, to complete tasks quickly, not leaving them undone or behind schedule. Finally, they must be very respectful of each other, able to recognize, accept, and build on each other's strengths, rather than competing in a destructive manner.

Teams that meet these criteria have a good chance to work effectively for a long while. Age is no factor. Some members can be young and others can be old. Gender does not matter, either, except insofar as a good model is presented to students who see their teachers working together on a basis of sexual equality and mutual respect and appreciation. What is essential is an attitude of working together with other teachers and many students to provide a quality educational experience, putting that experience at the forefront, ahead of egos and petty concerns.

Establishing Leadership

Like all groups working collaboratively toward attainment of goals, instructional teams require a leader, an acknowledged in-charge person who keeps things moving, structures the meetings, clarifies decisions and plans, and orchestrates the delegation of the various responsibilities that must be assumed by the members. In this case the leadership must come not from the principal but from within the team itself. This leadership needn't be voted on, as when people select chairpersons or presidents. Instead it is likely to be present when the group is formed, and it may be that the first act of leadership consists of one individual suggesting and pushing for formation of the group. Leadership is almost certain to emerge naturally, and if it does not one would have reason to question the team's prospects for success.

Building the Communication Bond

The team cannot function long without full and free communication among its members. Establishing such communication must be a matter of first priority, and the team leader has the main responsibility for seeing that it comes into being.

Within this bond of communication all team members must be helped to feel free to express themselves regarding all matters of consequence to the team, whether they be positive, negative, suggestive, critical, evaluative, or complimentary. When any individual begins to hold back out of fear of disapproval by other members, that person's effectiveness wanes. At the same time, it will be the leader's duty to see that the conversation remains pertinent to the concerns of the instructional team. That is, meetings must not be allowed to degenerate into gripe sessions or gossip about matters not related to the work of the team.

Free expression clears the air and helps generate new ideas, but it also leads to the necessity to make decisions. Some of these decisions will not suit all the members of the group. It is therefore necessary that all members retain an attitude of cohesiveness, and that they recognize the importance of winning and losing gracefully as well as compromising for the good of all.

If the group keeps certain operating principles in mind, it can avoid most of the win-lose situations. Thomas Gordon (1974) has described a no-lose approach, described earlier in this book, in which disputants learn to seek out solutions acceptable to both in such a way that both see themselves as winners. William Glasser's classroom meetings (1969), while intended for use by school students, also provide help in finding positive solutions to problems. The rules for those meetings require that participants seek only positive solutions to problems and that they refrain from complaining, backbiting, and finding fault with others. Again, the leader of the team must assume responsibility for maintaining this positive no-lose focus as the group makes its decisions, although this strategy should be discussed by the team members so that all can play a strong hand in its continual implementation.

Maintaining Morale

In teaching, as in all other areas, morale depends in large part on one's belief, whether accurate or not, that one is engaged in a worthwhile job, where there is relatively little threat, and where people in power and people being served think you are doing a good job. Other factors figure in, too, but on a lesser scale, such as salary, working conditions, social relations, and variety in activities associated with the job.

Teacher morale is very important because it seems to influence student attitude, excitement about learning, willingness to work, and in turn the overall morale of the student. Teachers with low morale tend to exhibit lack of enthusiasm and a negative attitude toward their work, impressions that seem to work against effective student learning. Those with good morale project an aura of enthusiasm and eagerness about their work which is also caught and reflected by students.

Within the team, teacher morale is just as important as in the self-contained classroom, because it can affect not only students but other team members as well. Fortunately, the team has a built-in control for morale. Unless conditions are bad indeed, the presence and cooperation of team members has an enlivening effect. When one person is down, the others provide a spark and boost, through sharing responsibilities and camaraderie. This occurs if the team is committed to a positive stance, agreeing not to succumb to the dampening effects of minor irritations. On the other hand, chronic complainers have deleterious effects on team morale and can be the rotten apple that spoils the barrel.

Thus it is important for team members to consider morale in general, to take pains to maintain morale at high levels, and to confront directly any problems that might lower morale. The members of the team present a strong front when united in their attitudes and predispositions. Outside forces seem to affect team morale to a lesser degree than is the case for individual teachers. On the other hand, irritations are more likely to occur among team members than among individual teachers. It is here that open communication is essential. The team leader must have the fortitude to call for an open airing, within the confines of the team, of interpersonal problems that might occur. The problems can be resolved rather than allowed to fester, and future problems of the same type can be forestalled.

It is important, too, that such problems be kept within the team. Airing dirty linen in public produces more problems than it solves, because its concerns infect others, cause them to take sides, and even look with disfavor on the team. An operating rule from the beginning should be that the team will resolve interpersonal matters internally; other people will not be brought into the matter.

PLANNING

The importance of planning in effective team teaching in loft settings cannot be overemphasized. Two types of planning must occur regularly, and both take time beyond that which other teachers must spend. The time, while inconvenient, is part of the price teachers must pay in order to enjoy the benefits of team teaching. The two types of planning are weekly formal planning on a given day at a given time, and daily informal planning done on the spur of the moment when unforeseen events affect the normal program. Each team will find its own way of taking care of the informal planning. This section gives attention to the formal, scheduled planning, since it is crucial to effective team instruction.

Formal planning should be arranged and conducted so that (1) it occurs on a regularly scheduled day at a regularly scheduled time;

(2) duties, clearly identified, are assigned to each team member, who then is responsible for keeping track of and discharging them; (3) records of important matters are kept for future reference; and (4) time is always allowed for airing problems and searching for positive solutions. Each of these conditions is discussed briefly in the following paragraphs.

Scheduled days and times are essential. They should be set, marked on the calendar, and kept religiously. Teams that decide on planning "only when necessary" usually end up neglecting matters needing attention and failing to plan ahead well enough. Runyon (1979) reports that her team found Monday afternoons immediately after school to be the best time for scheduled planning sessions. Team members are more rested, and at the beginning of the week they are more disposed to planning ahead even though that week's program would already have been planned except for minor details.

Duties are assigned to the extent possible in the planning sessions, so that each person understands individual requirements and functions and can then take responsibility for planning and discharging those responsibilities. For the most part, duties are assigned in various areas of the curriculum, with all members sharing in some, such as discipline. The nature of the duties is described further in the section entitled "The Act of Teaming."

Records are kept in brief format and reproduced for all members of the team by the person appointed secretary. Such records are very important in clarifying assignments, responsibilities, and division of duties. They provide reminders for each member, form the record should disagreements occur, comprise the history of the team's efforts, and serve as reference points for future planning.

Problems are given attention at each planning session. If there are none, that is fine, but if problems have begun to occur they are addressed during this scheduled time and resolved before they grow to greater proportions.

THE ACT OF TEAMING

The act of team teaching depends on the delegating and sharing of responsibilities. Runyon (1979) reports that her loft team assigns each teacher main responsibility for a given subject area, such as reading, math, language, or social studies. That teacher then plans each week's activities in that subject. Other teachers give input during the planning sessions held each Monday. This planning includes provisions for instruction in the subject—indicating which teachers will do what with which groups—as well as responsibilities for noninstructional tasks such as pre- and posttesting, record keeping, grouping, and regrouping when necessary. The teacher-in-charge of each subject grades all student work in that area and keeps the records.

The remaining subject areas, such as science, art, music, and physical education, are shared among the team members, allowing each to pursue special strengths and interests.

Team members share equally in providing instructional materials for all subject areas, remaining alert for useful worksheets, activities, games, books, objects, and other resources. These materials are kept in a central location so they are readily accessible to all.

Finally, all team members share responsibilities for discipline. This is potentially a difficult matter because there are many students to monitor. The amount of normal movement and noise can be high, and there are many opportunities, especially in transitions between lessons, for students to misbehave. To maintain effective discipline it is necessary that team members (1) have similar viewpoints regarding the amount of noise they will tolerate; (2) have similar philosophies concerning the allowable incidence of off-task behavior by students; and (3) arrange a workable system of discipline to which all subscribe and in which all participate equally. It is not effective to designate one teacher as the disciplinarian for the entire loft. All must present a united front.

Frank, who teaches in an upper-grade loft with four other teachers, describes his way of working with misbehaving students:

"I usually tell the student how this makes me feel. If the problem needs further discussion I take the student aside and ask, 'Why have I called you here?' If he doesn't answer I tell him to sit in the quiet corner until he is ready to discuss the problem. This takes the burden off my shoulders. When the child is ready to talk I ask him to tell why the behavior was inappropriate. Sometimes I have them write out the problem, how it can be solved, and what they are going to do about it in the future. This is put into a letter which I send home to parents; there it is signed and returned to me."

"Most confrontations can be avoided by sending a message to an individual student and letting the 'ripple effect' control the others. Positive reinforcement is the most effective tool. I provide it for work and good behavior as much as possible. This makes the students feel good and successful, and it encourages them to stay on task and make progress.

"Positive reinforcement, I-messages, and consistent treatment of misbehavior do the trick. I don't have to spend much time dealing with misbehavior. The students know what is expected of them and what will happen if they break the rules."

The physical arrangements of the loft make it difficult to employ assertive discipline. In self-contained classrooms the teacher put names and checks on the chalkboard, and that record is kept for the entire day. By contrast, the loft has three or four teachers working in different areas with groups whose membership changes several times each day. Chalkboard records thus become inefficient in controlling behavior.

Discipline in the loft can be made workable through an approach built on the elements advocated by Frederick Jones (1979). Those elements include posted rules, effective use of body language by teachers, and efficient methods of giving help to individual students during seatwork. Jones also suggests using incentive systems that allow students to earn, through good behavior, special or preferred activities at the end of the day. Even here it is not easy to maintain a consistent and even-handed incentive program where several teachers and groups of students are involved. Teachers must rely strongly on discussions with students about good and poor behavior, and use the force of their own personalities to prevent and correct inappropriate behavior.

MANAGING ROUTINES AND INCIDENTALS

Management of routines and incidentals in self-contained classrooms was discussed in an earlier chapter. For team teaching in lofts, additional considerations are required because of the numbers of students, teachers, and groups. Especially affected are matters of taking attendance, lunch count, cleaning the room, entering and exiting, grading and conferencing, rainy day activities, slush fund money, and class parties. Suggestions for managing each of these matters follow.

Attendance and Lunch Count

Calling the roll for one hundred or more students takes too much time and encourages misbehavior. Lofts need a system for quickly checking attendance. Greatest accuracy and efficiency are obtained when one teacher is placed in charge. That teacher appoints one student in each cluster or small group to report who is absent from that group. Names of absent students are recorded on the attendance sheet. This process requires only a couple of minutes to complete.

Lunch count is taken in a similar way. Students at each table are asked to stand if they are buying lunch. Teachers count the students standing and record the number for each group. If a problem occurs later, the difficulty can be traced quickly to a given group.

If lunch money must be held or collected, a safe procedure is to give each student a small white envelope, on which is written the student's name. Students put their money in the small envelopes which are then put into a larger brown envelope, one for each table. The large envelopes are kept until time to go to lunch, then students retrieve their money from their own envelopes. Should a problem occur, a student can be appointed to collect all money and return it. A second student is appointed to double-check the first. This procedure prevents the disappearance of money.

Keeping the Room Clean

One problem with a large open space monitored by several teachers is that a certain amount of debris seems to collect on tables and floors. This problem can be kept to a minimum by doing the following: (1) Teachers must be good models for the students, always picking up after themselves. (2) Student monitors are appointed to watch after the cleanliness of designated portions of the loft. (3) Teachers are assigned portions of the loft, and they help monitors control the neatness of that portion.

Entering and Leaving the Room

With such a large number of students attempting to enter and exit from the loft at the same time, great disorder can occur unless definite procedures are established. For entering the room in the morning, after recesses, and after lunch, students can be asked to form lines, one line for each teacher. Each teacher leads the line into the loft for the first few days. Thereafter, one teacher can bring in all the students. When students are dismissed from the room, they can form themselves into the same lines, or if that is impractical, they can be dismissed on a rotating basis by groups in which they are working at the time of dismissal.

Grading and Conferencing

At the beginning of the year, students are divided among the teachers so that they "belong" to a certain teacher, as they would in a homeroom. Students are helped to understand that they are responsible equally to all teachers, but that they are assigned to a particular teacher so the teachers can take care of certain matters more easily. Two of these matters are assigning grades and conferencing with parents.

Each teacher is responsible for filling out the report card for all students in his group, and then for conferencing with parents of those students. In actuality, grading in the various subjects is a group endeavor by all the teachers, since all participate in the various aspects of the curriculum. Thus, the teacher who teaches reading to Jason must report the grade Jason has earned to the teacher who fills out Jason's report card. Written comments and samples of work should be put into Jason's folder for use in the conference. Since the teacher conferencing with the parent will not know firsthand many of the details of Jason's work, pains must be taken to inform the conferencing teacher fully if there have been problems. The teacher must be able to explain the nature of the problem and describe plans being implemented to correct the problem.

Rainy Days

It is bad enough when rain keeps thirty restless students inside during recess, but when the number of students reaches one hundred and over careful planning must be done to prepare for such days. One effective plan is to use the four basic groups of students, as assigned to teachers for grading. Four separate activities are always ready, activities such as commercial games, pencil-and-paper games, blackboard games, and organized seat games such as Spello. The groups rotate through the different activities, engaging in a different one at each break. Since this is highly organized, and is planned and practiced in advance, one teacher can supervise everyone, allowing some relaxation time for each teacher.

Slush Fund Money

Teachers of self-contained classrooms spend money, whether their own or that furnished by the school, to purchase materials as they see fit until the money is gone. It is a matter of individual choice. But when four teachers are involved, the financial matters can become complex and can cause irritations within the team. This concern can be taken care of in the following way: At the beginning of the year each teacher puts into the common fund a certain amount of money, say $20. The team decides how they wish to spend money for supplies and incidentals. When the money is gone, each person puts in another \$20. One teacher is put in charge of the money to simplify matters of handling, spending, and accounting.

Parties

Class parties assume bigger-than-life proportions when you have over one hundred students. Runyon (1979) reports one of her first experiences:

I'll never forget my first loft valentine party. We had four teachers and 120 second- and third-grade students. They arrived at 8:30 and immediately began passing out their valentines, one here, one there. This continued at recess, at lunch, after lunch, and at the party. At the end of the day some students still had not passed out their valentines. Panic set in. What were we going to do? Well, we ate our cupcakes, drank our punch, and read our candy hearts. Then we collected every valentine that had not gotten to the right person and took them all home over the weekend. We bundled them into individual packets and had a belated Valentine's Day party on Monday morning.

Advance planning can help avoid such problems. The total group decides on choices of food, drink, and expenses. Room mothers or parent volunteers are contacted and asked to help with the party. They usually provide all that is needed. If there is time, group games can be played, with prizes of erasers, pieces of chalk, and pieces of bubble gum. It is important to select food that requires a minimum of preparation and party games in which all students can be involved at the same time. It is better to plan a little too much for the time available and then try to keep activities moving crisply.

BREAKING IN

Most teachers are reluctant to embark upon a team teaching experience in a loft setting. They fear that noise and discipline will become serious problems and they do not want to spend the amounts of time necessary for team planning. Many believe that students will not learn so well in very large groups. There are some grounds for all these concerns, but most teacher who choose loft teaching insist that the benefits outweigh the disadvantages.

When teachers decide to give loft teaching a try, they must be prepared to make three major adjustments. First, they must adjust to the fact that they are no longer the single dominant figure in the classroom. There are other teachers there and each will be aware of how well the other members teach. Second, there will indeed be a large number of students at hand, with the naturally attendant noise and movement. Third, team members must spend the time necessary for group planning, and they must be willing to assume and carry out the duties assigned them in the planning sessions. With these adjustments one becomes a smaller fish in a larger pond, but can count on much support from others in the situation.

Most teachers find the ideal way to break into loft teaching is to enter into an available position in an existing team. There, the routines are established and the myriad details arranged. Everything works. That allows one to concentrate on providing quality instruction without having to worry over things that might go wrong. Some, however, prefer to begin with a completely new team, feeling that in that way everyone starts on an equal footing and not as a junior member of an established firm. Problems naturally arise for new teams, but they are accepted and corrected, and one does not feel so much on display or on trial as with an established group. Either way, say advocates of team teaching, one eventually comes to feel comfortable and safe while making unique contributions. And that, they say, is one of the things that makes team teaching enjoyable.

WHEN THE MAGIC IS GONE

Good instructional teams do not have unlimited life. Like everything else they run their cycle, and members begin after a few years to tire and lose enthusiasm. This is only natural. Most people need some sort of change in their teaching every few years in order to keep fresh and vital.

No matter whether the team disbands for lack of enthusiasm or because one or more members relocate to other schools, it will not be easy to break up a closely knit team. But when one begins to feel stale or hear the call of new challenges, it is time to move on. The team will continue with a new member if it wishes, so one shouldn't be hesitant about moving on to something else.

CHECKPOINTS

Open space or loft teaching occurs in large rooms that usually contain three or four classes of students, with no interior walls to separate one group from another. Instructional team planning and some team teaching are required, and certain management questions require attention.

Advantages of open space
- more individual attention to students
- better variety of teaching activities
- high level of professional support
- flexibility in teaching through shared responsibilities
- permits multigrading and continuous progress

Disadvantages of open space
- high noise level
- excessive student movement
- requires sharing duties
- all activities must be coordinated
- much planning time required

The instructional team
- selection by mutual agreement (self-select)
- requires leadership
- requires a communication bond
- requires attention to morale

Team planning
- done on a regular schedule
- duties are assigned
- records are kept
- problems are aired as they occur

Team teaching
- each member has primary instructional responsibility
- members assist each other as necessary
- members share some of the instruction
- flexible student grouping is used
- all share equally in the discipline

Managing routines and incidentals
- attendance and lunch count: quick and accurate
- room cleanliness: assign students to areas
- traffic: routes and routines well established
- grading and conferencing: all teachers share in grading: conferencing with parents done by individual teachers, as assigned
- rainy days: plan ahead and keep students busy in groups
- money: pool resources with equal contributions; one person in charge
- class parties: plan, get parent help, operate efficiently

BIBLIOGRAPHY

Glasser, William. *Schools without Failure*. New York: Harper & Row, 1969.

Gordon, Thomas. *Teacher Effectiveness Training*. New York: McKay, 1974.

Jones, Frederick. "The Gentle Art of Classroom Discipline." *National Elementary Principal*, June 1979.

Runyon, Karen L. "Teaching in Open Space Schools." Unpublished Master's Paper, College of Education, San Diego State University, 1979.

12

Managing the Work of Paraprofessionals

WHAT ARE PARAPROFESSIONALS?

Para means alongside of, and paraprofessional means someone who works alongside the professional. In classroom teaching, the professional is the teacher and the paraprofessional is a person who assists the teacher. This paraprofessional may be student or adult, salaried or volunteer. Usually they are paid aides, parent volunteers, or cross-age tutors. Whatever the status, the paraprofessional has a recognized place in the educational program and performs a recognized service. More and more teachers have come to rely on contributions of paraprofessionals. They have found them invaluable not only in preparing materials and doing clerical work, but in monitoring the work of small groups of students, giving one-to-one help, and in some cases providing basic instruction under teacher supervision.

Paraprofessionals have been used informally for decades, but they did not receive widespread attention until the teacher shortages of the 1950s. In one famous effort, the 1953 Bay City Michigan Project financed by the Ford Foundation, teacher aides were paired with teachers to work with groups of forty-five students at the elementary level. The aides worked mainly in menial tasks such as correcting papers, taking roll, and preparing instructional materials. After two years, evaluations were made of student achievement, parent opinion, and student reactions. No differences were found between classes with aides and control groups so far as achievement, but students reported that they liked having the aides; teachers reported that the aides helped reduce the amount of time ordinarily spent in correcting papers, preparing lessons, disciplining students, and assisting individual students; and parents also reported favorable reactions (Park, 1956).

The Bay City Project received its share of criticism, however. Most frequently expressed were concerns about students working under the direction of less-qualified adults. Many feared that aides would begin to undermine and replace certificated teachers. Both fears proved groundless. Paraprofessionals are now extensively used throughout the country. Student achievement has not fallen as a result of their presence in the classroom, and aides have never been used to replace teachers.

WHAT AIDES CAN DO

Paraprofessionals may have originally been used for collecting papers and helping children on with their coats, but their value has since expanded greatly. One can almost say that paraprofessionals are good for whatever kind of help the teacher needs. They still do their share of clerical work, but increasingly they are given quasi-instructional duties, such as supervising instructional games, monitoring and assisting students during art work and seatwork, and working with small groups to provide practice in basic skills of reading, spelling, and mathematics. They also help teachers prepare instructional materials such as flash cards, art materials, visual aids, and worksheets. They organize bulletin boards, administer tests, and serve as another adult with whom children can relate.

Brownley (1981) lists a number of valuable functions performed by paraprofessionals within the following categories: (1) instructional activities, such as tutoring, testing, monitoring groups, and supervising learning centers; (2) clerical services, such as correcting papers, helping with lesson planning, recording scores, and filing papers; (3) housekeeping duties, such as watering, keeping the room neat, and taking care of animals; and (4) auxiliary services, such as helping with special projects, programs, and field trips.

It is clear from such lists of paraprofessional activities that aides' duties are helpful and supplementary, but not intended to provide basic instruction in place of the teacher. Their help relieves the teacher of many time-consuming tasks that while necessary to the overall instructional program do not require the skills of a trained teacher. Thus, valuable time is made available to teachers for planning and for working more effectively with students who have special needs. At least that is how the picture is presented on paper. If one observes in classrooms, however, it is not uncommon to see skilled aides provide much or even all of the direction and supervision in activities such as art, music, physical education, and project work in science and social studies.

Are Paraprofessionals Worth the Trouble?

Paraprofessionals add to the complexity of teachers' lives. This prompts questions about whether they are worth the extra trouble they bring. Most teachers insist that they are well worth it, pointing out that while planning is necessary in order to derive high value from aides, instructional programs can become much fuller, richer, and more student oriented than when the teacher works alone with a class of students. Some teachers go so far as to describe aides as worth their weight in gold (Wood, 1981). At the price of gold that might be a slight exaggeration, but the sentiment is often expressed by teachers who have enjoyed the benefits of skilled, committed aides.

OBTAINING PARAPROFESSIONALS

The main categories of paraprofessional help are paid instructional aides, parent volunteers, cross-age tutors, and senior citizens. Usually, only the instructional aides are paid a salary, and they are recruited, selected, and often trained by the personnel departments of the school districts. Most teachers do not have a paid aide because the money for aides' salaries usually comes from the special funds of federal or state programs, such as those in special education, Title I reading and mathematics, and certain school improvement programs. Some school districts still furnish aides out of their instructional budget, but as school revenues decrease this practice is becoming more rare.

Other paraprofessionals—parents, student tutors, and senior citizens—volunteer their services. Their pay consists only of the pleasure they derive from working with students and making a contribution to the educational program. One might think that without pay few people would be willing to serve, but surprising numbers of skilled, willing people are there for the asking. Brown and Stahl (1981) list several sources of volunteer paraprofessionals. Some of their suggestions are incorporated into the sections that follow.

Parents and Relatives

The prime source of volunteer help is from parents and other relatives of students in the class. Grandparents especially are excellent, since they have available time and work well with the young. Relatives tend to be reticent about volunteering, however, so some recruitment may be necessary. This can be done at the beginning of the year by sending notes home with the students asking for volunteer help. The notes should specify the sort of assistance needed, together with the days and times. Attached should be forms for making application to volunteer in the school. In most cases this will yield all the help a teacher can use.

Colleges and High Schools

Nearby colleges and high schools can provide excellent volunteer help. Often students there will have already decided on teaching as a career and they welcome the opportunity to work in classrooms. These institutions can be contacted to determine whether they have Future Teachers of America or similar organizations, or in other manners offer service to the community. Volunteers from colleges and high schools are usually people of high personal qualities and they are fine role models for younger students. Teacher education departments within colleges and universities are also excellent sources. Many teacher education programs require that applicants have experience working with children before they are admissible to training programs. Such people bring skill, desire to do well, and positive attitudes toward children and education.

Older Elementary Students

Many teachers over the years have found older elementary students to be among their most valuable aides in the classroom. Research has shown that the use of these cross-age tutors helps increase achievement and attitudes toward school for both the children being helped and the children helping. Details about how cross-age tutors are selected and used are presented later in this chapter.

PTA Bureaus

In schools that have active Parent-Teacher Associations, there may exist bureaus run by parents that furnish qualified parent volunteers to aid in the classroom. Some organizations even provide training for the volunteers to help them develop understanding of the school program and basic skills for working effectively with children.

SELECTING PARAPROFESSIONALS

Stringent criteria are seldom used in selecting paraprofessionals. Most teachers look for only three things in people whom they consider: (1) a sincere desire to work with students and help provide a quality educational experience; (2) a personality suited to working with children and other adults in the school; and (3) an assurance of reliability, that is, that the person can and will appear regularly as scheduled. This third factor is extremely important, because it is devastating to a program to plan experiences and activities that depend on the presence of an aide only to have the person not show up when expected.

HOW MANY AIDES ARE NEEDED?

While one or two aides can provide invaluable services to teacher and students, more than two can become cumbersome and counterproductive. The number needed for optimal effectiveness varies according to the curriculum. If most of the instruction is presented by the teacher in large groups, one aide may be sufficient. This person can do clerical work while instruction is presented and then can monitor and assist individual students during seatwork and group activities.

If the daily program is set up around learning centers, choosing areas, and small-group activities, then as many as four aides can be used to advantage. Such is often the case in primary classrooms, where small-group work and careful monitoring of students are emphasized. There, one may see the teacher directing the program, a paid aide in charge of a group activity, a parent volunteer doing clerical work or assisting individual students, and two cross-age tutors circulating to help students.

Classrooms require fewer aides as the children get older. One seldom sees more than one aide in intermediate grades, but will often see several adults in early primary grades. While the assistance of paraprofessionals is helpful, their work has to be planned and monitored by the teacher, thus adding in that way to the burden of teaching. Each teacher must decide where the point of diminishing returns begins to make paraprofessionals more trouble than they are worth.

ANOTHER WORD ABOUT CROSS-AGE TUTORS

It is very motivating to younger children to have older students from the same school sit beside them, play with them, read to them, and help them with their work. For that reason alone many teachers like to use cross-age tutors on a regular basis. Those teachers usually report that cross-age tutors are among their most reliable, conscientious, patient, and valued paraprofessionals. This comes as a surprise to many teachers, and the use of cross-age tutors is often seen as a very recent innovation.

However, use of older students has a long and valued tradition in the United States. Students were always used that way in the one-room school house, where older students expected that part of their time in school was to be spent helping younger students. This role expanded during the Depression when thousands of students were given small amounts of pay by the National Youth Administration for their assistance as paper graders, library aides, and tutors. Today, cross-age tutors receive no pay for their services, but their value has become more widely recognized. As Thelan (1969) points out, student aides bring benefits to teaching that should be sought for their own good, not simply out of necessity. Among them are giving more individual attention to students, improving the social climate of the classroom, increasing meaning for younger students, and building the self-concept of both older and younger students.

The use of cross-age tutors must be planned and monitored by the teacher, and this necessitates an investment of time. For that reason teachers would not wish to use large numbers of such students. One to three students, used for an hour each a few times per week yields advantages that far outweigh the cost of planning and monitoring.

ESTABLISHING GROUND RULES

When teachers use paraprofessionals, certain ground rules must be established at the outset. If the school district has a handbook for aides and volunteers, a copy should be given to the paraprofessional and each of its points covered in a special conference. If such a handbook is not available, teachers should be sure to discuss authority, reliability, instruction, discipline, communication, professionalism, and legal requirements, which are discussed briefly in the sections that follow.

Authority

The paraprofessional should be aware of the chain of authority within the school. Especially should it be clarified that the teacher maintains authority in the classroom. The paraprofessional has authority over children and other matters in the classroom only in the extent to which that authority is delegated by the teacher. It should be clearly understood that the teacher has the final say in all matters related to the instructional program, the learning environment, and the dealings with students and their parents.

Reliability

It should be established that reliability is of the essence in teaching. That means that everyone, teachers and paraprofessionals alike, must be where they are supposed to be at the appointed time, that they have done the necessary preparation, that they do what they say they are going to do, and that they let nothing except emergency situations interfere with their obligations. Sometimes people are ill and unable to go to work, or emergencies occur that require their attention. In such cases, paraprofessionals should understand that it is their responsibility to inform the teacher as early as possible so the teacher can make other arrangements. Teachers, for their part, must remember two obligations: they should not spring surprise duties on the paraprofessional that cannot be handled well or gracefully, and they should always anticipate the possibility that the aide might be absent or might not be able to perform an assigned task, and therefore they should have a back-up plan in mind.

Instruction

The teacher is the professional, authorized and expected to provide the instructional program. This does not mean that the aide cannot carry out certain instructional tasks. But when doing so, the tasks should be ones planned by the teacher, with instructions on how the aide is to work with the students. In other words, the classroom teacher is not to turn over portions of the curriculum to the paraprofessional expecting that person to do the planning, instructing, monitoring, preparation of materials, and evaluation of students. Aides may provide instruction; indeed many are very adept at doing so. But the teacher is always in charge and always responsible for the outcomes.

Discipline

Technically, aides are not to discipline students. That is the province of the classroom teacher, school principal, or other credentialed person who might legally be in charge of the group. In practice, of course, it is sometimes necessary for the paraprofessional to use mild forms of control, such as telling students to stop misbehavior and providing reinforcement for desired behavior. They may also participate in the discipline system established by the teacher provided they have the teacher's permission. Paraprofessionals may not spank students, hurt them physically, berate them, make them stay after school, or force them to do onerous tasks such as copying from the encyclopedia. When punishment is in order, it is to be provided by the teacher.

Communication

Paraprofessionals should be instructed in two areas of communication. First, they should be taught how to speak with young students, in calm reassuring tones of voice, using words that the students understand. They should serve as models for students, and use correct grammar and polite language. They can learn to do this by observing and imitating the teacher's method of talking with students. Second, teachers should stress the necessity for open communication between aide and teacher when problems occur. Such openness, provided the matter is handled tactfully without putting either person on the defensive, enables people to resolve problems far more easily than if a matter is left to fester.

Professionalism

Paraprofessionals, certainly those who are paid for their services, should be shown how to behave in a "professional" manner. This professionalism refers to an attitude about one's status and work, an attitude that reflects a sincere intent to work in the best interests of the educational program. It is shown in the way one talks, dresses, assumes responsibility, and shows dependability.

It has been reported that over 97 percent of the informal talk that occurs in teachers' lounges is negative in nature. Few experienced teachers would dispute that contention. But negative talk is often counterproductive. It seems to encourage further negativism and divert energy from productive work. Paraprofessionals should understand that, in the best interests of students and adults, what they say about students, teachers, administrators, parents, and colleagues should be positive. On rare occasions frank talk is called for and sometimes is critical of others, but even then comments should be couched in terms that point to positive solutions, to better ways' of doing things without denigrating the character of others. When teachers hear their paraprofessionals speak derogatorily of the school, program, or personnel, they should take immediate steps to correct the situation.

Professionalism is also shown in the way one dresses. Adult paraprofessionals should be encouraged to dress in a style similar to that of the teachers in the school. Ordinarily that would mean not wearing shorts, dungarees, or sweatshirts. When a teacher accepts a paraprofessional, paid or volunteer, dress regulations or accepted styles should be discussed. For cross-age tutors, of course, this is not necessary, but for adults it should be specifically discussed or presented in writing.

Responsibility and dependability are additional aspects of professionalism. Responsibility refers to using common sense, such as paying attention to children when on playground duty, not reading or going into the faculty room for coffee. It refers to assuming routine duties without waiting to be asked by the teacher in such matters as helping students with clothing, lunches, illness, and other personal matters. Dependability refers to living up to expectations—doing what you are supposed to do when you are supposed to do it. Teachers are better off without aides who are undependable, because they may fail to come through when counted on most. Of course, it is the teacher's responsibility to inform the aide clearly of expectations, routines, and duties.

Legal Requirements

While teachers and paraprofessionals are not always subject to the same legal requirements and restrictions, paraprofessionals should be informed about the law as it relates to what teachers can and cannot do. Areas of greatest concern are those having to do with dismissal, liability, and freedom of expression.

Teachers and paraprofessionals can be dismissed from their jobs if they are shown to be incompetent, insubordinate, or to have engaged in immoral conduct. Incompetence refers to the inability to perform satisfactorily those duties normally expected. This inability must occur repeatedly over a period of time, and it must be documented. Insubordination means continual refusal to follow a direct, reasonable order given by a person in authority, or repeatedly breaking a valid school rule in a willful and defiant manner. Immoral conduct generally includes matters of sex, alcoholism, obscene language, and serious crime. In some of these matters, distinction is made as to whether the act is done publicly or privately. For example, sexual matters between consenting adults in private rarely receive attention. Sexual activity between teacher and student, however, is almost always grounds for dismissal. In other matters consideration is given to whether one's performance on the job is affected, such as in the case of alcohol. Conviction of a serious crime is almost always grounds for dismissal.

Liability for student injury or other loss is a matter requiring attention since so many children are injured at school. Teachers and paraprofessionals have a legal responsibility to protect students from harm and injury. If suit is brought to show teacher negligence, the courts try to determine two things: first, did the supervisor exercise reasonable foresight in anticipating danger to the student, and second, did the supervisor act in a reasonable and prudent way. Teachers and aides will not be found negligent in student injury if they meet these two criteria. Therefore it is necessary that paraprofessionals be clearly informed that they must be present and attentive when assigned supervisorial duties, and that they make sure equipment used by students is safe and in good working order. In addition, they should not let children move out of their line of sight.

Freedom of expression for teachers has become greatly liberalized since a Supreme Court decision in 1969 guaranteed teachers and students freedom of expression in the schools. Teachers are allowed to speak out on controversial matters, including conditions and policies of the schools in which they work. They may not, however, make false or reckless accusations that disrupt the educational process, or make abusive and scornful attacks on school officials (Fischer, Schimmel, and Kelly, 1981). Paraprofessionals should be cautioned that they may not use the classroom as a forum for expressing personal conviction in sensitive matters of religion, politics, sex education, and the like.

TRAINING PARAPROFESSIONALS

Some school districts provide training programs for the paid aides who work in their classrooms. Such training was a requirement for people hired within the provisions of the Elementary and Secondary Education Act. The training typically deals with rules and responsibilities, discipline procedures, professionalism, lines of authority, communication, and legal responsibilities. It also includes some elements of child development, instruction, record keeping and filing, and use of school equipment and supplies.

Most paraprofessionals, however, are trained on the job, in the classroom, by the teacher. This is almost always so for volunteers and cross-age tutors. On-the-job training is acceptable—even preferable in most cases—since the duties of the paraprofessional vary from classroom to classroom. Usually, teachers include an orientation to the classroom; show where supplies are kept and where children work; indicate specific duties of the aide; show where the aide is to be stationed, work, or circulate; and demonstrate how the duties are to be performed. Then as the paraprofessional works in the manner indicated, the teacher provides necessary feedback.

After a time, the aide comes to understand the work and can discharge it without direct supervision. Still, it is the teacher's duty to plan all work included in the instructional program. Many write on cards what the aide is expected to do. These notations need not be made in detail, but there should be indications of duties, sequences, materials, and approximate time allocations.

When the aide's duties are mostly clerical, such as grading and filing or preparation of instructional materials, verbal instructions at the beginning of the day may be sufficient. Even so, it helps to prevent misunderstandings between teacher and aide to have a list of duties written on a work card.

ASSIGNING WORK AREAS AND TIMES

All paraprofessionals, whether paid, volunteer, or cross-age, should have a place in the classroom designated as their own. There the teacher places notes, materials, or other items for the paraprofessional. A table or desk with a chair of appropriate height should be provided. Adults should not be asked to sit in small chairs at low tables used by young children.

Work times are scheduled according to teacher need. Paid aides are assigned to the classroom for a designated number of hours, usually two, three, or five. Volunteer aides are scheduled on the basis of agreements with the teacher. The volunteers usually can be there only on certain days or for certain times. The teacher arranges work that allows them to make the greatest contribution while they are present. Volunteers should not be left simply to "hang around" and observe, not knowing what to do with themselves. If a parent volunteers unexpectedly to help during a morning, the teacher should not automatically accept the offer, especially if the person is going to be in the way and have nothing to do. If there are papers to be checked, materials to be prepared, children to be worked with individually, and so forth, the teacher can accept the offer and put the parent quickly to work. If not, the teacher should thank the parent and ask if he or she could come back on a subsequent day.

MAINTAINING PARAPROFESSIONAL MORALE

Good morale is as necessary to paraprofessionals as to teachers. It affects the quality of their work and the degree to which they provide assistance to teacher and students. Yet it is a matter that can easily be overlooked.

The morale level of the paraprofessional is affected by the following: acceptance, belonging, meaningful work, clear directions and expectations, sense of accomplishment and closure, and evidence of appreciation.

Acceptance is a sense that grows out of personal attention and communication from the teacher. It shows pleasure and appreciation. A sense of belonging is established by assigning specific work space and tasks and otherwise making the paraprofessional feel part of the instructional team. Meaningful work has clear relation to student learning and is not always menial or tedious. Clearly stated objectives and directions are important. When one is carrying out duties planned by another person, it is disconcerting not to know what is intended or expected. A sense of accomplishment and closure contributes to good morale in that it allows one to note steps taken and work completed. Some people are made uncomfortable when they see no clear evidence of progress or when they feel that their work does not move forward. Finally, evidence of appreciation is something all of us need in abundance. It does not take much effort to say "well done." A sincere thank you does wonders. An occasional token gift or award is greatly appreciated.

WHAT HAPPENS WHEN PARAPROFESSIONALS ARE ABSENT?

Absenteeism by paraprofessionals can be most disconcerting to teacher and students, and damaging to the educational program. It is therefore important to keep aides on the job and to have the program organized so that it can continue when they must be absent.

Some aides take all the absences to which they are entitled without loss of pay. The harm that this does to the program can be reduced by maintaining good morale as described previously and by making paraprofessionals such an integral part of the program that they feel a strong stake in the students' progress. This commitment, together with the pleasure that comes from working with students and faculty, reduces absences to matters of illness or absolute necessity.

Still, there will be days when an aide is too ill to come to work. All too often those days seem to be ones for which the aide's duties are indispensible, and the teacher is left making rapid changes in the day's activities. Such times can be anticipated, and when they occur the program can move ahead as planned with the help of substitute aides, cross-age tutors, or alternate instructional plans.

Substitute aides are seldom available on call as are substitute teachers. Finding a substitute falls to the teacher, although often the aide who is ill will call a friend to go in as a replacement. Teachers often have acquaintances among retired teachers who can be called on short notice and will come to school to help for the day. When this is not possible, one can obtain older students from the school or from a junior or senior high school who can help in the room for an hour or two. In addition, the teacher should always have a back-up plan in mind, in which the day's activities are modified so that the aide's services are not needed. This can be done by assigning project or library work to some of the students while the teacher works with others, or by doing total-class activities instead of grouped activities that require the aide's presence.

HOW TO ATTRACT RELIABLE AIDES

Some teachers are known for their ability to attract and maintain an unending supply of quality aides and volunteers eager to work in their rooms. How do they do this? Basically, they treat people well and supply a sense of fulfillment. Parents talk among themselves about teachers, their programs, and their desires and abilities. There seem to be a number of people who like to work in elementary classrooms—people who are retired or who enjoy and have the time to work with children. Those people hear about certain teachers and seem to gravitate to them.

Parents and others also take notice of teachers who have exciting but demanding programs for learners, who maintain discipline with kindness and consideration, and who are simply enjoyable people with whom to associate. They respond to teachers who go out of their way to communicate and make them partners in the educational program. They watch for teachers who provide quality extracurricular activities with plays, concerts, and field days. They notice teachers who go out of their way to relate warmly with children and adults. They hear about those who do the little things that establish good morale.

Some teachers would rather work without aides, preferring to rely on their own abilities in providing a sound educational program. This is perfectly acceptable. There is nothing wonderful about having an aide, unless the program is improved thereby. An over-supply of aides can get in the way of instruction, and some teachers get bogged down in dealing with them and attending to their assorted trials and troubles. But for those who find that one or two good aides help enliven their program, make it more complete, and enable them to manage more easily, good aides are available. It is simply a matter of making contact with them.

CHECKPOINTS

Paraprofessionals are nonteachers who work in the classroom with the teacher to help provide the educational program. They usually fall into the category of paid aide, parent volunteer, or cross-age tutor.

What paraprofessionals can do
- tutoring, testing, and supervising
- correcting papers, recording, and filing
- assisting with special programs and projects

How paraprofessionals are obtained
- recruited by schools for funded programs
- recruited by teachers, from sources such as
  - parents and relatives
  - high schools and colleges
  - older elementary students
  - bureaus of parent-teacher associations
  - senior citizens' groups
- qualities desired
  - desire to work in the classroom
  - suitable personality
  - reliability

Groundrules that must be established
- authority: belongs to the teacher, but can be delegated to the aide
- reliability: absolutely essential in aides
- instruction: can be provided by paraprofessionals, but always under supervision of the teacher
- discipline: the sole province of the teacher
- communication: needed for good relationships
- professionalism: standards explained and required by the teacher
- legal requirements: attention given to
  - incompetence, insubordination, immorality
  - liability for student injury or loss
  - freedom of expression, and restrictions thereon

Training of paraprofessionals
- by schools, for funded programs
- by teachers for in-class assistance

Work areas and assigned times
- a designated "post" or assigned area
- times arranged according to school plan or teacher need

Morale of paraprofessionals maintained through
- acceptance
- sense of belonging
- meaningful work
- clear directions and expectations
- sense of accomplishment
- evidence of appreciation

When paraprofessionals are absent
- substitute
- cross-age helper
- revised program

BIBLIOGRAPHY

Brown, W., and Stahl, N. "Help Is Out There—Here's How to Find It." *Instructor*, August 1981.

Brownley, M. "Aides Mean Aid—To You." *Instructor*, August 1981.

Fischer, L. et al. *Teachers and the Law*. New York: Longman, 1981.

Park, C. et al. "The Bay City, Michigan Experiment: A Cooperative Study for the Better Utilization of Teacher Competencies." *Journal of Teacher Education*. June 1956.

Thelan, H. "Tutoring by Students," *School Review*. September-December 1969.

Wood, J. "Volunteers Worth Their Weight in Gold." *Instructor*, August 1981.

13

Classroom Management for Substitute Teachers

In all of teaching there is no job more difficult than that of the substitute teacher. The substitute must provide on-going instruction in an unfamiliar setting to an unknown group of students, involved in a curriculum planned by another person. Most classes of students find sport in working against rather than with the substitute, in degrees ranging from subtle playfulness to overt hostility. The substitute's difficulties lie only in small part with the unfamiliar curriculum. The major difficulty is management of time, materials, activities, and especially of student behavior so that the day's efforts are productive rather than wasted in ceaseless confrontation with uncooperative students.

While this picture is forbidding, and indeed it is more often accurate than not, the substitute's life need not be eternally dreary. To the contrary, many teachers find substituting a rewarding and pleasantly varied experience. Those people, many of whom consider substitute teaching a full-time job, have learned that effective classroom management makes the difference between providing an interesting experience for students and serving only as a baby sitter, or worse, as a jail warden.

This chapter focuses on management skills that make that difference for substitute teachers. It establishes the need for mutual responsibilities, then begins with the phone call in the morning and leads through a day on the job. It suggests ways of becoming acquainted quickly with the school surroundings. It offers ideas for useful activities at each grade level, and it provides plans for emergencies or unexpected situations. This information can help

216

Roberta, an experienced substitute teacher, explains her role:

"As a substitute teacher I have two main duties. The first is to maintain class control. The second is to see that the students get their work done. The plan I use to fulfill my duties is as follows:

1. Write my name on the board and tell how to pronounce it.
2. Pass out cards for nametags, if they aren't on students' desks. Know all students' names by recess.
3. Have the class read the room standards. If none are posted, they read these from my chart:
   - Raise your hand to speak.
   - Follow directions the first time.
   - Finish all work.
   - Treat others as you want to be treated.
   - No pencil sharpening.
4. Explain the consequences for both breaking these rules and for complying with them. (I use Canter's system of consequences.)
5. Appoint a pencil monitor. The monitor collects a pencil from each student and gives a sharpened pencil in return. I carry a supply of sharpened pencils with me.
6. Reward system: Grades 1–3—give star to table or cluster of students for paying attention, working quietly, cleaning up, and finishing the assignment. Stars earn extra benefits. Grades 4–6—incentive of 15 minutes free time at end of day. Time is lost for misbehavior. This brings good peer pressure.
7. At the end of the day I write a letter to the teacher. I mention by name all the students who worked hard, behaved well, and were helpful to me."

bring substitute teaching into a practical, business-like operation that moves through the day effectively and pleasantly.

MUTUALITY: THEIR WAY/YOUR WAY

Teachers often complain that substitutes do not follow the plans, and that the students get behind in their work. Substitute teachers, on the other hand, complain that they are never allowed to use their own special skills and that they can neither have fun nor even teach in a classroom of students who do not respect them. Whether substitute teachers should follow a lesson plan exactly or whether they can introduce an occasional activity of their own is a common concern.

If effective instruction is to occur, a reciprocal relationship must be established between the classroom teacher and the substitute. Teachers and substitutes have obligations toward each other to make the classroom run smoothly. Those obligations fall into three major areas: teaching the curriculum, allowing for creativity and individuality, and maintaining discipline. The following suggestions help clarify responsibilities in those three areas.

Teaching the Curriculum

The teacher's obligation is to plan lessons carefully. Needed materials should be kept neatly ordered and close at hand. If no alterations are to be allowed in the plans, leave a note for the substitute and stress how important this is.

The substitute's obligations are first to have an adequate grounding in the curriculum at all grade levels, and second to follow the teacher's lesson plans as carefully as possible. The day goes easier when one keeps to the regular routine. Children do not like to have their schedules disrupted too much. Of course there will be times when the daily plan cannot be followed to the letter. Then the substitute may rely on the "prepackaged curriculum" which is introduced later in this chapter.

Allowing Creativity and Individuality

Many teachers plan out special days for the substitute teacher when they know they are going to be absent. For instance, instead of proceeding with group work in social studies, the class might read the *Junior Scholastic*. When teachers make such special plans, they should specify which parts are open to alterations by the substitute. Then the substitute will have an opportunity to teach a favorite lesson, perhaps, in art or creative writing. If the substitute does not wish to teach a special lesson, the original plans are followed.

Substitute teachers should be ready to teach a creative or favorite lesson at any time. They should take with them any materials that might not be available in the classroom. Even when requested to stick closely to the teacher's plans, they can do some of their favorite short activities, especially in those odd moments between lessons or when a breather is needed between difficult tasks. These mini-lessons can be just as creative as longer, more complicated ones, and they help keep students attentive and on-task. Here are a few samples of such activities:

1. Name a group, such as dogs, cars, famous people, or vegetables. Ask students to name a certain number of members that belong in that group. In lower grades name some members and ask students to identify the group to which they belong.

2. When students finish their work early, ask them to write lists that encourage divergent thinking. Topics for these lists might be things you can wear on your feet, yellow objects, happy events, or things to do to celebrate a holiday. Reward the student who makes the longest list.

3. To strengthen map reading and research skills have students break up into groups of four or five. Give each group a map of the state and have them find as many towns or cities as they can with animals or birds in the name. Set a time limit to see which group can come up with the most. Change the topic and try a second time.

4. For diversity try doing "hink-pinks," a puzzle activity that builds vocabulary and synonym recognition. State two words, with one describing the other. Students must find a synonym, consisting of rhyming words.

Example: unhappy father   (*Answer*: sad dad).

5. Form a circle with the class and begin counting. When you come to a number with five in it or a multiple of five say "fizz." When you come to a number with seven in it or a multiple of seven say "buzz." An example would be: . . . 12, 13, buzz, fizz, 16, buzz, 18. . . . If a player makes a mistake he has to sit down. The last player remaining is the winner.

These are a few examples of good activities for short periods of time. A large collection of this type allows the substitute to follow the teacher's plans and at the same time insert a few favorite activities.

Maintaining Discipline

Teachers know that substitutes are considered fair game. Control is made much easier if the class is taught how to behave with a substitute teacher. For their part, teachers should train their students to work with, rather than against substitutes. Monitors should be assigned to assist the substitute, and students should be held accountable for their behavior.

Substitutes, for their part, must learn how to establish a climate of effective discipline during the first few minutes of the day. Standards should be spelled out, as should any special system of discipline. Then the substitute should determine how the class handles pencil sharpening, drinks of water, and trips to the restroom. If an established discipline pattern exists, follow those rules; doing so will save headaches. If there is none, have consequences for breaking rules clearly thought out ahead of time. Canter's assertive discipline, discussed in Chapter 4, is a useful system. Be sure it incorporates positive reinforcement for good behavior, as in the examples that follow:

1. For primary grades, pass out brightly colored tagboard fish (laminated for durability) to students who are behaving appropriately. Announce that if they receive a certain number by the end of the day they will be able to turn them in for a special Good Citizen award. Their names can be put on a list of good workers to show to their regular teacher.

2. For intermediate grades, cut small squares of construction paper. Have good behavior award recipients write their names on them. Leave a container near the door so the tickets can be deposited at the end of the day. Have a drawing to pick one or two winners who may choose from a "goodie box" that contains stickers, erasers, pencils, decals, and so forth. Students with more tickets in the container have better odds of being chosen. Students work hard for these rewards, which they earn for completing assignments, helping the substitute, and displaying their best behavior.

Summary of the Reciprocal Relationship

Teacher
- Plan lessons well.
- Allow time for the substitute to teach a favorite lesson if possible.
- Teach students how to work with a substitute, and hold them accountable for their behavior.

Substitute
- Unless otherwise allowed, follow the teacher's plans carefully.
- Have a special lesson ready to use at all times, and if you cannot use it, be creative with good time-filler activities.
- For discipline, establish standards early, have consequences determined in advance, and use a good system of positive reinforcement.

BEFORE THE DAY BEGINS

Phone Call

When the phone rings early in the morning, you may be fuzzy-headed no matter how long you have been substituting. So that you do not miss anything that is said, keep a folder of materials permanently beside your phone:

- pencil and pad of paper
- list of schools and their beginning times
- map of the school district(s)
- rules and regulations for the substitute, furnished by the schools
- telephone number for the substitute teacher office.

When answering the call, keep your conversation brief. The substitute clerk will provide key pieces of information. Be sure you have notations for the following:

- name of school to which assigned
- classroom teacher's name
- grade
- room number
- time school begins
- any special information that might be needed about the room or class.

If the clerk mentions abbreviations such as EH, TMR, or MGM, be sure you know what they mean; ask if you are unsure. Enter the school name on your calendar as a means of keeping records of dates and sites where you have worked.

Checking In

It is important that you make a good impression when you first arrive at school. Get there early. Check in at the office. Fill out necessary forms, such as sign-in sheets or pay vouchers. Be sure the head secretary knows you have arrived. Ask her to inform the principal. Greet the principal if possible, but do not use valuable time for lengthy conversation. While in the office get the key to your classroom. Check the teacher's mailbox, which may contain the attendance folder for the class and possibly a message for you. Make a point of checking the mailbox again later in the day.

Knowing the School

When business in the office is completed, take a couple of minutes to learn the layout of the school. Locate places that affect you, such as the library, cafeteria, auditorium, and appropriate playground. Locate another teacher or early arriving student. Ask these questions:

- Do you meet the students on the playground or at the classroom door?
- At noon do you walk them to the lunch area or simply dismiss them from the room?

Other places you need to locate are the supply room, the work room, and the teachers' lounge. Look through the supply room quickly to see what is available to you, because you may find you need some of the supplies on the spur of the moment. Later you can send a student to the office to obtain materials you might need. Take note of the equipment available in the workroom. Plan to have your lunch in the faculty lounge, if that is where other teachers eat. Introduce yourself to them and be friendly.

Preparing for the Day

When you enter your classroom the first thing to locate is the lesson plan book. Find out first if you have scheduled duties on the playground, lunch area, or bus area. You may have morning duty that no one has told you about. If not, check the plan book to see what it contains for the day:

- Is there a time schedule?
- Does the schedule take you through the entire day?
- Is there time for you to teach one of your own favorite lessons?
- Do you understand the instructions? If not, ask a student as soon as possible about that part of the routine.
- Are needed materials at hand?
- Can you locate the teachers' manuals?

If there are no lesson plans, and this often happens, look around the room. There may be a time schedule posted on the chalkboard or wall. If not, open the room and invite some of the "peekers" to come in. Ask them about the daily schedule, how long each subject lasts, and the times of recesses and lunch period. Have them show you where books and materials are located. Ask them how the class behaves; they are not at all reticent to say. Thank them and ask them to leave the room so you can prepare. Outline a schedule of lessons. Make up your mind that you will not falter in presenting them, because students will likely test you at such times. When the lessons are outlined, take a trip around the room. Open cupboards and drawers to check on materials. Be sure the lights are on and the temperature and ventilation adjusted to the weather. Write your name on the board and get ready for the bell.

THE PREPACKAGED CURRICULUM

As indicated, it often happens that the substitute arrives at the classroom and finds no lesson plans. The initial reaction might be to panic, but if you are prepared this is an opportunity to teach in your own way. To make this easily possible, you should prepare in advance a full day's curriculum, prepackaged, for any grade level. Materials for this curriculum should be light, compact, and easy to carry. The trick is to be ready for any one of seven grade levels, with five or six strong activities for each and the materials necessary for carrying them out. The following sections describe how such a prepackaged curriculum can be prepared and organized.

Organizing the Package

Substitutes should make their materials as compact and light weight as possible. They must literally weigh a lesson before deciding whether to include it. Carrying a five pound book for a two minute lesson isn't practical. Here are two means of packaging that work well:

1. Develop a folder of work for each grade level. When assigned a grade, you simply have to take that folder with you. The benefit is that what you need to carry is light and convenient. The drawback is that many of the materials might be used in more than one grade. If you begin switching materials from one folder to another, you are bound to lose track of some of them.

2. Another means of packaging is to choose lessons that can be used across several grade levels. The better you accomplish this, the lighter your load will be. Make thoughtful decisions about what you want to teach and then pack all of your materials in one container.

The container may even be used for motivation. Davis (1980) recommends using a basket with a big bow, placed in a prominent position, with the mysterious promise that exciting activities will pop out during the day. Another convenient carry case is a cardboard filing box. It has space to file worksheets and other materials. It keeps everything at your fingertips, but you have to be careful that it does not become so large and heavy you cannot manage it.

No matter which packaging system you select, you must keep yourself familiar with the contents and where they are located. Go over the lessons regularly. Remove those that you do not use and replace them with new ones you finding interesting. Even if the students have not seen a particular lesson before, you may have become bored with it. Adding new material can enliven matters for you.

Activities

To illustrate what might be included in the prepackaged curriculum, the following describes a complete day's curriculum for fourth, fifth or sixth grade. The lessons are fairly creative, they cover the basic subject areas, and they require relatively few materials. The same general format can be used for primary grades, although several allowances must be made for kindergarten activities.

1. *Reading/Creative Writing*: Read a familiar fairy tale that children like. Discuss with the students the characteristics of each personality in the story. Have the students rewrite the story so that the characters act just the opposite of how they did in the original. For example, in *Cinderella* students would change the heroine into a contemptible girl and her stepmother into a loving person. Finished stories can be shared with the class. Materials needed are fairy tale; students furnish paper and pencils.

2. *Mathematics*: Demonstrate and discuss with the students three different types of graphs—bar, line, and circle. Divide the students into groups and assign each group a topic on which to gather information. Have them graph the information using all three methods. The topics could be as simple as hair color or height of students in the room. Materials needed are graph models and graph paper; students furnish pencils or crayons.

3. *Language*: Use word hunts as a means of providing meaningful practice in the use of the dictionary. Words can come from the spelling list. Call out a word and ask questions about it, such as:

- How many definitions does it have?
- What is the plural of the word?

- From what language is it derived?
- What part of speech is it?

Reward the first person who can answer all the questions, and follow with a class discussion. Materials needed are available in the classroom: dictionaries, paper, pencil.

4. *Social Studies*: Provide activities having to do with skills related to maps. Have each student make a map of his or her route to school. Have them devise a way of indicating turns, distances, and landmarks along the way. They can label streets, stores, parks, and so forth. Map legends can be discussed and included. Materials needed are all available in the classroom: paper, pencil, rulers, crayons.

5. *Art*: Making "spinning pictures" is an activity of high interest to students. Have them cut out a cardboard circle and draw a picture on one side. Then turn the circle over and draw a related picture on the other side. A circle, for example, might have a bird on one side and a tree on the other, or a horse and a barn. Attach a loop of string to each side of the circle as shown in Figure 7. Hold the strings and twirl the circle to wind them. Then gently pull the strings outward. The circle turns rapidly and the pictures seem to merge together. This can lead into a discussion of how motion pictures work. Materials needed are available in the school: cardboard, string, drawing materials.

6. *Physical Education*: KSB (kickball, softball, basketball) is an excellent game to teach students during physical education. The object of this game is for a kicker to kick the ball and run around the four corners of a basketball court before the pitcher can retrieve the ball and make a basket. If the runner succeeds, a point is scored. There are no outs. Sides change as soon as each person on a team has had

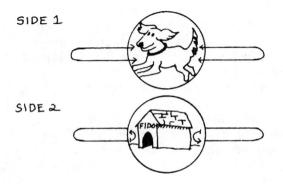

SIDE 1

SIDE 2

FIGURE 7   Example of a spinning picture.

a chance to kick. The team in the field should rotate so that there is a new pitcher for each new kicker.

The activities described in this prepackaged curriculum provide an enjoyable, worthwhile day's learning experience. Each subject area contains a topic that can be completed in one day. The projects can be done with a minimum of preparation and materials.

PREPARING FOR THE UNEXPECTED

Substitute teachers must always be prepared for unexpected occurrences. Occasionally, situations occur that cause even the most capable to doubt their ability to find solutions on the spur of the moment. These unforseen circumstances do not occur often, but they can be devastating when not planned for in advance. The following sections present ideas and suggestions for helping deal with such times.

Illnesses and Accidents

When illnesses and accidents occur, the first thing to do is to fall back on one's resource of common sense. Minor emergencies can be handled by the teacher. For more serious matters a student monitor can be sent to the office for help.

If a student comes to you with complaints of headache, stomach ache, tooth ache, and so forth, do not be too quick to send the child to the nurse. Ask him to put his head down on the desk for a while, until he begins to feel better. In many cases children will forget they even felt ill. Sometimes they do have minor pains that cause discomfort, so one should not challenge the authenticity of the illness. When students are very ill you can usually see it in their face, body, or actions. In such cases send them to the nurse immediately, and if they need help send another student along with them.

Other problems, such as bumps, scrapes, and bruises occur continually. These types of accidents can be taken care of in the room with soap and water. Older children like to administer their own first aid, and they should be allowed to do so.

Serious accidents happen most often on the playground. There the teacher should remain composed and calm but act quickly. Stay with the injured student and send another to the office for help. Reassure the injured student that help will be there soon, and it is best to remain perfectly still. When the nurse arrives try to describe how the accident occurred, with as much detail as possible.

Assemblies

It is good practice to ask about assemblies when you check in the office in the morning. If there is an assembly that day remind the students of it when you make the morning announcements. End the lesson in plenty of time to prepare to leave for the assembly. Before the assembly begins remind the class that whatever discipline program you are using will remain in effect in the auditorium. If you feel the class is unusually active, have them line up alternating boys and girls. Tell the students that the quicker they line up and get quiet the sooner they will get to the assembly for the better seats. Sit with your students, not at the back of the room. Your presence reminds them of the behavior that is expected.

Visitors and Speakers

Occasionally you will be asked to host a guest speaker or a visitor scheduled by the teacher. Sometimes an extra adult in the room means more work for you, but it may help the day pass well. Welcome the guest and introduce yourself. Let him or her know that you will provide as much help as needed. Even when the other person is in charge you may still be needed for discipline. Usually a speaker is interesting enough to hold class attention, but you may have to help out with certain students.

Other visitors may pop in at any time, scheduled or unscheduled. Most often they will be parents of students in the class. It is not a good idea to push them into the back of the room and ignore them. It is better to involve them with the lesson if possible. They can drill children with flash cards, read a story, or even give a spelling test. Often they appreciate being included. If not, they will tell you, but will appreciate being asked in any case.

Field Trips

When you arrive at school you may see the bus parked in front and realize that some lucky class gets to go on a field trip. When you find out it is for your class, it may leave you thoroughly unnerved unless you have anticipated the possibility. Davis (1981) has provided suggestions that can help make the trip more enjoyable for the substitute:

1. Collect all permission slips or medical releases. Put them quickly into alphabetical order so that in case of emergency you can find one easily. Take them with you.

2. Know the phone number of the school and an alternative number for emergencies. Have with you the exact change necessary for a phone call.

3. See that students who are not going know exactly where to go and what to do during the day.

4. Before you leave go over the rules with the students. Remind them that they must set a good example for their school. That means using their best behavior, staying together, cleaning up their litter, and always being courteous. Field trip rules may be available at the school. If not, tell the students that your regulations are rules for the group.

5. If the group consists of primary age children, they should wear name tags. These can be made quickly from construction paper, and should show the name of the child and the number of the bus. Take a head count before the trip begins and then recount every time you change an activity and especially before you leave to return.

6. Take notes on the trip. The teacher will need and appreciate them for follow-up lessons, and if time remains you can use them for discussion before the students are dismissed.

Rainy Days

For substitute teachers, rainy days bring double jeopardy. Not only do the students have to adjust to a new teacher, but they have to stay in at lunch and recess, too. This will make them more difficult to manage than usual. Here are examples of two interesting and exciting activities that can keep the children occupied.

Primary: Find the Bell. One player stands with eyes closed or blindfolded in the center of a circle of seated children. The center player counts to twenty as a bell is passed around the circle of students, ringing as it travels. When the counter reaches twenty the bell stops and all hands go behind the students' backs. The player in the center has three guesses as to who has the bell. The player who has the bell takes the next turn in the center of the circle.

Intermediate: Quiet Ball. The class is asked to sit quietly on top of their desks. A soft sponge ball is tossed back and forth between them. A judge stands in front of the room and makes the decision as to who is out—the catcher if the ball is dropped or the thrower if it is a bad throw. Students who make an out have to sit in their chairs. The judge has the final say in the decisions. The last player left is the winner and new judge.

Rainy day activities are a way for students to relax from their studies, but what about the substitute? Some schools provide aides to give the teacher a short break. In others, teachers share watching adjoining rooms so each teacher can have a break.

Holidays

Holidays are exciting times of the year, and the substitute can share in the exhuberance. The following are good activities for typical holiday seasons (Pavlich and Rosenast, 1974):

1. *Halloween (continuation story)*: Ask a student to begin a Halloween story. Each student thereafter adds another sentence. Record the story on a ditto master and give a copy to each student. Leave one for the teacher.

2. *Thanksgiving (Thanksgiving menu)*: A menu can be made by having the students list foods that begin with letters in the word Thanksgiving. Follow with an art project in which students draw the foods or clip them from magazines and glue them to a place setting.

3. *Christmas (word game)*: Write "Christmas Day" on the board and have students make as many words as possible from the letters contained therein. Letters may be used only as many times as they appear in the two words.

4. *Spring (spring flowers)*: Have students do a spring flowers art project using felt pens and watercolor. They do this by outlining one or more flowers with the felt pen, then applying a watercolor wash. Do not stay within the lines.

5. *Valentine's Day (love puzzles)*: Have the students cut out large hearts from red construction paper. Write messages on them and decorate them with cupids and arrows. Trace a jigsaw puzzle pattern over it and cut it out on the lines. Exchange hearts with a friend and try to put the puzzles back together.

END OF THE DAY

When the students leave at the end of the day, you can relax but your work is not yet down. Certain final tasks should be completed carefully if you are to be of best help to the teacher and leave a good impression. Four main tasks are included: checking papers, writing notes to the teacher, closing up the room, and checking out from the office.

The substitute teacher is responsible for checking papers assigned during the day. Do not leave them for the regular teacher. Sort the papers into stacks. Check those that you were in charge of.

Record the scores at the top of each page and restack them neatly at the top of the teacher's desk where they will be easily found.

Notes left for the teacher are very helpful. For each assignment, the teacher should know what was attempted and what was completed. Jot down notes as the day goes along. For instance, under the heading *Reading* indicate pages covered along with what was not completed. Don't worry if an assignment was not completed. Often the teacher will plan more than usual to be sure that you have something to do all day.

Comments about citizenship should be included in the notes. Be positive. Include some of the fine things that happened that day. If a student helped you, mention that. On the other hand be careful when describing discipline problems. In most cases you should handle the problem yourself so that it is not carried over to the next day. If you must comment, refrain from making judgements about the students. Simply list the behaviors that occurred. At the end of the note thank the teacher for the day and leave your telephone number.

Try to leave the room in the same order in which you found it. Do a quick check of the following:

- Is the floor clean?
- Are the chairs put up?
- Are the cupboards closed?
- Are the windows closed and locked?
- Is the bookshelf straightened?
- Is the chalkboard erased?
- Is the sink wiped dry?
- Do you have all of your belongings?

When you leave, lock the classroom door. Check it to be sure it is secure.

The final step is to check out at the office. You must return the classroom key to the secretary. Sometimes you may have to sign out. Find out from the secretary whether you get your release from the substitute list at that time or the following morning. While in the office visit the principal if possible. If you are looking for regular employment have with you a personal résumé which you can leave. If you are a professional substitute, have some business cards prepared and leave three or four with the principal. If you cannot speak personally with the principal, leave a thank-you note that includes something about how the day went. Remember to be positive.

SUBSTITUTE TEACHING AS A PROFESSION

Classroom teachers consider themselves professionals, but they do not have to attract clientele, nor do they have to scramble continually for jobs. Life is different for the substitute. Substitute teaching more than any other aspect of teaching can be thought of as a business. Substitutes cannot work until they sell themselves. They must establish a good reputation if they are to be requested more than once. If they are to be successful, they must know the business angle of substituting, be a self-promoter, and have a positive, professional attitude toward all people with whom they work (Davis, 1981).

Knowing the Ropes

Understanding the business particulars in substitute teaching is very important. When you begin in a district you should check on certain points so that you will not become confused later (Davis, 1981):

- What is the daily rate of pay?
- When do pay periods begin and end?
- Does one receive more money on long-term positions?
- Are substitutes eligible for health and other benefits?
- Is there sick leave or holiday pay?
- Can one substitute at individual teachers' requests, or is it necessary to wait for a call from the district office?

These questions should be answered for each district in which you work, since policies vary considerably from one place to another.

Selling Yourself

People in sales know the value of advertising their products. In the business of substitute teaching, your product is yourself, and you must learn how to promote that product. You will want your face and name to become familiar to principals, teachers, and the district substitute clerk, so they will automatically think of you when a need arises. As you are requested more often, you will become able to select certain schools and rooms that you like and where you have learned the routines.

The best and easiest way to build a good reputation is to do work of the highest quality. If you provide a good program, students and teachers will be pleased, and you will be requested repeatedly. This makes it worthwhile to put extra work and effort into the job.

Another way to make yourself known is to prepare attractive fliers about yourself and post them in the faculty rooms of the schools you prefer. Mention any specialties you have, and if you wish add a catchy slogan. You can have your picture duplicated on the flier. Have some business cards prepared, too. Pass them out to teachers and principals who you hope will request you again.

Call attention to yourself by joining professional organizations where you interact with teachers. Visit schools in your area and perhaps volunteer to provide some special lessons. Visit with the teachers in their lunch room. This will help them remember your face and name.

BE PROFESSIONAL

The attitude you project as a substitute teacher is crucial. You will be placed in many different situations, some of which will not be as you would like them. Yet almost all situations provide invaluable learning experiences. Learn to work in those places with a positive outlook. Let that outlook carry over into any situation where you share experiences and anecdotes with students, teachers, and administrators. No one wants to request, hire, or be taught by a person who continually grumbles and criticizes the people with whom they work. In teaching, do the job right, that is, do your best to teach in the way you would want a substitute to teach your own child. In short, be competent, positive, and friendly. That is the best way to make a lasting positive impression.

CHECKPOINTS

Substitute teaching is possibly the most difficult job in all of teaching. The substitute faces an unknown group of students who are often uncooperative or even hostile, and is expected to provide instruction in an unfamiliar setting with activities and materials planned by someone else. Management problems for substitutes are formidable, but certain procedures have emerged that help with the task.

>   Mutuality: reciprocal relationship between teacher and substitute

- curriculum: cover teacher needs, but leave some space for substitute
- creativity: substitutes need a repertoire of high-interest activities for various lengths of time
- discipline: teachers should teach class how to behave, with built-in accountability; substitutes must have workable strategies well prepared

Beginning the day

- morning telephone call: get all necessary information—name of school, teacher, grade, room number, time school begins (keep beside the phone: pad and pencil, map of schools, phone number of substitute clerk)
- checking in: report to office, sign forms, get key
- learn school layout: locate library, cafeteria, auditorium, playgrounds; also teachers' supply and workroom.
- prepare for day: locate or prepare schedules, plans, materials

The prepackaged curriculum (a full day's curriculum, ready for use)

- organize in folders or file box
- activities: for all subjects, worthwhile and with a minimum of materials

Preparing for the unexpected

- illnesses and accidents
- assemblies
- visitors and speakers
- field trips
- rainy days
- holidays

End of the day

- check papers
- leave positive note for teacher
- leave room in good order
- check out with principal or secretary

Substitute teaching as a profession

- know the particulars of salary and benefits
- selling oneself
- the professional demeanor

BIBLIOGRAPHY

Charles, C. M. *Building Classroom Discipline: From Models to Practice*. New York: Longman Inc., 1981.

Davis, Diane. "Sub Center: Have a Good Trip!" *Instructor* 90 (1981), no. 10, p. 24.

Davis, Diane. "Sub Center: The Business of Substitute Teaching." *Instructor* 91 (1981), no. 2, p. 36.

Davis, Diane. "Sub Center: The Magic Basket." *Instructor* 90 (1980), no. 5, p. 38.

Pavlich, V., and Rosenast, E. *Survival Kit for Substitutes*. New York: Citation Press, 1974.

14

Stress Management for Teachers

As recently as the 1950s it was not uncommon for teachers to work effectively until age sixty-five. They were expected to retire then, but many continued happily beyond that age. Today, it is a rare teacher who remains effective until sixty-five. Increasingly, teachers look to early retirement, and many end their careers between the ages of fifty-five and sixty. They accept reduced retirement benefits so they may escape the pressures of teaching, preferring to work at part-time jobs or even begin new careers. The problem is not limited to the aging, for thousands of teachers are abandoning their careers in their early thirties.

This situation is unfortunate because experienced teachers have much to contribute to the education of the young. Previously they were able to work until retirement with dignity, respect, and success. Now, they say it isn't worth it, because teaching exacts too great a toll. While the public may still consider teaching a plush job, evidence shows that it is one of the more pressure-packed professions. Psychologist and psychiatrists report rising incidences of battle fatigue among teachers, an emotionally disabling condition formerly seen mainly in military men during combat.

What has caused this remarkable change in such a short time? The formerly rather sedentary occupation of teaching has been affected by changes from all quarters. Students have grown increasingly restive, and are generally acknowledged to be more difficult to deal with than ever before. They are lured by myriad interests other than school learning, and they have become less responsive to adult authority. The curriculum has undergone great modification since the middle 1950s, with very different content and teaching methods in mathematics, natural science, foreign language, English, social science, physical education, and other areas. These changes require continual retooling by teachers. Along with the curriculum changes has come pressure for accountability, which has increased the levels of teacher anxiety. Its paper work jams a day already short on time. Student achievement has declined, bringing public criticism of schools and teachers. Financial support for schools has not kept pace with that of former years, leaving teachers feeling pinched for supplies, salaries, and fringe benefits. New demands are put on teachers regularly, without their consent or involvement, such as the mainstreaming of exceptional students into regular classrooms and the large scale implementation of bilingual and bicultural programs. All of these new programs require teacher retraining. School districts expect teachers to participate in training programs and numerous meetings in which new requirements are taught and explained. Teachers find it increasingly difficult to find the time for such efforts.

In short, teachers feel with some justification that they are expected to accomplish more and more, necessitating greater amounts of time investment, while given fewer resources and less appreciation and support from the public. When you add to that picture a few hostile students and an occasional parent eager to abuse or sue the teacher, it is no wonder that so many are looking for something else to do with their lives.

The picture presented here is austere. Teachers will agree that it is fairly accurate, although most quickly point out that teaching still has its rewards, too. It is a high-quality occupation that brings one close to fine students and adults. Not all teachers are willing to throw the baby out with the bathwater. They don't expect everything to be rosy, without problems of any sort. They would simply like to have some of the heavy stress removed from their work.

STRESS AND ITS EFFECTS

Teacher reactions to matters such as those mentioned here are commonly referred to as "stress." Stress is being blamed for a variety of physical and emotional ailments in teachers—nervous breakdown, migraine headaches, skin rashes, cardiovascular disease, and more frequently though less dramatically, nervousness, fatigue, anxiety, escapism, apathy, and general sense of purposelessness. Seen in this light, stress appears to be a demon to be avoided at all costs. Such is not the case, for stress can be helpful as well as hurtful.

Webster's New Intercollegiate Dictionary defines stress as intense pressure or strain. In living organisms, stress is better understood as an emotional response to conditions that are traumatic, threatening, or unusually exciting. This emotional response produces chemical changes that prepare the body for action, and those changes are accompanied by various observable behaviors such as rapid pulse, increased blood pressure, muscle tension, trembling, and perspiration. Stressful conditions also produce reactions that are obscure and go unnoticed until they manifest themselves in headache, upset stomach, and insomnia. On the other hand, certain stressful situations produce neither anxiety or noticeable nervousness, and serve to energize and happily excite the individual.

Thus, stress has its good side as well as its bad. Life without some stress would be dull at best. Indeed, surprising numbers of people require high levels of stress in order to meet the levels of creativity or productivity they have set for themselves (Forbes, 1979). Such stress may be the same thing that is commonly called "challenge." People seek this stress or challenge as a way of bringing excitement, direction, and purpose to their lives.

Stress, then, serves a useful function when it exists in moderate degree or when the individual feels able to deal with the challenge of the situation. It becomes harmful when it reaches proportions that seem unmanageable, when the individual feels unable to succeed in the situation or even contend with it. This double-edged nature of stress was described by Hans Selye (1956) in his book *The Stress of Life*. Selye described stress as consisting of two parts—distress and eustress. Distress is negative, and occurs when the individual feels unable to cope. It tends to disable the individual and produce a variety of illnesses and side effects. Eustress is positive. It occurs in the presence of interesting problems which the individual finds challenging but feels capable of resolving. It energizes, enlivens, and excites. Thus, we would be wrong to say that teachers do not need stress in their lives. They need and seek what Selye calls eustress, and they need freedom from what he calls distress.

WHAT BOTHERS TEACHERS MOST

Regardless of where they teach, or at what level, teachers are bothered by the same sets of problems. Donald Cruickshank and his associates (1982) have conducted eight studies to determine what teachers see as their main professional problems. He reports that teachers everywhere share five unfulfilled goals: (1) affiliation, the need to establish and maintain positive relationships with pupils and colleagues; (2) control, the need to have students behave appropriately—relatively quiet, orderly, and courteous; (3) parent relationships, the desire for mutually supportive relationships with parents; (4) student success; and (5) time, sufficient time to accomplish necessary personal and professional tasks. Stress is associated with each of the five areas identified by Cruickshank, and that stress becomes counterproductive when teachers feel unable to deal with conditions that exist.

Tim Young (1980), in reporting the Tacoma, Washington School District's implementation of a program of stress reduction for teachers, showed a list of concerns among Tacoma teachers that was similar to that found by Cruickshank. The most frequent problem areas reported by teachers were (1) managing disruptive children; (2) talking to parents about their child's problem; (3) evaluating student performance or giving grades; and (4) teaching students who are below average in achievement level. Time constraint was not included as a problem in the Tacoma program, but in a study by Elizabeth Manera and Robert Wright (1980), their sample of classroom teachers ranked time management as the most significant source of stress.

WHAT ENERGIZES TEACHERS?

Major sources of stress for teachers seem to stem from pressures of too little time, student misbehavior, dealing with parents, and teaching and evaluating students. Truly devastating distress occurs occasionally over matters of poor teacher evaluations, reassignments, and dismissals. If these are the things that bring greatest stress to teachers, what then are their opposites, those things that bring contentment and energy?

One might think that teachers would be energized by the opposites of conditions that bring stress—that is, adequate time, good student behavior, cooperative work with satisfied parents, and good student achievement. Research indicates, however, that while removal of major stressors results in job satisfaction, it does not in itself motivate teachers to invest greater amounts of effort into their work (Silver, 1982).

The Tacoma project mentioned previously organized for teachers such activities as aerobics, seminars on diet and exercise, and inservice workshops on self-image, assertive discipline, and legal and financial matters. Such efforts make teachers' lives more comfortable, but it is questionable that they bring about greater professional satisfaction.

Thus, when we look for conditions that energize teachers and cause them to work more diligently at their jobs, we can see that it is not enough merely to remove stressors. As noted, some stress is desirable because it increases interest and excitement. If teachers are to find their work stimulating and purposeful, there must occur certain conditions that engender positive stress, a seeking, a challenge that allows success and brings recognition.

Research on teacher motivation has identified several factors in teaching that lead to satisfaction and motivate teachers to invest more of themselves into their jobs. Those factors include achievement, recognition, interesting work, responsibility, advancement, and growth possibility (Silver, 1982). Unfortunately, few schools have provided organized means of giving recognition to teachers who have done outstanding work. There is the occasional "teacher of the year" award, but it goes to only one person and therefore brings little reward for good teaching in general. There are the reputations that grow by word of mouth, the occasional parents who express gratitude, the occasional students who thank their teacher, and the occasional comments from administrators and fellow teachers. But all in all, recognition for teaching well done is too scarce to provide incentive for most teachers.

Many teachers seek reward in either self-satisfaction or advancement through the ranks. Unfortunately, both of these options are weak. Self-satisfaction runs thin for most people if others take no notice of their attempts at excellence. Slowly they begin to question the value of their efforts, especially when frustrations come anyway, and gradually some begin to do little more than what is necessary to get by. For those who wish to advance professionally, few options are open other than movement into administration. While diligence, perseverence, and good human relations help them along, there is little to suggest that excellence in teaching serves as a springboard into administration. Besides, the vast majority of teachers have no interest in administrative work, and so this option does little to motivate them.

It seems fair to conclude that the betterment of working conditions and salaries can reduce the amount of stress teachers experience; however, removal of that stress, while certainly important for teachers' mental health, does not itself encourage teachers to invest greater effort into their work. It also seems fair to conclude that schools have poor mechanisms for providing those conditions that motivate teachers toward excellence. This condition should be addressed forthrightly by those who seek to improve the quality of teaching.

STRESS MANAGEMENT FOR TEACHERS

The emotional state of teachers in general calls for attention. Many find conditions in the schools so unpleasant that they are leaving for more attractive jobs. Large numbers have reached burnout—have become emotionally troubled and have seen their effectiveness with students greatly diminished—but stay on in teaching because they are unable or unwilling to enter a new profession. Many teachers still find pleasure, excitement, and reward in teaching, but their numbers are declining. The majority drift uneasily between the extremes, having their good moments and their bad, but generally feeling more and more overwhelmed by the circumstances surrounding their work.

Even though most teachers feel increasing amounts of stress, and feel less and less in control of their professional lives, there is much that can be done to improve their condition. These steps can be taken personally, by oneself, but better results are likely to occur when teachers take them together. Best results are possible when entire school districts decide that for the sake of teachers and students alike they must reduce teacher stress and at the same time energize their efforts. Thus, there exist two aspects of teaching that require attention. The first has to do with job comfort vs. discomfort, in which the sources of great stress are identified and reduced. The second aspect has to do with positive direction vs. aimlessness, which calls for identification and strengthening of those factors that energize teachers and bring quality to their professional lives.

JOB COMFORT VS. JOB DISCOMFORT

Teachers who speak of stress and burnout are referring to conditions in their employment that are very burdensome, threatening, unpleasant, and unmanageable. Teachers commonly identify fifty to one hundred separate conditions that contribute to their discomfort. Those most frequently mentioned are too much to do, too little time, student misbehavior, and dealing with unappreciative parents and students. When these conditions occur infrequently they present little problem. They do not become highly troublesome until they occur in such quantity and with such frequency that the teacher begins to feel unable to contend with them. The means of reducing stress in the job setting, then, are first to reduce the occurrence of these stressors and second to acquire skills for dealing with those that occur anyway.

Major approaches to reducing and dealing with stressors in teaching include the following: prioritizing, selective avoidance, time

Carolyn tells about the joys of playground supervision:

"While on the subject of yard duty, I can say that it can be a rewarding experience. May I also say that under certain conditions it can be hell. Briefly, rules are broken, fights break out over disputed game rules, and children ignore all the safety rules. You are asked to listen to one sad story after another as to who took cuts, who hit whom, and now a kid's crying because a disparaging remark was made about his mother. Balls land on roof tops or roll into the street and children fall and scrape knees. A written note is required or else the damaged child will not be allowed to see the nurse. If it's a windy day, you get nose bleeds, more notes to write, and ubiquitous uneasiness. Those are the rewarding experiences. Now let me tell you about. . . ."

"No, really, on yard duty it seems like you and 400 kids. How I pray for the wisdom, which so often eludes me, to know not to pick on the wrong child for a deviant act of another. To be wise enough to single out the initiator, and not the innocent bystander. When there is a confrontation, the kids frequently don't know themselves who started it. I usually ask them to shake hands. Kindergartners love to do that, and they go away hand in hand. First and second graders comply, but fourth graders don't go for it too readily. I go on to step two: since they are not smiling, I suggest they at least smile. The power of suggestion works wonders. I bet them they can't smile by the time I count to three. That rarely fails. If it does, I am alerted to a problem that may have deep roots, one that has little to do with the situation at hand."

management, discipline skills, parent communication, and maintaining physical well-being. Suggestions for practical steps that can be taken in these areas are presented in the sections that follow.

Prioritizing

To prioritize simply means to put things in order of importance. The reason for prioritizing is to help oneself deal with important matters first and leave the less important for later. Most people function the other way around—they attend to inconsequential matters first, feeling they can get them out of the way and then concentrate fully on the important matters. Unfortunately, given the limited amounts of available time, the inconsequential matters receive attention but the important matters are left undone.

The way to correct this condition is obvious: take care of important matters first. If there remains time (or inclination) one can take care of the unimportant later, and if not, little damage is done. We seldom feel pressure if we do not get around to reading junk mail. Pressure comes from not getting done the things that we really need to do, or that others expect us to get done on time.

Prioritizing, then, helps people deal with essential matters by making sure that there is time for them. If we can get only so much done during the day, as teachers so often lament, then what we get done ought to be that which is important in our professional lives.

Selective Avoidance

At a recent conference on the major problems of teachers, one of the speakers insisted that the best way for teachers to deal with stress was simply to avoid it. The audience laughed, but the speaker was serious. He meant that teachers can learn to say no, as a way of preventing their becoming overburdened with things to do. They can avoid association with people who are chronic complainers, who find fault with everyone and everything and affect the attitudes of those around them. They can put aside the trivial matters that consume so much time, and leave them aside forever. They can learn not to take work home with them at night, so that they can enjoy the luxury of thinking about nonschool topics. They can give students greater responsibility in helping manage the classroom and the instructional program. These are examples of what the speaker meant by avoiding stress.

Of course, there are areas that must not be avoided. Teachers are obliged to prepare, obtain materials, do a good job of teaching, control student behavior, evaluate students, attend necessary meetings, keep records, file reports, and communicate with parents. But if one were to analyze the incredible number of tasks that routinely fall to the teacher, one would find that a large portion of them could be left aside without negative consequences of any sort.

Time Management

Time is a precious commodity, and unfortunately there is only so much of it. "Too much to do and not enough time to do it," is one of teachers' most often heard complaints. The point is granted—it is certainly obvious to anyone who bothers to look—that teachers are overwhelmed with things to do and people to report to. But for the moment, let us acknowledge another important fact: Teachers could save great amounts of time simply by not wasting what they have available to them.

Many time-robbers eat away at teachers' time every day. One of them has been mentioned already, the tendency to deal with matters that could just as well be left aside indefinitely. Suppose that Mr. Johnson works in his room for two hours each day after school. Two hours of concentrated work should be more than enough to take care of all the matters that have significant impact of teaching and learning. But it is not difficult to spend two full hours, occupied all the while, without tending to matters of planning activities, obtaining and preparing instructional materials, or evaluating student work. Mr. Johnson uses his time reading all the memos, notices, advertisements, and other pieces of mail he receives at school. He goes to the faculty room to get coffee and on the way stops to talk with the custodian about yesterday's ball games. In the lounge he meets the principal. They chat, tell jokes, and talk about politics. After he returns to his room, he waters all his plants and feeds the rat, hamsters, and rabbits. He dislikes messiness so he picks up scraps, arranges books, cleans the sink, and tidies his desk. While looking for reference material for the next day's lesson on Mexico, he comes across interesting material on money, coins, mints, and various monetary systems, which he reads. Before he knows it, it is five o'clock, but few of his necessary tasks have been done. He still has papers to grade, so he takes them home.

Mr. Johnson fell prey to three of teachers' greatest time robbers—dealing with the trivial, talking instead of working, and working in a disorganized way. Most of his time was lost in completing nonessential matters, most of which could have been taken care of by student monitors. He wasted a half-hour talking with the custodian and the principal. His work style shows that he has given little thought to organizing his time. He takes care of matters that catch his eye rather than following a planned sequence.

The poor self-discipline shown by Mr. Johnson causes him to work inefficiently, thereby losing a good deal of the limited time he has available outside of class. This problem is made more serious by two other factors: The first is that his principal, wishing to be very democratic, calls numerous faculty meetings. There time is spent discussing matters that often concern only two or three teachers. Since discussion is kept open, other teachers who are not involved with the issue ask questions and give input, thereby causing the meeting to last longer than necessary. Mr. Johnson goes along docilely because he is a good friend of the principal, but privately he decries the numerous meetings and the amount of time they require.

The second factor that cuts into Mr. Johnson's time is the vast quantity of paper work required in the mathematics program the school has adopted. The program is individualized, and it requires that every student be diagnosed for strengths and weaknesses and then given instructional activities to remediate weaknesses. These activities are for the most part done individually by students, monitored by Mr. Johnson and an instructional aide. The students' work must be scored, and for the errors noted, the students must receive further corrective activities. Periodically, all students are tested to obtain evidence of progress. Their test papers must be filed and all scores must be plotted on a master chart. Extensive time is used in the paper work.

Time savers, as opposed to the time robbers described, help teachers to get their work done in minimum time. The most valuable time-savers are work efficiency, delegating work to students, reducing paper checking, and controlling the number and agendas of meetings.

Efficiency permits teachers to accomplish great amounts of work in short periods of time. It begins with prioritizing tasks, giving attention to those that are absolutely necessary, such as planning, scoring papers, preparing for conferences, and preparing instructional materials and activities. Also high on the list should come those tasks that are difficult or boring, leaving for later those that are most enjoyable. One should give last attention to flyers, memos, advertisements, and so forth that are not urgent or important.

One should then make sure to work during work time, avoiding all temptation to chat, gossip, daydream, or gaze out the window. Chatting with others is important, but it should be done during breaks, not during time scheduled for work. Thinking, too, is important, but the mind should be kept on the matter at hand rather than being allowed to range far afield.

As for routine tasks such as watering plants, cleaning the room, feeding animals, and dusting, those should go to students. A system of classroom monitors was described in Chapter 5 for attending to such matters. If the students are too young for such tasks, the work can be done by aides or volunteers. Older students in the school are usually eager to help.

Paper checking, which consumes such vast amounts of time, can be cut back drastically without harmful consequences. Most teachers believe that if they assign work to students they are bound to mark every single paper carefully. There are at least two strong counter-arguments to this view. First, many tasks given to students are for practice only. Teachers can circulate and observe students at work. Afterward, the practice sheets can be discarded. A second argument against careful marking of students' papers is that students profit little from marks on papers that they completed one or more days previously. If the purpose of correction is to help students do better, then correction should be given at the time of the error. Paper correcting is reduced, then, by designating much work as practice, to be observed by teacher and aide but not marked. Following adequate practice, some work is submitted for checking. Any papers sent home with students should be carefully checked and marked.

Record keeping is another type of paper work that teachers consider time consuming and nonproductive. This task can be reduced in three ways—by keeping only those records that are truly necessary; by training students to keep many of the records; and by obtaining the assistance of a parent volunteer to help with checking, recording, and filing.

With regard to meetings, teachers have much more control than they suspect over their number, length, and nature. They can ask that meetings be held only at scheduled times, which for many faculties is once per week, that the principal prepare in advance a written agenda, that the agenda be followed, and that the meeting be ended when the agenda is completed. The faculty can request that the entire staff not convene when matters concern only a few of the teachers. Minutes of the meetings can be distributed to the other teachers. And the staff can agree that each and every matter need not be discussed ad nauseum. Most decisions should be made by the principal and designated committees, with the remainder of the staff being informed and having the opportunity to vote if the matter affects them.

Discipline Skills

Teachers everywhere identify discipline as one of their main concerns in working with students. Not only does student misbehavior take away great amounts of time available for teaching and learning—somewhere around fifty percent in most classrooms, according to some research (Jones, 1979)—but the clashes of wills between teacher and students over misbehavior are often emotional and highly draining. This is a major source of frustration and one of teaching's greatest stressors.

In recent years, however, powerful new systems of behavior control have been developed. Three such systems are behavior modification, assertive discipline, and Frederick Jones's classroom management program, all described in Chapter 4. Each of these programs is comprised of a set of specific teacher skills that can be fairly easily learned and used in a manner that eliminates most of the confrontations between teacher and students. Teachers cannot automatically apply these skills. Training is required, but it is available and the results are known to be effective.

A second factor that can work to the teacher's advantage is the growing concern among parents that children learn and behave properly in school. The permissive attitude of former years has given way to insistence on structure, standards, and discipline. Teachers can now expect increased parental support and cooperation in working for better student learning and behavior.

Parent Communication

Good cooperation between parents and teachers does not occur automatically, simply because parents are becoming more concerned. Once again it is the teacher's responsibility to initiate and build strong communication with parents, as a means of engendering active support and cooperation. Suggestions have been made previously about ways to initiate and maintain such communication. To reiterate, teachers can use notes, newsletters, phone calls, and personal conferences as means of describing the educational program, reporting on individuals' strengths and weaknesses, describing special events, listing special needs for the class, and asking directly for help, support, and cooperation. The tone of all communications should be positive, deal with matters of obvious educational import, be addressed to the needs of the individual child or the class, and be specific and concise. Establishing good communication might appear at first to be another drain on precious time, but in the long run it pays off handsomely in support and cooperation, with reduced frustration, anxiety, and work load.

Physical Well-Being

Authorities on stress and stress management emphasize the importance of adequate rest, good nutrition, and recreation. Some go so far as to assert that health is the key to the management of stress (Swick and Hanley, 1980). The purpose of this chapter is not to suggest ways of managing one's total life, but it must be recognized that teachers' physical health figures strongly in their ability to deal with the enormous stress in their lives. Teachers should realize, therefore, that good diet, rest, exercise, and recreation are matters requiring attention.

POSITIVE DIRECTION

The point was made earlier that teacher stress called for attention to two aspects of teaching—job comfort as opposed to discomfort, and positive direction as opposed to aimless drifting. The previous section focused on job comfort, identified conditions in teaching that produce undue stress, and made suggestions for rearranging job conditions to remove as much of the stress as possible.

This section deals with the second of the two aspects, and it gives attention to things teachers can do to increase positive, useful stress, referred to as eustress. Moderate amounts of eustress energize teachers, provide a sense of direction, make them pleased with their jobs, and give them a feeling of importance and accomplishment, conditions that profoundly affect morale. Clearly, this is stress too, but of a positive sort rather than negative. In seeking eustress teachers should consider group efforts, student achievement, newsletters, public performances, shared responsibility with students, and building *esprit de corps.*

Group efforts refer to projects undertaken by a group of teachers who wish to collaborate on a given idea or plan, such as putting on a field day or art exhibit, organizing and implementing a cardiovascular fitness program, teaching principles of archeology through simulated digs, or arranging Saturday work-play days for parents and children at school. Excitement and enjoyment grow out of such group activities, and they provide a forum for sharing ideas and expertise.

Genuine *student achievement* provides much positive stimulation for teacher and students. Such is especially the case when progress is graphed and when products are publicly displayed. When students are urged to achieve, when achievement is made possible, when progress is documented, and when students are motivated to surpass their previous levels of individual and group achievement, student motivation and achievement snowball. Teacher motivation snowballs along with it.

Newsletters prepared by students as part of their language arts program furnish a marvelous vehicle for accomplishing several things that enliven teaching and learning. First, the fact that the work is done by the students and that all students make contributions motivates them to write well. They have to use correct spelling, grammar, and handwriting. Parents read student-produced newsletters avidly, take pride in their child's work, and express support for teacher and class. The newsletter gives the class a means of expressing the excitement of their curriculum and the progress they are making. The teacher gets credit and recognition for the newsletter and the accomplishments it documents.

Public performances and exhibits also provide high levels of excitement and desire to do well. Most schools encourage teachers and their classes to present performances such as plays, readers' theatre, holiday skits, musicals, and so forth. Students work hard to prepare for such events, and parents take great interest and give much support. Less frequently, classes arrange exhibits, often in conjunction with performances, in which samples of student work are put on display. Most often these exhibits display work in arts and crafts. Occasionally, a class puts on an exhibit of science projects. There are, however, numerous other possibilities for such exhibits, and most can deal with subjects central to the curriculum. For example, students can make their own books, which they write, illustrate, and bind. Since the work will be on display, students are motivated to produce an attractive product of high quality. Possibilities for exhibits of student projects in language, mathematics, and social studies are endless.

Most people think of exhibits as being displays for parents as a part of evening performances, open houses, and so forth. But displays of student work set up on the corridors of the school, or even outside the individual classroom, where they are viewed only by students and adults who work in the school, can be very useful. The student motivation, spirit, and desire to achieve that naturally accompany such activities energize teachers and bring the class much favorable attention.

From the outset of each school year, teachers should impress on students the role and responsibility they have in their own educational process, that they, like the teacher, have to do their part if best learning is to occur. They can be shown how to take an active stance in learning, help the teacher and each other, and assume duties in the on-going management of the classroom. As they begin to see themselves as active participants in learning, rather than passive recipients of whatever the teacher makes them do, they adopt an attitude of *shared responsibility*—that is, of working together with the teacher and each other for the well-being of all. When this attitude develops, there comes with it a spirit of togetherness that is motivating and satisfying to teachers and students alike.

If teachers are able to bring about this attitude of shared responsibility, and then add to it a sense of great accomplishment, of being special, and of setting new marks of excellence, there will occur that elusive condition referred to as *esprit de corps*, group spirit, that binds students together and makes school a time of pleasure and fulfillment. This group spirit is one of the best things that can happen to a teacher, for the work becomes joyful instead of laborious and the students supportive instead of lethargic or resistant. The days end with a satisfied glow instead of wretched fatigue. As students rally, they provide immense rewards to the teacher. Word and feelings spread, and parents become supportive and rewarding, too. *Esprit de corps* does not automatically occur, even when teachers work hard for it. Sometimes the mix of student personalities is simply not right. But usually it can be made, or allowed, to happen when teacher and students go beyond normal expectations of effort, responsibility, and concern for each other. And when it does, it provides the greatest reward and the greatest motivation that are available in teaching.

CHECKPOINTS

Teaching seems to produce more stress than ever before, which contributes to job dissatisfaction and early burnout. Recent attention to this problem has identified sources of stress and has provided suggestions for dealing with it more effectively.

Stress: some is needed, but too much is harmful
- "eustress": a challenge, interesting, helpful
- "distress": inability to cope: overwhelming, hurtful

What bothers teachers most
- lack of affiliation with students and colleagues
- student misbehavior
- poor relationships with parents
- lack of student success
- lack of time

What energizes teachers
- achievement by students
- recognition
- interesting work
- responsibility
- possibilities for advancement
- growth possibilities

Stress management for teachers
- prioritizing: take care of important matters first
- selective avoidance: learn to say no
- time management: work efficiently; use time-savers

- discipline skills: new, effective systems have been developed
- parent communication: rally parents to teachers' side
- physical well-being: health and recreation are important

Positive direction in teaching: building spirit and meaning
- group efforts: teachers working together
- student achievement
- newsletters
- public performances
- shared responsibility: teacher and students
- *esprit de corps*

BIBLIOGRAPHY

Cruickshank, Donald R. "Five Areas of Teacher Concern." *Phi Delta Kappan*, March 1982.

Forbes, Rosaline. *Life Stress*. New York: Doubleday, 1979.

Jones, Frederick. "The Gentle Art of Classroom Discipline." *National Elementary Principal*. June 1979.

Manera, Elizabeth S. and Wright, Robert E. "Stress Factors in Teaching." *Action in Teacher Education*, Fall 1980.

Selye, Hans. *The Stress of Life*. New York: McGraw Hill, 1956.

Silver, Paula F. "Synthesis of Research on Teacher Motivation." *Educational Leadership*, April 1982.

Swick, Kevin J. and Hanley, Patricia E. *Stress and the Classroom Teacher*. Washington D.C.: National Education Association, 1980.

Young, Tim. "Teacher Stress: One School District's Approach." *Action in Teacher Education*, Fall 1980.

Index